Unwindi...

Adventure Awaits

906.632.3366   800.647.2858

www.saultstemarie.com

SCAN ME

Sault Ste Marie
PURE MICHIGAN

Contents

Front Cover: Eye-catching Viking Octantis
on the St. Marys River. (Roger LeLievre)

Back Cover: Algoma Intrepid at South
Chicago, IL. (Stephen Sostaric)

This https://www.facebook.com/
photo/?fbid=5770005846650088&

4

Great Lakes Fleet
TRANSPORTERS OF BULK CARGOES

With 20 million tons of annual carrying capacity, and reliable vessels able to deliver 15,000 to 75,000 tons in all seasons, our professional staff and crews can customize service to your specific needs.

cn.ca/greatlakesfleet

5

KNOW YOUR SHIPS

64th EDITION

**Annual Guide to Boats & Boatwatching
on the Great Lakes & St. Lawrence Seaway**

ISBN: 978-1-891849-30-5

© **2023** No part of this book may be published, broadcast, rewritten or redistributed without permission.

Marine Publishing Co. Inc.
523 N. Ashley St., Ann Arbor, MI 48103
knowyourships@gmail.com / 734-276-3299

Editor/Publisher: Roger LeLievre
Crew: Graham Grattan, Samuel Hankinson, Jack Hurt, Kathryn Lau (Advertising), Nancy Kuharevicz, Matt Miner, Wiliam Moran, Isaac Pennock, John Philbin, William Soleau and Nick Stenstrup. **Founder:** Tom Manse (1915-1994)

The information in this book was obtained from the U.S. Army Corps of Engineers, the U.S. Coast Guard, Lake Carriers' Association, Lloyd's Register, Transport Canada, St. Lawrence Seaway Management Corporation, Great Lakes Tugs & Workboats, Shipfax, Tugfax, Boatnerd.com and vessel owners operators.

This issue is dedicated to the late **Audrey LeLievre**, whose behind-the-scenes commitment over many years helped this book evolve into the indispensible directory and shipping yearbook it is today. Thanks Mom! - RL

KNOWYOURSHIPS.COM

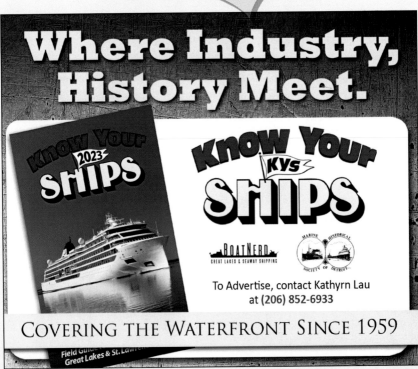

SCAN ME

Where Industry, History Meet.

2023

Know Your SHIPS

Know Your KYS SHIPS

BoatNerd GREAT LAKES & SEAWAY SHIPPING

MARINE HISTORICAL SOCIETY OF DETROIT

To Advertise, contact Kathyrn Lau
at (206) 852-6933

COVERING THE WATERFRONT SINCE 1959

Field Guide
Great Lakes & St. Lawr

Passages

Roger Blough being towed to Conneaut, OH, by tug Meredith Ashton.
(Samuel Hankinson)

Arriving

The big story of 2022 was the debut, with much deserved fanfare, of the versatile Interlake Steamship Co. self-unloader *Mark W. Barker* (read the full story on page 160). The *Barker* is the first non-tug-barge combination built for U.S. Great Lakes service since 1981. Named for Interlake's president, it is the latest to be christened after family members. James R. Barker is Mark's father and Kaye E. Barker is his mother.

Mark W. Barker on christening day. *(Andrea Guerriero)*

The second-biggest head-turner of 2022 was the Great Lakes debut of the impressive passenger liner *Viking Octantis*, which will be joined this year by her sister ship *Viking Polaris*. At 672 feet long and a true sight to behold, the gleaming white vessels mark a major commitment by Viking Cruises in the Great Lakes market. The *Octantis* wasn't the only new face on the cruising side this season: Read more about the burgeoning Great Lakes passenger industry on page 168.

Viking Octantis and Hon. James L. Oberstar share the harbor at Duluth, MN, June 27, 2022. *(Gus Schauer)*

Algoma Central Corp. brought two, 2007-built saltwater tankers into the fold in late 2022, *Chantaco* and *Chiberta*, which have been renamed *Algotitan* and *Algoberta*, respectively. The pair replaces two other tankers in the fleet, *Algoma Hansa* and *Algonorth*, both of which headed overseas in early 2023. The fleet has also bought the Norwegian tanker *Birgit Knutson*, which may come to the lakes in 2023.

Algoma Hansa has already left the lakes. *(Andrew Russell)*

Canada Steamship Lines' self-unloader *Nukumi* entered service in spring 2022 on the Canadian East Coast delivering deicing salt, which will be her main cargo (more on her on page 162).

The Canadian Coast Guard officially announced that its newest icebreaker would be named *Judy LaMarsh*. The icebreaker was acquired in 2021 and spent most of 2022 undergoing a refit before entering the icebreaking fray late in the season.

Continued on Page 10

Manistee and St. Clair at Marine Recycling Corp.'s scrapyard in Port Colborne, ON. (Ted Wilush) Right: Manistee with Ojibway's severed stack nearby. (Janey Anderson)

Departing

Three vessels arrived at the Marine Recycling Corp. scrapyard in Port Colborne, ON, in 2022. The long-idle, World War II-vintage *Manistee* made port March 30 under tow from Toledo, OH. Next up was her former fleetmate, *Ojibway*, which came in under her own power on April 5. Finally, on September 29, the veteran cement carrier *S.T. Crapo* was towed from Green Bay, WI, where she had served as a cement storage barge for many years. *Ojibway*, built in 1952 as *Charles L. Hutchinson* (ii) and which later sailed as *Ernest R. Breech* and *Kinsman Independent* (iii), operated through the 2021 season but needed expensive steel renewal. Built at Great Lakes Engineering Works, River Rouge, MI, in 1927, the *Crapo* was retired as a steamer in 1996. Finally, demolition of the *St. Clair*, destroyed in a winter lay-up fire in February 2019, was completed in 2022.

S.T. Crapo scrap tow leaving Green Bay, WI. The tug Texas is assisting. (Korey Garceau)

Changing

In mid-March 2022, Sarter Marine Towing Co. of Sturgeon Bay, WI, was sold to The Great Lakes Towing Co. Sarter is the former Selvick Marine Towing Co., dating back to 1969 and sold to Sarter in 2019. Early in 2023, Port City Marine Services of Muskegon, MI, took over management of the St. Marys Cement tugs and barges by forming a Canadian subsidiary.

On the Horizon

McKeil Marine bolstered its dry-bulk fleet with the acquisition of the shallow-draft self-unloader *Da Shen* in spring 2022. The vessel is being rebuilt at a shipyard in China and was expected on the Great Lakes this year under the name *Northern Venture (ii)*.

In 2022, Algoma Central Corp. announced a joint venture with Furetank AB to build eight dual-fuel, ice-class tankers in China. Delivery is expected between 2023 and 2025. On the dry-bulk side, Algoma is building another Equinox-class vessel in China, to be named *Algoma Bear*. She will replace the 1979-vintage *Algoma Transport* in 2024.

McAsphalt Marine is building a bitumen tanker at Wuhu Shipyard in China for Great Lakes/Seaway/East Coast service. The new ship, *McAsphalt Advantage*, was expected to join the fleet in 2023 and will be McAsphalt's first powered (non-tug/barge) vessel.

Casualties

On November 2, 2022, *Algoma Compass* struck a bridge abutment as it entered the Welland Canal downbound. She continued to Hamilton, ON, where her cargo of sand was unloaded and repairs were made. The vessel is the former *Roger M. Kyes* and *Adam E. Cornelius* (iiii).

On the morning of February 27, 2023, fire broke out in the engine room of *Algoma Discovery* while she was in winter quarters at Port Colborne, ON. The blaze was quickly extinguished, but at press time the extent of damage to the 1987-built bulker was unknown.

Port Colborne firefighters alongside Algoma Discovery. *(Bobby Davidson)*

Marine Museums

The 1905-built museum tug *James Whalen*, docked at Heritage Park in Thunder Bay, ON, sank May 1, 2022. She was raised in early September and placed on a dock, but her future remains unclear.

The Milwaukee, WI-based Discovery World Museum sold its flagship schooner *Denis Sullivan* to an organization in Boston. She left the lakes in fall 2022. A two-year period of inactivity caused by the COVID-19 pandemic left it without a captain or maintenance crew.

Museum tug James Whalen on the bottom at Thunder Bay, ON. *(Michael Hull)*

Continued on Page 12

High-quality bar steel being loaded aboard the Paul R. Tregurtha at Monroe, MI. *(Samuel Hankinson)*

Innovations

Three unusual cargoes moved to the western end of Lake Superior from Monroe, MI, in 2022 aboard Interlake Steamship Co. vessels. In August, a trial load of 400 tons of special bar quality steel was brought to Duluth in the cargo hold of the *Paul R. Tregurtha*, the first backhaul load ever for the vessel that usually returns to Lake Superior in ballast after delivering coal to lower lakes power plants. Then, in October, *Mark W. Barker* loaded 4,000 more tons of bar steel, followed by another 2,000 tons in December. The steel is used to manufacture grinding balls for the mining industry.

Lay-ups

The former *American Valor* is still tied up at Toledo, OH, awaiting repowering and reactivation. Interlake Steamship Co.'s long-idle *John Sherwin* remains tied up at DeTour, MI, waiting for the resumption of a self-unloader/dieselization project that was abandoned in 2008. *McKee Sons* continues to languish at a dock in Muskegon, MI. Two Great Lakes Fleet vessels remain in long-term lay-up: The fire-damaged *Roger Blough* was towed to Conneaut, OH, in fall 2022, and the steamer *Cason J. Callaway* remains docked at Sturgeon Bay, WI. The Pelee Island ferry *Jiimaan* remains sidelined at Sarnia, ON, being evaluated for future use. The ferry *Spartan* remains laid up at Ludington, MI, as does the tug *LT-805*, which was acquired by Interlake last fall. Great Lakes Fleet's 1952-built steamer *Philip R. Clarke*, which had been in indefinite lay-up at Toledo since 2020, was reactivated in July 2022.

Continued on Page 14

Cason J. Callaway and Walter J. McCarthy Jr. under tow at Sturgeon Bay, WI, by tug William C. Selvick, February 2023. *(Paul C. LaMarre III)*

Badger (left), Spartan and tug LT-805 at Ludington, MI, in 2022. (Stephen Sostaric)

Philip R. Clarke on a foggy Detroit River with the Renaissance Center appearing to float in the clouds. (Gerry Kaiser)

A Sleeping Giant Awakens?

Fast Eddie struts her stuff in 1978. (Roger LeLievre)

Ryerson's iconic stack. (Kevin Skow)

Since the magnificent *Edward L. Ryerson* laid up in May 2009 during an economic tumble, ship fans have been hoping the streamlined vessel would someday return to service. Against pretty much all odds and a nearly 14-year lay-up, their dreams may be coming true. As 2023 dawned, workers were scurrying around the 1959-built, non-self-unloading, steam-powered vessel, poking, prodding and working to bring the *Ryerson* back.

But what makes the boat so special? Chris Winters, author of the forthcoming book *Ironboat* and resident *Ryerson* expert, has an idea. "In the late 1950s, it was difficult to imagine a world where the demand for iron ore was stagnant or in decline," he said. "From the drafting board onward, the *Ryerson*, was a 'pure play,' purpose-built ironboat, a streamlined workhorse emblematic of mid-century American industrial elan, and the high-water mark of the shipbuilder's art."

Dreams can come true, so it's good to know the *Ryerson*'s graceful lines, flared bow, a pilothouse that looks like it means business, a signature stainless steel funnel and a throaty steam whistle that can be heard for miles may soon be back thrilling boat nuts wherever she roams. "There's been nothing like her, before or since," said Winters of the vessel often referred to by her fans by just the initials ELR, which, as we all know, is the measure of a real star.

FAMOUS

SOO LOCKS BOAT TOURS

Join us for:
Lock Tours • Lighthouse Cruises • Sip N' Sail Cruises

515 E. Portage Ave., Sault Ste. Marie, MI • (906) 632-2512
(next to the Museum Ship Valley Camp)

Book Your Tour at: famoussoolocks.com

STEWART J. CORT

Edwin H. Gott headed across Lake Superior at dusk.

Our Beautiful Great Lakes

KYS was lucky enough to get two trips on lakers in 2022, on the Edwin H. Gott (this page) and the Herbert C. Jackson (facing). As has often been said, the work aboard ship can be hard, but you can't beat the view from the office! (All photos, Roger LeLievre)

Supermoon on the St. Marys River.

Herbert C. Jackson's emergency steering wheel and stack.

Jackson above the Soo Locks as dawn breaks.

17

18

Vessel Index

Walter J. McCarthy Jr. off Two Harbors, MN, Jan. 1, 2023.
(Gus Schauer)

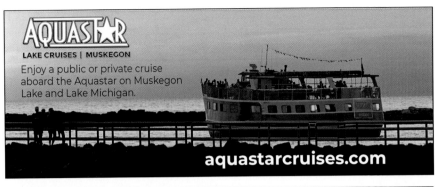
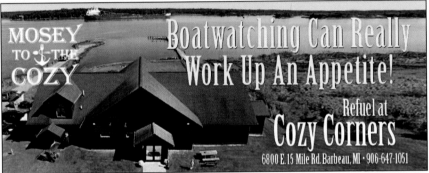

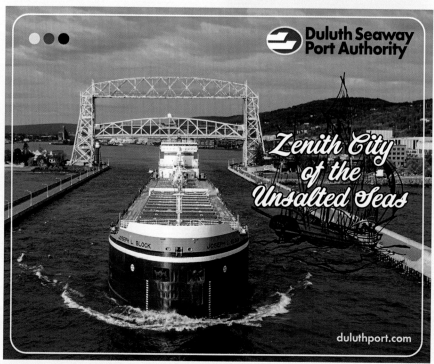

Fleet Listings

Cuyahoga on the Detroit River. (Samuel Hankinson)

LAKES / SEAWAY FLEETS

Listed after each vessel in order are Type of Vessel, Year Built, Type of Engine, Maximum Cargo Capacity (at midsummer draft in long tons) or Gross Tonnage*, Overall Length, Breadth and Depth (from the top of the keel to the top of the upper deck beam) or Draft*. Only vessels over 30 feet long are included. The figures given are as accurate as possible and are for informational purposes only. Vessels and owners are listed alphabetically as per American Bureau of Shipping and Lloyd's Register of Shipping format. Builder yard and location, as well as other pertinent information, are listed for major vessels. Former names of vessels and years of operation under the former names appear in parentheses. A number in brackets following a vessel's name indicates how many vessels, including the one listed, have carried that name.

KEY TO TYPE OF VESSEL

2B	Brigantine	DS	Spud Barge
2S	2-Masted Schooner	DV	Drilling Vessel
3S	3-Masted Schooner	DW	Scow
4S	4-Masted Schooner	ES	Excursion Ship
AC	Auto Carrier	EV	Environmental Response
AT	Articulated Tug	FB	Fireboat
ATB	Articulated Tug/Barge	FD	Floating Dry Dock
BC	Bulk Carrier	GC	General Cargo
BK	Bulk Carrier/Tanker	GL	Gate Lifter
BT	Buoy Tender	HL	Heavy Lift Vessel
CA	Catamaran	IB	Ice Breaker
CC	Cement Carrier	IT	Integrated Tug
CF	Car Ferry	MB	Mailboat
CO	Container Vessel	MU	Museum Vessel
CS	Crane Ship	PA	Passenger Ship
DB	Deck Barge	PB	Pilot Boat
DH	Hopper Barge	PF	Passenger Ferry
DR	Dredge	PK	Package Freighter

PV	Patrol Vessel
RR	Roll On/Roll Off
RT	Refueling Tanker
RV	Research Vessel
SB	Supply Boat
SC	Sand Carrier
SR	Search & Rescue
SU	Self-Unloader
SV	Survey Vessel
TB	Tugboat
TF	Train Ferry
TK	Tanker
TS	Tall Ship
TT	Tractor Tugboat
TV	Training Vessel
TW	Towboat
WB	Workboat

KEY TO PROPULSION

B	Barge	R	Steam – Triple Exp. Compound Engine
D	Diesel	S	Steam – Skinner "Uniflow" Engine
DE	Diesel Electric	T	Steam – Turbine Engine
E	Electric	W	Sailing Vessel (Wind)

Fleet Name Vessel Name	Vessel IMO #	Vessel Type	Year Built	Engine Type	Cargo Cap. or Gross*	Overall Length	Vessel Breadth	Vessel Depth

A

ALGOMA CENTRAL CORP., ST. CATHARINES, ON (algonet.com)

Algoberta	9333814	TK	2007	D	11,799	469' 02"	75' 06"	38' 09"

Built: RMK Marine Shipyard, Istanbul, Turkey (Chiberta '07-'23)

Algocanada	9378591	TK	2008	D	11,453	426' 01"	65' 00"	32' 08"

Built: Eregli Shipyard, Zonguldak, Turkey

Algoma Bear	N/A	SU	2024	D	39,400	740' 00"	78' 00"	48' 02

Built: Yangzijiang Shipbuilding Group Ltd., Jingjiang City, China

Algoma Buffalo	7620653	SU	1978	D	24,300	634' 10"	68' 00"	40' 00"

Built: Bay Shipbuilding Co., Sturgeon Bay, WI (Buffalo {3} '78'-'18)

Algoma Compass	7326245	SU	1973	D	29,200	680' 00"	78' 00"	42' 00"

Built: American Shipbuilding Co., Toledo, OH (Roger M. Kyes '73-'89, Adam E. Cornelius {4} '89-'18)

Algoma Conveyor	9619268	SU	2018	D	39,400	740' 00"	78' 00"	48' 03"

Built: Nantong Mingde Heavy Industry Co. Ltd., Nantong City, China; completed by Yangzijiang Shipbuilding Group Ltd.

Algoma Discovery	8505848	BC	1987	D	34,380	729' 00"	75' 09"	48' 05"

Built: 3 Maj Brodogradiliste d.d., Rijeka, Croatia (Malinska '87-'97, Daviken '97-'08)

Algoma Equinox	9613927	BC	2013	D	39,400	740' 00"	78' 00"	48' 03"

Built: Nantong Mingde Heavy Industry Co. Ltd., Nantong City, China

Algoma Guardian	8505850	BC	1987	D	34,380	729' 00"	75' 09"	48' 05"

Built: 3 Maj Brodogradiliste d.d., Rijeka, Croatia (Omisalj '87-'97, Goviken '97-'08)

Algoma Harvester	9613939	BC	2014	D	39,400	740' 00"	78' 00"	48' 03"

Built: Nantong Mingde Heavy Industry Co. Ltd., Nantong City, China

Algoma Innovator	9773375	SU	2017	D	24,900	650' 08"	78' 00"	44' 09"

Built: 3 Maj Brodogradiliste d.d., Rijeka, Croatia

Fleet Name / Vessel Name	Vessel IMO #	Vessel Type	Year Built	Engine Type	Cargo Cap. or Gross*	Overall Length	Vessel Breadth	Vessel Depth
Algoma Intrepid	9773387	SU	2020	D	24,900	650' 08"	78' 00"	44' 09"

Built: 3 Maj Brodogradiliste d.d., Rijeka, Croatia; laid down as Algoma Endurance

Algoma Mariner	9587893	SU	2011	D	37,399	740' 00"	77' 11"	49' 03"

Built: Chengxi Shipyard Co. Ltd., Jiangyin City, China (Laid down as Canadian Mariner {2})

Algoma Niagara	9619270	SU	2017	D	39,400	740' 00"	78' 00"	48' 02"

Built:Yangzijiang Shipbuilding Group Limited, Jingjiang City, China

Algoma Sault	9619282	SU	2017	D	39,400	740' 00"	78' 00"	48' 02"

Built:Yangzijiang Shipbuilding Group Limited, Jingjiang City, China

Algoma Strongfield	9613953	BC	2015	D	39,400	740' 00"	78' 00"	48' 03"

Built: Nantong Mingde Heavy Industry Co., Ltd., Nantong City, China (CWB Strongfield '15-'17)

Algoma Transport	7711737	SU	1979	D	32,678	730' 00"	75' 11"	46' 07"

Built: Port Weller Dry Docks, Port Weller, ON (Canadian Transport '79-'11)

Algonova {2}	9378589	TK	2008	D	11,453	426' 01"	65' 00"	32' 08"

Built: Eregli Shipyard, Zonguldak, Turkey (Eregli 04 '07-'08)

Algoscotia {2}	9273222	TK	2004	D	19,160	488' 03"	78' 00"	42' 00"

Built: Jiangnan Shipyard (Group) Co. Ltd., Shanghai, China

Algosea {3}	9127198	TK	1998	D	17,258	472' 07"	75' 04"	40'08"

Built: Alabama Shipyard Inc., Mobile, AL (Aggersborg '98-'05)

Algoterra	9442249	TK	2010	D	16,000	473' 00"	75' 05"	40' 08"

Built: Jiangnan Shipyard Corp., Shanghai, China (Louise Knutsen '10-'19, Louise K '19-'19)

Algotitan	9333802	TK	2007	D	11,799	469' 02"	75' 06"	38' 00"

Built: RMK Marine Shipyard, Istanbul, Turkey (Chantaco '07-'23)

Birgit Knutsen	9483516	TK	2010	D	16,000	473' 00"	75' 05"	40' 08"

Built: Jiangnan Shipyard Corp., Shanghai, China; currently operating on saltwater (Louise Knutsen '10-'19, Louise K '19-'19)

Captain Henry Jackman {2}	9619294	BC	2021	D	39,400	740' 00"	78' 00"	48' 03"

Built: Yangzijiang Shipbuilding Group Ltd., Jingjiang City, China

John D. Leitch	6714586	SU	1967	D	34,127	730' 00"	77' 11"	45' 00"

Built: Port Weller Dry Docks, Port Weller, ON; rebuilt with new mid-body, widened 3' by the builders in '02 (Canadian Century '67-'02)

Radcliffe R. Latimer	7711725	SU	1978	D	36,668	740' 00"	77' 11"	49' 03"

Built: Collingwood Shipyards, Collingwood, ON; rebuilt with a new forebody at Chengxi Shipyard Co. Ltd., Jiangyin City, China, in '09 (Algobay '78-'94, Atlantic Trader '94-'97, Algobay '97-'12)

**Algoma Intrepid and USCG
Hollyhock in Mackinac
Straits ice.** (Nathan Poppink)

Fleet Name / Vessel Name	Vessel IMO #	Vessel Type	Year Built	Engine Type	Cargo Cap. or Gross*	Overall Length	Vessel Breadth	Vessel Depth
Tim S. Dool	6800919	BC	1967	D	31,054	730' 00"	77' 11"	39' 08"

Built: Saint John Shipbuilding & Drydock Co., Saint John, NB; widened by 3' at Port Weller Dry Docks, St. Catharines, ON, in '96 (Senneville '67-'94, Algoville '94-'08)

OPERATED BY ALGOMA CENTRAL CORP. FOR G3 CANADA LTD. (g3.ca)

G3 Marquis	9613941	BC	2014	D	39,400	740' 00"	78' 00"	48' 03"

Built: Nantong Mingde Heavy Industry Co. Ltd., Nantong City, China (CWB Marquis '14-'16)

ALPENA SHIPWRECK TOURS, ALPENA, MI (alpenashipwrecktours.com)

Lady Michigan		ES	2010	D	90*	65' 00"	19' 00"	11' 00"

AMERICAN STEAMSHIP CO., WILLIAMSVILLE, NY – SEE RAND LOGISTICS INC.

AMHERSTBURG FERRY CO. INC, AMHERSTBURG, ON

Columbia V		PA/CF	1946	D	46*	65' 00"	28' 10"	8' 06"

Built: Champion Auto Ferries, Algonac, MI (St. Clair Flats, Crystal O)

Columbia VII		PA/CF	1951	D	145*	75' 00"	35' 00"	7' 00"

Built: Erieau Shipbuilding & Drydock Co. Ltd., Erieau, ON (Daldean '51-'20)

Ste. Claire V		PA/CF	1997	D	82*	86' 06"	32' 00"	6' 00"

Built: Les Ateliers Maurice Bourbonnais Ltée, Gatineau, QC (Courtney O., M. Bourbonnais)

ANDRIE INC., MUSKEGON, MI (andrietg.com)

A-390		TK	1982	B	2,346*	310' 00"	60' 00"	17' 00"

Built: St. Louis Shipbuilding & Steel Co., St. Louis, MO (Canonie 40 '82-'92)

A-397		TK	1962	B	2,928*	270' 00"	60' 01"	22' 05"

Built: Dravo Corp., Pittsburgh, PA (Auntie Mame '62-'91, Iron Mike '91-'93)

Endeavour		TK	2009	B	7,232*	360' 00"	60' 00"	24' 00"

Built: Jeffboat LLC, Jeffersonville, IN

Karen Andrie {2}	6520454	AT	1965	D	516*	120' 00"	31' 06"	16' 00"

Built: Gulfport Shipbuilding, Port Arthur, TX; paired with barge Endeavour (Sarah Hays '65-'93)

Rebecca Lynn	6511374	TB	1964	D	433*	112' 07"	31' 06"	16' 00"

Built: Gulfport Shipbuilding, Port Arthur, TX; paired with barge A-397 (Katherine Clewis '64-'96)

Sarah Andrie	7114032	TB	1970	D	190*	99' 05"	32' 04"	6' 07"

Built: Main Iron Works, Houma, LA; paired with barge A-390 (Seminole Sun '70-'97, Declaration '97-'99, Caribe Service '99-'15)

OPERATED BY ANDRIE INC. FOR HOLCIM U.S.

G.L. Ostrander	7501106	AT	1976	D	198*	140' 02"	40' 01"	22' 03"

*Built: Halter Marine, New Orleans, LA; repowered, '91 and '02; paired with barge Integrity, length together 544' 00"
(Andrew Martin '76-'90, Robert L. Torres '90-'94, Jacklyn M '94-'04)*

Innovation	9082336	CC	2006	B	7,320*	460' 00"	70' 00"	37' 00"

Built: Bay Shipbuilding Co., Sturgeon Bay, WI; paired with tug Samuel de Champlain, length together 544' 00"

Integrity	8637213	CC	1996	B	14,000	460' 00"	70' 00"	37' 00"

Built: Bay Shipbuilding Co., Sturgeon Bay, WI; paired with tug G. L. Ostrander, length together 544' 00"

Samuel de Champlain	7433799	AT	1975	D	299*	140' 02"	39' 02"	20' 00"

Built: Mangone Shipbuilding, Houston, TX; paired with barge Innovation (Musketeer Fury '75- '78, Tender Panther '78- '79, Margarita '79- '83, Vortice '83- '99, Norfolk '99-'06)

OPERATED BY ANDRIE INC. FOR OCCIDENTAL CHEMICAL CORP., LUDINGTON, MI

Spartan	7047461	AT	1969	D	190*	121' 01"	32' 01"	10' 09"

*Built: Burton Shipyard, Port Arthur, TX; paired with barge Spartan II
(Lead Horse '69-'73, Gulf Challenger '73-'80, Challenger {2} '80-'93, Mark Hannah '93-'10)*

Spartan II		TK	1980	B	8,050	407' 01"	60' 00"	21' 00"

Built: Sturgeon Bay Shipbuilding Co., Sturgeon Bay, WI (Hannah 6301 '80-'10)

OPERATED BY ANDRIE INC. FOR U.S. OIL, A DIVISION OF U.S. VENTURE INC., APPLETON, WI (usoil.com)

Albert	7517686	AT	1979	D	249*	114' 05"	35' 00"	18' 08"

Built: American Gulf Shipyard Inc., Larose, LA (Hercules '79-'81, El Bronco Grande '81-'06, Craig Eric Reinauer '06-'18)

Great Lakes {2}		TK	1982	B	5,024*	414' 00"	60' 00"	30' 00"

Built: Bay Shipbuilding Co., Sturgeon Bay, WI; paired with tug Michigan (Amoco Great Lakes '82-'85)

Margaret	1588140	TK	2005	B	7,311*	391' 00"	74' 00"	27' 00'

Built: SENESCO Marine, North Kingstown, RI; paired with tug Albert (RTC-101 '05-'18)

Michigan {10}	8121795	AT	1982	D	292*	107' 08"	34' 00"	16' 00"

Built: Bay Shipbuilding Co., Sturgeon Bay, WI; sank at dock Milwaukee, WI, 1-5-'23 (Amoco Michigan '82-'85)

APOSTLE ISLANDS CRUISES INC., BAYFIELD, WI (apostleisland.com)

Archipelago		ES	2018	D	55*	64' 08"	28' 00"	8' 00"
Ashland Bayfield Express		PA	1995	D	13*	49' 00"	18' 05"	5' 00"
Superior Princess		ES	2012	D	90*	64' 09"	19' 00"	11' 00"

ARNOLD FREIGHT COMPANY, ST. IGNACE, MI

Corsair		CF/PK	1955	D	98*	94' 06"	33' 01"	8' 01"

Built: Blount Marine Corp., Warren, RI

Senator (The)		PK	1959	D	98*	94' 10"	31' 00"	9' 09"

Built: Sturgeon Bay Shipbuilding Co., Sturgeon Bay, WI; rebuilt in '11; (Put-In-Bay '59-'94, Sacre Bleu '94-'20)

Fleet Name / Vessel Name	Vessel IMO #	Vessel Type	Year Built	Engine Type	Cargo Cap. or Gross*	Overall Length	Vessel Breadth	Vessel Depth

ASHTON MARINE CO., NORTH MUSKEGON, MI (ashtontugs.com)

AM 2100		DH	2018	B	879*	200′ 00″	35′ 00″	15′ 00″
Built: Jeffboat LLC, Jeffersonville, IN								
AM 2101		DH	2018	B	879*	200′ 00″	35′ 00″	15′ 00″
Built: Jeffboat LLC, Jeffersonville, IN								
Candace Elise	8016380	TB	1981	D	199*	100′ 00″	32′ 00″	14′ 08″
Built: Modern Marine Power Inc., Houma LA (Perseverance '81-'83, Mr. Bill G '83-'90, El Rhino Grande '90-'97, Stephen Dann '97-'15)								
Meredith Ashton {2}	8964460	TB	1999	D	151*	95′ 03″	32′ 00″	13′ 07″
Built: Thoma-Sea Boat Builders Inc., Houma, LA (Nutmeg State '99-'99, C. Angelo '99-'20)								

ASI GROUP LTD., STONEY CREEK, ON (asi-group.com)

ASI Clipper		SV	1939	D	64*	70′ 00″	23′ 00″	6′ 06″
Built: Port Colborne Iron Works, Port Colborne, ON (Stanley Clipper '39-'94, Nadro Clipper '94-'08)								

ATLAS MARINE SERVICES LLC, FISH CREEK, WI

Atlas		PA	1992	D	12*	30′ 04″	11′ 05″	5′ 04″
Northern Lighter		GC	1973	D	5*	36′ 00″	9′ 09″	1′ 06″

B

B & L TUG SERVICE, THESSALON, ON

C. West Pete		TB	1958	D	29*	65′ 00″	17′ 05″	6′ 00″
Built: Erieau Shipbuilding & Drydock Co. Ltd., Erieau, ON								

BABCOCK WELDING & SHORELINE SERVICES, SARNIA, ON

Lime Island		TB	1953	D	13*	42′ 02″	12′ 00″	5′ 05″
Built: Knudsen Brothers Shipbuilding, Superior, WI								

BAY CITY BOAT LINES LLC, BAY CITY, MI (baycityboatlines.com)

Islander		ES	1946	D	39*	53′ 04″	19′ 09″	5′ 04″
Built: Knudsen Brothers Shipbuilding Co., Superior, WI (Nichevo '46-'72)								
Princess Wenonah		ES	1954	D	96*	64′ 09″	31′ 00″	7′ 03″
Built: Sturgeon Bay Shipbuilding Co., Sturgeon Bay, WI (William M. Miller '54-'98)								

BAY SHIPBUILDING CO., DIV. OF FINCANTIERI MARINE GROUP LLC., STURGEON BAY, WI (fincantieribayshipbuilding.com)

Bay Ship		TB	1943	D	19*	45′ 00″	12′ 04″	5′ 03″
Built: Sturgeon Bay Shipbuilding Co., Sturgeon Bay, WI (Sturshipco)								

BAYSAIL, BAY CITY, MI (baysailbaycity.org)

Appledore IV		2S/ES	1989	W/D	48*	85′ 00″	18′ 08″	8′ 08″
Built: Treworgy Yachts, Palm Coast, FL								
Appledore V		2S/ES	1992	W/D	34*	65′ 00″	14′ 00″	8′ 06″
Built: Treworgy Yachts, Palm Coast, FL (Westwind, Appledore)								

BEAUSOLEIL FIRST NATION TRANSPORTATION, CHRISTIAN ISLAND, ON (chimnissing.ca)

Indian Maiden		PA	1987	D	91.5*	73′ 06″	23′ 00″	8′ 00″
Built: Duratug Shipyard & Fabricating Ltd., Port Dover, ON								
Sandy Graham		PA/CF	1957	D	212*	125′ 07″	39′ 09″	8′ 00″
Built: Barbour Boat Works Inc., New Bern, NC								
Waaseyaagmik		CF	1970	D	175*	113′ 09″	34′ 00″	8′ 00″
Built: New Bern Shipyard Inc., New Bern, NC								

BEAVER ISLAND BOAT CO., CHARLEVOIX, MI (bibco.com)

Beaver Islander		PF/CF	1963	D	95*	96′ 03″	27′ 02″	8′ 03″
Built: Sturgeon Bay Shipbuilding, Sturgeon Bay, WI								
Emerald Isle {2}	8967840	PF/CF	1997	D	95*	130′ 00″	38′ 00″	12′ 00″
Built: Washburn & Doughty Associates Inc., East Boothbay, ME								

BIG LAKE MARINE LLC, MILWAUKEE, WI

Capt. Kollin		TB	1960	D	44*	47′ 00″	17′ 00″	7′ 00″
Built: Main Iron Works, Houma, LA (Little Tim, Amber, Capt. Babin)								
Miss K		TB	1947	D	19*	37′ 05″	11′ 02″	4′ 06″
Built: Peterson Builders Inc., Sturgeon Bay, WI (Jas L. Ferebee)								

BLUE HERON CO. LTD., TOBERMORY, ON (blueheronco.com)

Blue Heron 8		ES	2015	D	90*	63′ 08′	23′ 00″	6′ 05″
Blue Heron V		ES	1983	D	24*	54′ 06″	17′ 05″	7′ 02″
Flowerpot		ES	1978	D	39*	47′ 02″	15′ 08″	5′ 06″
Flowerpot Express		ES	2011	D	59*	49′ 07″	16′ 05″	4′ 01″

Fleet Name / Vessel Name	Vessel IMO #	Vessel Type	Year Built	Engine Type	Cargo Cap. or Gross*	Overall Length	Vessel Breadth	Vessel Depth
Great Blue Heron		ES	1994	D	112*	79' 00"	22' 00"	6' 05"

BRENNAN MARINE, LACROSSE, WI (jfbrennan.com)

Bulldog	8651879	TB	1944	D	142*	86' 00"	23' 00"	10' 03"

Built: Equitable Equipment Co., Madisonville, LA (ST-707 '44-'60, Forney '60-'07, Edward H. '07-'17, Jean C. '17-'18)

BRIGANTINE INC., KINGSTON, ON (brigantine.ca)

St. Lawrence II		TV	1954	W/D	34*	72' 00"	15' 00"	8' 06"

BRIGS YOUTH SAIL TRAINING, HAMILTON, ON (brigs.ca)

Playfair		TV	1973	D/W	33*	59' 08"	15' 00"	8' 00"

BUFFALO DEPARTMENT OF PUBLIC WORKS, BUFFALO, NY (emcotter.com)

Edward M. Cotter		FB	1900	D	208*	118' 00"	24' 00"	11' 06"

Built: Crescent Shipbuilding, Elizabeth, NJ (W. S. Grattan 1900-'53, Firefighter '53-'54)

BUFFALO RIVER HISTORY TOURS, BUFFALO, NY (buffaloriverhistorytours.com)

Harbor Queen		PA	2016	D	48*	63' 00"	24' 00"	10' 00"
River Queen		PA	2014	D	5*	45' 00"	12' 00"	3' 02"

BUFFALO SAILING ADVENTURES INC., BUFFALO, NY (spiritofbuffalo.com)

Spirit of Buffalo		2S/ES	1992	D/W	34*	73' 00"	15' 06"	7' 02"

Built: Rover Marine Lines, Norfolk, VA (Jolly Rover '92-'09)

BURROWS MARINE INC., WEBSTER, NY (burrowsmarine.com)

Donald Sea		TB	1964	D	39*	48' 05"	16' 05"	6' 02"

Built: Allied Shipyard Inc., Larose, LA (Brianna Brynn)

BUSCH MARINE INC., CARROLLTON, MI (buschmarine.com)

Edwin C. Busch		TB	1935	D	18*	42' 06"	11' 11"	5' 00"

Built: Manitowoc Shipbuilding Co., Manitowoc, WI (Stella B '35-'79, Paul L. Luedtke '79-'98, Joanne '98-'09)

Gregory J. Busch	5156725	AT	1919	D	299*	151' 00"	27' 06"	14' 07"

Built: Whitney Bros. Co., Superior, WI (Humaconna '19-'77); laid up at Saginaw, MI

C

CALUMET RIVER FLEETING INC., CHICAGO, IL (calumetriverfleeting.com)

Aiden William		TB	1954	D	120*	82' 00"	23' 06"	9' 09"

Built: Defoe Shipbuilding Co., Bay City, MI (John A. McGuire '54-'87, William Hoey {1} '87-'94, Margaret Ann '94-'08, Steven Selvick '08-'14)

John Marshall	7223261	TB	1972	D	199*	111' 00"	30' 00"	9' 07"

Built: Main Iron Works, Houma, LA (Miss Lynn '72-'78, Newpark Sunburst '78-'83, Gulf Tempest '83-'89, Atlantic Tempest '89-'89, Catherine Turecamo '89-'14)

John M. Selvick	8993370	TB	1898	D	256*	118' 00"	24' 03"	16' 00"

Built: Chicago Shipbuilding Co., Chicago, IL; laid up at Chicago, IL (Illinois {1} 1898-'41, John Roen III '41-'74)

Kimberly Selvick		TW	1975	D	93*	57' 07"	28' 00"	10' 00"

Built: Grafton Boat Co., Grafton, IL (Scout 1 '75-'02)

Lake Trader		DB	1982	B	2,262*	250' 00"	72' 00"	17' 00"

Built: Forked Island Shipyard Inc., Abbeville, LA (TJ 2501, Primary 1)

Nathan S	8841967	TB	1962	D	194*	91' 00"	29' 00"	11' 06"

Built: Main Iron Works, Houma, LA (Donald C. Hannah '62-'09, Donald C. '09-'17)

Niki S		TB	1971	D	39*	42' 00"	18' 00"	6' 00"

Built: Scully Bros. Boat Builders, Morgan City, LA (Miss Josie '71-'79, Matador VI '79-'08)

Terry D		TB	1954	D	76*	66' 00"	19' 00"	9' 00"

Built: Liberty Dry Dock Inc., Brooklyn, NY (Sanita '54-'77, Soo Chief '77-'81, Susan M. Selvick '81-'96, Nathan S. '96-'02, John M. Perry '02-'08, Zuccolo '08-'12, Carla Selvick '12-'14)

CANADA STEAMSHIP LINES INC., MONTREAL, QC – DIVISION OF THE CSL GROUP INC. (cslships.com)

Atlantic Huron {2}	8025680	SU	1984	D	34,860	736' 07"	77' 11"	46' 04"

Built: Collingwood Shipyards, Collingwood, ON; converted to a self-unloader in '89 and widened 3' in '03 at Port Weller Dry Docks, St. Catharines, ON (Prairie Harvest '84-'89, Atlantic Huron {2} '89-'94, Melvin H. Baker II {2} '94-'97)

Baie Comeau {2}	9639892	SU	2013	D	37,690	739' 10"	77' 11"	48' 05"

Built: Chengxi Shipyard Co. Ltd., Jiangyin City, China

Baie St. Paul {2}	9601027	SU	2012	D	37,690	739' 10"	77' 11"	48' 05"

Built: Chengxi Shipyard Co. Ltd., Jiangyin City, China

CSL Assiniboine	7413218	SU	1977	D	36,768	739' 10"	78' 00"	48' 05"

Built: Davie Shipbuilding Co., Lauzon, QC; rebuilt with a new forebody at Port Weller Dry Docks, St. Catharines, ON, in '05; repowered in '15 (**Stern section:** Jean Parisien '77-'05)

CSL Laurentien	7423108	SU	1977	D	37,795	739' 10"	78' 00"	48' 05"

Built: Collingwood Shipyards, Collingwood, ON; rebuilt with new forebody in '01 at Port Weller Dry Docks, St. Catharines, ON; repowered in '15 (**Stern section:** Louis R. Desmarais '77-'01)

Tug Michigan and cement-carrying barge Innovation. (Paul C. LaMarre III)

Edgar B. Speer making the turn at Mission Point on the St. Marys River. (Eric Treece)

Fleet Name / Vessel Name	Vessel IMO #	Vessel Type	Year Built	Engine Type	Cargo Cap. or Gross*	Overall Length	Vessel Breadth	Vessel Depth
CSL Niagara	7128423	SU	1972	D	37,694	739'10"	78'00"	48'05"

*Built: Collingwood Shipyards, Collingwood, ON; rebuilt with a new forebody in '99 at Port Weller Dry Docks, St. Catharines, ON; repowered in '14 (**Stern section: J. W. McGiffin '72-'99**)*

CSL St-Laurent	9665281	BC	2014	D	35,529	739'10"	77'11"	48'05"

Built: Yangfan Shipbuilding Co. Ltd., Zhoushan City, China

CSL Tadoussac	6918716	SU	1969	D	30,051	730'00"	77'11"	41'11"

Built: Collingwood Shipyards, Collingwood, ON; rebuilt with new mid-body, widened 3' at Port Weller Dry Docks, St. Catharines, ON, in '01 (Tadoussac {2} '69-'01)

CSL Welland	9665279	BC	2014	D	35,529	739'10"	77'11"	48'05"

Built: Yangfan Shipbuilding Co. Ltd., Zhoushan City, China

Ferbec {2}	9259848	SU	2002	D	28,910	615'02"	101'08"	54'11"

Built: COSCO KHI Ship Engineering Co. Ltd., Nantong, China; vessel is too large for the St. Lawrence Seaway but is a frequent visitor to the St. Lawrence River (Orientor 2 '02-10, CSL Melbourne '10-'17)

Frontenac {5}	6804848	SU	1968	D	26,822	729'07"	75'00"	39'08"

Built: Davie Shipbuilding Co., Lauzon, QC; converted to a self-unloader by Collingwood Shipyards, Collingwood, ON, in '73

Nukumi	9914711	SU	2022	D	25,800	738'11"	78'00"	N/A

Built: Chengxi Shipyard Co. Ltd., Jiangyin City, China

Oakglen {3}	7901148	BC	1980	D	35,067	729'11"	75'10"	47'01"

Built: Boelwerf Vlaanderen Shipbuilding N.V., Temse, Belgium (Federal Danube '80-'95, Lake Ontario '95-'09)

Rt. Hon. Paul J. Martin	7324405	SU	1973	D	37,694	739'07"	77'11"	48'04"

*Built: Collingwood Shipyards, Collingwood, ON; rebuilt with a new forebody in '00 at Port Weller Dry Docks, St. Catharines, ON; repowered in '14 (**Stern section: H. M. Griffith '73-'00**)*

Spruceglen {2}	8119261	BC	1983	D	33,824	730'01"	75'09"	48'00"

Built: Govan Shipyards, Glasgow, Scotland (Selkirk Settler '83-'91, Federal St. Louis '91-'91, Federal Fraser {2} '91-'01, Fraser '01-'02)

Thunder Bay {3}	9601039	SU	2013	D	37,690	739'10"	77'11"	48'05"

Built: Chengxi Shipyard Co. Ltd., Jiangyin City, China

Whitefish Bay {2}	9639880	SU	2013	D	37,690	739'10"	77'11"	48'05"

Built: Chengxi Shipyard Co. Ltd., Jiangyin City, China

CANADIAN COAST GUARD (FISHERIES AND OCEANS CANADA), OTTAWA, ON (www.ccg-gcc.gc.ca)
CENTRAL AND ARCTIC REGION, MONTREAL, QC

A. LeBlanc	9586060	PV	2014	D	253*	141'07"	22'09"	9'09

Built: Irving Shipbuilding Inc., Halifax, NS; stationed at Quebec City, QC

Amundsen	7510846	IB	1978	D	5,910*	295'09"	63'09"	31'04"

Built: Burrard Dry Dock Co., North Vancouver, BC (Sir John Franklin '78-'03); stationed at Quebec City, QC

Cape Chaillon, Cape Commodore, Cape Discovery, Cape Dundas, Cape Hearne,								
Cape Providence, Cape Rescue		SR	2004	D	34*	47'09"	14'00"	4'05"
Cape Lambton, Cape Mercy, Thunder Cape		SR	2000	D	34*	47'09"	14'00"	4'05"
Cape Storm		SR	1999	D	34*	47'09"	14'00"	4'05"
Caporal Kaeble V.C.	9586045	PV	2012	D	253*	141'07"	22'09"	9'09"

Built: Irving Shipbuilding Inc., Halifax, NS; stationed at Quebec City, QC

Tank barge Margaret and tug Albert on the St. Clair River.
(George Haynes)

Fleet Name Vessel Name	Vessel IMO #	Vessel Type	Year Built	Engine Type	Cargo Cap. or Gross*	Overall Length	Vessel Breadth	Vessel Depth
Caribou Isle		BT	1985	D	92*	75' 06"	19' 08"	7' 04"

Built: Breton Industrial & Marine Ltd., Port Hawkesbury, NS; stationed at Prescott, ON

Constable Carrière	9586069	PV	2012	D	253*	141' 07"	22' 09"	9' 09"

Built: Irving Shipbuilding Inc., Halifax, NS; stationed at Quebec City, QC

Cove Isle		BT	1980	D	80*	65' 07"	19' 08"	7' 04"

Built: Canadian Dredge & Dock Co. Ltd., Kingston, ON; stationed at Parry Sound, ON

Des Groseilliers	8006385	IB	1983	D	5,910*	322' 07"	64' 00"	35' 06"

Built: Port Weller Dry Docks, St. Catharines, ON; stationed at Quebec City, QC

F.C.G. Smith	8322686	SV	1985	D	439*	114' 02"	45' 11"	11' 02"

Built: Georgetown Shipyard, Georgetown, PEI; status is listed as decommissioned at Quebec City, QC

Griffon	7022887	IB	1970	D	2,212*	234' 00"	49' 00"	21' 06"

Built: Davie Shipbuilding Co., Lauzon, QC; stationed at Prescott, ON

Île Saint-Ours		BT	1986	D		75' 05"	23' 00"	4' 04"

Built: Breton Industrial & Marine Ltd., Port Hawkesbury, NS; stationed at Sorel-Tracy, QC

Judy LaMarsh	9560120	IB	2010	D	1828*	217' 51"	53' 80"	14' 04"

Built: STX RO Offshore, Braila, Romania; rebuilt as an icebreaker in '22 (Mangystau-2 '10-'22)

Kelso		RV	2009	D	63*	57' 07"	17' 01"	4' 09"

Built: ABCO Industries Ltd., Lunenburg, NS; stationed at Burlington, ON

Limnos	6804903	RV	1968	D	489*	147' 00"	32' 00"	12' 00"

Built: Port Weller Dry Docks, St. Catharines, ON; stationed at Burlington, ON

Martha L. Black	8320432	IB	1986	D	3,818*	272' 04"	53' 02"	25' 02"

Built: Versatile Pacific Shipyards, Victoria, BC; stationed at Quebec City, QC

Pierre Radisson	7510834	IB	1978	D	5,910*	322' 00"	62' 10"	35' 06"

Built: Burrard Dry Dock Co., North Vancouver, BC; stationed at Quebec City, QC

Private Robertson VC	9586033	PV	2012	D	253*	141' 07"	22' 09"	9' 09"

Built: Irving Shipbuilding Inc., Halifax, NS

Samuel Risley	8322442	IB	1985	D	1,988*	228' 09"	47' 01"	21' 09"

Built: Vito Steel Boat & Barge Construction Ltd., Delta, BC; stationed at Parry Sound, ON

Vincent Massey	9199622	IB	2000	D	3,382*	274' 06"	57' 00"	27' 09"

Built: Havyard Leirvik AS, Leirvik, Norway; stationed at Quebec, QC (Tor Viking '00-'03, Tor Viking II '03-'20)

CANAMAC BOAT CRUISES, TORONTO, ON *(torontoboatcruises.com)*

Stella Borealis		ES	1989	D	356*	118' 00"	26' 00"	7' 00"

Built: Duratug Shipyard & Fabricating Ltd., Port Dover, ON

CARGILL LIMITED, BAIE COMEAU, QC *(cargill.ca)*

L'Anse du Moulin	8668248	TT	2007	D	350*	90' 05"	36' 07"	13' 08"

Built: Shanghai Harbor Foxing, Shanghai, China; operated by Groupe Océan (Hai Gang 107 '07-'14, Svitzer Wombi '14-'15, Svitzer Cartier '15-'17, Océan Cartier '17-'18)

CARMEUSE NORTH AMERICA (ERIE SAND & GRAVEL), ERIE, PA *(carmeusena.com)*

J.S. St. John	5202524	SC	1945	D	415*	174' 00"	31' 09"	15' 00"

Built: Smith Shipyards & Engineering Corp., Pensacola, FL (USS YO-178 '45-'51, Lake Edward '51-'67)

John J. Boland navigating the narrow Sturgeon Bay Ship Canal. (Korey Garceau)

Fleet Name Vessel Name	Vessel IMO #	Vessel Type	Year Built	Engine Type	Cargo Cap. or Gross*	Overall Length	Vessel Breadth	Vessel Depth
CEMBA MOTOR SHIPS LTD., PELEE ISLAND, ON								
Cemba		TK	1960	D	17*	50'00"	15'06"	7'06"

CENTRAL MARINE LOGISTICS INC., GRIFFITH, IN *(centralmarinelogistics.com)*
   MANAGER FOR CLEVELAND-CLIFFS INC., CLEVELAND, OH *(clevelandcliffs.com)*

Edward L. Ryerson	5097606	BC	1960	T	27,500	730'00"	75'00"	39'00"

    Built: Manitowoc Shipbuilding Co., Manitowoc, WI; in long-term lay-up at Superior, WI, since May 2009; indications are a return to service in '23 is possible

Joseph L. Block	7502320	SU	1976	D	37,200	728'00"	78'00"	45'00"

    Built: Bay Shipbuilding Co., Sturgeon Bay, WI

Wilfred Sykes	5389554	SU	1949	T	21,500	678'00"	70'00"	37'00"

    Built: American Shipbuilding Co., Lorain, OH; converted to a self-unloader by Fraser Shipyards, Superior, WI, in '75

CENTRAL MICHIGAN UNIVERSITY, COLLEGE OF SCIENCE & TECHNOLOGIES, MOUNT PLEASANT, MI

Chippewa		RV	2013	D	17*	34'09"	12'00"	6'03"

CHAMPION'S AUTO FERRY, ALGONAC, MI *(hiferry.com)*

Champion		CF	1941	D	69*	65'00"	25'09"	5'08"
Middle Channel		CF	1997	D	81*	79'00"	30'00"	6'05"
North Channel		CF	1967	D	67*	75'00"	30'04"	6'01"
South Channel		CF	1973	D	94*	79'00"	30'03"	6'01"

CHARITY ISLAND TRANSPORT INC., AU GRES, MI *(charityisland.net)*

North Star		PA	1949	D	14*	50'05"	14'06"	3'06"

    Built: J.W. Nolan & Sons, Erie, PA

CHICAGO DEPARTMENT OF WATER MANAGEMENT, CHICAGO, IL

James J. Versluis		TB	1957	D	126*	83'00"	22'00"	11'02"

    Built: Sturgeon Bay Shipbuilding Co., Sturgeon Bay, WI

CHICAGO FIRE DEPARTMENT, CHICAGO, IL

Christopher Wheatley		FB	2011	D	300*	90'00"	25'00"	12'02"
Victor L. Schlaeger		FB	1949	D	350*	92'06"	24'00"	11'00"

CHICAGO FIREBOAT TOURS, CHICAGO, IL *(fireboattours.com)*

Fred A. Busse		ES	1937	D	99*	92'00"	22'04"	9'06"

    Built: Defoe Boat & Motor Works, Bay City, MI; former Chicago fireboat offers cruises at Chicago, IL

CITY CRUISES INC., CHICAGO, IL *(cityexperiences.com)*

Odyssey Chicago River		ES	2018	D	93*	133'10"	31'10"	9'20"
Odyssey Lake Michigan		ES	1993	D	81*	162'50"	40'00"	23'50"
Spirit of Chicago		ES	1988	D	92*	156'70"	35'00"	7'01"
Spirit of Navy Pier		ES	1998	D	97*	138'09"	36'00"	10'05"

CITY OF TORONTO, TORONTO, ON *(toronto.ca/parks)*

Ned Hanlan II		TB	1966	D	22*	41'06"	14'01"	5'05"

    Built: Erieau Shipbuilding & Drydock Co. Ltd., Erieau, ON

Thunder Bay departing her namesake port. (Michael Hull)

Fleet Name / Vessel Name	Vessel IMO #	Vessel Type	Year Built	Engine Type	Cargo Cap. or Gross*	Overall Length	Vessel Breadth	Vessel Depth
Ongiara	6410374	PA/CF	1963	D	180*	78' 00"	36' 01"	9' 09"
Built: Russel Brothers Ltd., Owen Sound, ON								
Sam McBride		PF	1939	D	387*	129' 00"	34' 11"	6' 00"
Built: Toronto Dry Dock Co. Ltd., Toronto, ON								
Thomas Rennie		PF	1951	D	387*	129' 00"	32' 11"	6' 00"
Built: Toronto Dry Dock Co. Ltd., Toronto, ON								
Trillium		PF	1910	R	564*	150' 00"	30' 00"	8' 04"
Built: Polson Iron Works, Toronto, ON; last sidewheel-propelled vessel on the Great Lakes								
William Inglis		PF	1935	D	238*	99' 00"	24' 10"	6' 00"
Built: John Inglis Co. Ltd., Toronto, ON (Shamrock {2} '35-'37)								
CJC CRUISES INC., GRAND LEDGE, MI *(detroitprincess.com)*								
Detroit Princess		PA	1993	D	1,430*	222' 00"	62' 00"	11' 01"
Built: Leevac Shipyards Inc., Jennings, LA (Players Riverboat Casino II '93-'04)								
CLEVELAND FIRE DEPARTMENT, CLEVELAND, OH								
Anthony J. Celebrezze		FB	1961	D	42*	66' 00"	17' 00"	5' 00"
Built: Paasch Marine Services Inc., Erie, PA								
COBBY MARINE (1985) INC., KINGSVILLE, ON								
Vida C.		TB	1960	D	17*	46 '03"	15' 05"	3' 02"
COLLINGWOOD CHARTERS INC., COLLINGWOOD, ON *(collingwoodcharters.ca)*								
Huronic		PA	1999	D	60	56' 03"	19' 00"	6' 04"
COOPER MARINE LTD., SELKIRK, ON								
Ella G. Cooper		PB	1972	D	21*	43' 00"	14' 00"	6' 05"
Janice C. No. 1		TB	1980	D	33*	57' 00"	20' 00"	6' 00"
J.W. Cooper		PB	1984	D	25*	48' 00"	14' 07"	5' 00"
Kimberley A. Cooper		TB	1974	D	17*	40' 00"	13' 05"	4' 05"
Mrs. C.		PB	1991	D	26*	50' 00"	14' 05"	4' 05"
Stacey Dawn		TB	1993	D	14*	35' 09"	17' 04"	3' 05"
Wilson T. Cooper		DB	2009	D	58*	56' 08"	23' 06"	5' 08"
CORPORATION OF THE TOWNSHIP OF FRONTENAC ISLANDS, WOLFE ISLAND, ON *(frontenacislands.ca)*								
Howe Islander		CF	1946	Cable	13*	53' 00"	12' 00"	3' 00"
Built: Canadian Dredge & Dock Co. Ltd., Kingston, ON; ferry offers service from Kingston, ON, to Howe Island, ON								
Simcoe Islander		PF	1964	D	24*	47' 09"	18' 00"	3' 06"
Built: Canadian Dredge & Dock Co. Ltd., Kingston, ON; ferry links Wolfe Island, ON, to Simcoe Island, ON								
CROISIÈRES AML INC., QUEBEC CITY, QC *(croisieresaml.com)*								
AML Alize		ES	1980	D	39*	41' 00"	15' 01"	6' 01"
AML Cavalier Maxim	5265904	ES	1962	D	752*	191' 02"	42' 00"	11' 07"
Built: John I. Thornycroft & Co., Wollston, Southampton, England (Osborne Castle '62-'78, Le Gobelet D' Argent '78-'88, Gobelet D' Argent '88-'89, Le Maxim '89-'93)								

U.S. Navy's Blue Angels perform at Chicago's Air & Water Show, with USCG Katmai Bay in the foreground. *(Matt Adamski)*

Fleet Name / Vessel Name	Vessel IMO #	Vessel Type	Year Built	Engine Type	Cargo Cap. or Gross*	Overall Length	Vessel Breadth	Vessel Depth
AML Grand Fleuve		ES	1987	D	499*	145' 00"	30' 00"	5' 06"
Built: Kanter Yacht Co., St. Thomas, ON								
AML Levant	9056404	ES	1991	D	380*	112' 07"	29' 00"	10' 02"
Built: Goelette Marie Clarisse Inc., LaBaleine, QC (Famille Dufour)								
AML Louis Jolliet	5212749	ES	1938	R	2,436*	170' 01"	70' 00"	17' 00"
Built: Davie Shipbuilding Co., Lauzon, QC								
AML Suroît		ES	2002	D	171*	82' 00"	27' 00"	6' 00"
Built: RTM Construction, Petite Rivière-St-François, QC (Le Coudrier de l'Isle '02-'14)								
AML Zephyr		ES	1992	D	171*	82' 00"	27' 00"	6' 00"
Built: Katamarine International, Paspebiac, QC (Le Coudrier de l'Anse '92-'14)								

CRUISE TORONTO INC., TORONTO ON (cruisetoronto.com and greatlakesschooner.com)

Fleet Name / Vessel Name	Vessel IMO #	Vessel Type	Year Built	Engine Type	Cargo Cap. or Gross*	Overall Length	Vessel Breadth	Vessel Depth
Challenge		ES	1980	W/D	76*	96' 00"	16' 06"	8' 00"
Built: Kanter Yachts Co., Port Stanley, ON								
Kajama		ES	1930	W/D	263*	128' 09"	22' 09"	11' 08"
Built: Nobiskrug, Rendsburg, Germany								
Obsession III		ES	1967	D	160*	66' 00"	25' 00"	6' 01"
Built: Halter Marine, New Orleans, LA (Mystique)								

C.T.M.A., CAP-AUX-MEULES, QC (ctma.ca)

Fleet Name / Vessel Name	Vessel IMO #	Vessel Type	Year Built	Engine Type	Cargo Cap. or Gross*	Overall Length	Vessel Breadth	Vessel Depth
C.T.M.A. Vacancier	7310260	PA/RR	1973	D	11,481*	388' 04"	70' 02"	42' 03"
Built: J.J. Sietas KG Schiffswerft, Hamburg, Germany (Aurella '80-'82, Saint Patrick II '82 '98, Egnatia II '98-'00, Ville de Sete '00-'01, City of Cork '01-'02)								
C.T.M.A. Voyageur 2	9119402	PA/RR	1996	D	7,606*	368' 11"	64' 11"	42; 32"
Built: Astilleros de Huelva, Huelva, Spain (Dart 7 '96-'99, Lembitu '99-'00, RR Challenge '00-'07, Challenge '07-'08, Clipper Ranger '08-'19)								
Madeleine II	9430105	PA/RR	2008	D	5,893	415' 00"	72' 02"	26' 09"
Built: Factorias Vulcano S.A., Vigo, Spain								

D
___

DAN MINOR & SONS INC., PORT COLBORNE, ON

Fleet Name / Vessel Name	Vessel IMO #	Vessel Type	Year Built	Engine Type	Cargo Cap. or Gross*	Overall Length	Vessel Breadth	Vessel Depth
Andrea Marie I		WB	1986	D	87*	75' 02"	24' 07"	7' 03"
Built: Ralph Hurley, Port Burwell, ON								
Jeanette M.		WB	1981	D	31*	70' 00"	20 01"	6' 00"
Built: Hike Metal Products, Wheatley, ON								

DEAN CONSTRUCTION CO. LTD., WINDSOR, ON (deanconstructioncompany.com)

Fleet Name / Vessel Name	Vessel IMO #	Vessel Type	Year Built	Engine Type	Cargo Cap. or Gross*	Overall Length	Vessel Breadth	Vessel Depth
Annie M. Dean		TB	1981	D	58*	50' 00"	19' 00"	5' 00"
Built: Dean Construction Co., LaSalle, ON								
Bobby Bowes		TB	1944	D	11*	37' 04"	10' 02"	3' 06"
Built: Russel Brothers Ltd., Owen Sound, ON								
Canadian Jubilee		DR	1978	B	896*	149' 09"	56' 01"	11' 01"
Neptune III		TB	1939	D	23*	53' 10"	15' 06"	5' 00"
Built: Herb Colley, Port Stanley, ON								

DEAN MARINE & EXCAVATING INC., MOUNT CLEMENS, MI (deanmarineandexcavating.com)

Fleet Name / Vessel Name	Vessel IMO #	Vessel Type	Year Built	Engine Type	Cargo Cap. or Gross*	Overall Length	Vessel Breadth	Vessel Depth
Andrew J.		TB	1950	D	25*	47' 00"	15' 07"	8' 00"
Built: J.F. Bellinger & Sons, Jacksonville, FL								
Enduring Freedom		TB	2001	D	88*	59' 08"	22' 00"	8' 00"
Built: Orange Shipbuilding, Orange, TX (ST-911)								
Kimberly Anne		TB	1965	D	65*	55' 02"	18' 08"	8' 00"
Built: Main Iron Works, Houma, LA (Lady Lisa, Lucy, Miss Alma)								
Madison R.	5126615	TB	1958	D	194*	103' 00"	26' 06"	12' 00"
Built: Gulfport Shipbuilding, Port Arthur, TX (Alabama '58-'77, Ares '77-'09, Nels J '09-'17)								
Megan J.		TB	1967	D	22*	41' 09"	12' 04"	6' 06"
Built: Equitable Equipment Co., Madisonville, LA (Miss Jaclyn, Dottie-Do, Jaclyn)								
West Wind		TB	1941	D	53*	60' 00"	17' 01	7' 06"
Built: Lester F. Alexander, New Orleans, LA (West Wind '41-'51, Russell 2 '51-'61)								

DEEP WATER MARINE, HOLLAND, MI (deepwatermarine.net)

Fleet Name / Vessel Name	Vessel IMO #	Vessel Type	Year Built	Engine Type	Cargo Cap. or Gross*	Overall Length	Vessel Breadth	Vessel Depth
G.W. Falcon		TB	1936	D	22*	49' 07"	13' 08"	6' 02"
Built: Fred E. Alford, Waukegan, IL (Lillie B. '36-'57)								
James Harris		TB	1943	D	18*	41' 09"	12' 05"	5' 00"

DETROIT CITY FIRE DEPARTMENT, DETROIT, MI

Fleet Name / Vessel Name	Vessel IMO #	Vessel Type	Year Built	Engine Type	Cargo Cap. or Gross*	Overall Length	Vessel Breadth	Vessel Depth
Curtis Randolph		FB	1979	D	85*	77' 10"	21' 06"	9' 03"
Built: Peterson Builders Inc., Sturgeon Bay, WI								

Fleet Name Vessel Name	Vessel IMO #	Vessel Type	Year Built	Engine Type	Cargo Cap. or Gross*	Overall Length	Vessel Breadth	Vessel Depth
Sivad Johnson		FB	2020	D		32' 00"	10' 06"	11' 06"

Built: Silver Ships, Mobile, AL; named in honor of a Detroit firefighter who died while saving two girls from drowning in the Detroit River in 2020

DETROIT CRUISE CO., DETROIT, MI

Samuel D. Buchanan		PA	1949	D	10*	63' 07"	15' 03"	4' 08"
(Clinton '49-'21)								

DIAMOND JACK'S RIVER TOURS, DETROIT, MI *(diamondjack.com)*

Diamond Belle		ES	1958	D	93*	93' 06"	25' 00"	7' 00"

Built: Hans Hansen Welding Co., Toledo, OH (Mackinac Islander {2} '58-'90, Sir Richard '90-'91)

Diamond Queen		ES	1956	D	94*	92' 00"	25' 00"	7' 02"

Built: Marinette Marine Corp., Marinette, WI (Mohawk '56-'96)

DK CONSTRUCTION INC., HOLLAND, MI *(dkconstruction.com)*

Haskal		TB	1937	D	19*	37' 00"	10' 04"	5' 01"

DISCOVERY CRUISES, TRAVERSE CITY, MI *(discoverycruisestc.com)*

Discovery		ES	1974	D	57*	62' 03"	22' 00"	7' 01"

Built: Blount Marine Corp., Warren, RI (Charles Town Belle, River Rose)

DONKERSLOOT MARINE DEVELOPMENT CORP., NEW BUFFALO, MI *(donkerslootmarine.com)*

Miss Jamie Lynn		DR	1989	D	254*	120' 00"	34' 00"	5' 06"

DOORNEKAMP LINES, PICTON, ONTARIO *(doornekamplines.ca)*

Amy Lynn D.	9688659	TB	2013	D	327*	106' 00"	29' 10"	10' 01"

Built: Damen Shipyards, Hardinxveld, Netherlands (Otago '13-'18, MSC Allianz Explorer '18-'20)

Dowden Spirit		DB	2014	B	2,130*	250' 02"	72' 01"	16' 04"

Built: Glovertown Shipyards Ltd., Glovertown, ON

Jacob Joseph C	9642631	DB	2020	B	2,076*	233' 08"	77' 09"	14' 09"

Built: Damen Shipyards, Hardinxveld, Netherlands

Sheri Lynn S		TB	2017	D	55*	52' 03"	18' 02"	9' 05"

Built: Damen Shipyards, Yichang City, China

DREW HARRISON HAULAGE LTD., PICTON, ON

A.L. Killaly		TB	1942	D	36*	55' 06"	14' 06"	5' 10"

Built: Russel Brothers Ltd., Owen Sound, ON (Ward '32-'47)

DRUMMOND ISLAND TALL SHIP CO., DRUMMOND ISLAND, MI *(ditallship.com)*

Huron Jewel		ES	2017	W/D	8*	78' 00"	14' 70"	2' 00"

DUC D'ORLEANS CRUISE BOAT, CORUNNA, ON *(ducdorleans.com)*

Duc d'Orleans II		ES	1987	D	120*	71' 03"	23' 02"	7' 07"

Built: Blount Marine Corp., Warren, RI (Spirit of Newport '87-'06)

DULUTH FIRE DEPARTMENT, DULUTH, MN *(duluthmn.gov/fire)*

Marine 19		FB	2019	D	N/A	31' 00"	10' 05"	N/A

The name honors the 19 firefighters who have died in the line of duty since the department's inception.

E

EASTERN UPPER PENINSULA TRANSPORTATION AUTHORITY, SAULT STE. MARIE, MI *(eupta.net)*

Drummond Islander III		CF	1989	D	96*	108' 00"	37' 00"	7' 02"

Built: Moss Point Marine Inc., Escatawpa, MS; ferry offers service from DeTour, MI, to Drummond Island, MI

Drummond Islander IV		CF	2000	D	97*	148' 00"	40' 00"	12' 00"

Built: Basic Marine Inc., Escanaba, MI; ferry offers service from DeTour, MI, to Drummond Island, MI

Neebish Islander II		CF	1946	D	89*	89' 00"	25' 09"	5' 08"

Built: Lock City Machine/Marine, Sault Ste. Marie, MI; laid up at Barbeau, MI (Sugar Islander '46-'95)

Neebish Islander III		CF	2022	D	N/A	92' 00"	33' 00"	7' 04"

Built: Burger Boat Co., Manitowoc, WI; ferry offers service from Barbeau, MI, to Neebish Island, MI

Sugar Islander II		CF	1995	D	90*	114' 00"	40' 00"	10' 00"

Built: Basic Marine Inc., Escanaba, MI; ferry offers service from Sault Ste. Marie, MI, to Sugar Island, MI

ECOMARIS, MONTREAL, QC *(ecomaris.org)*

Ecomaris		TV/2S	1999	W/D	28*	65' 02"	17' 07"	8' 03"
(Roter Sand '99-'18)								

EMPRESS OF CANADA ENTERPRISE LTD., TORONTO, ON *(empressofcanada.com)*

Empress of Canada		ES	1980	D	399*	116' 00"	28' 00"	6' 06"

Built: Hike Metal Products, Wheatley, ON (Island Queen V {2} '80-'89)

Fleet Name / Vessel Name	Vessel IMO #	Vessel Type	Year Built	Engine Type	Cargo Cap. or Gross*	Overall Length	Vessel Breadth	Vessel Depth
ERIE ISLANDS PETROLEUM INC., PUT-IN-BAY, OH								
Cantankerus		TK	1955	D	43*	56' 00"	14' 00"	6' 06"
Built: Marinette Marine Corp., Marinette, WI								
ESSROC CANADA, PICTON, ON								
Metis	5233585	CC	1956	B	5,800	331' 00"	43' 09"	26' 00"
Built: Davie Shipbuilding Co., Lauzon, QC; lengthened 72', deepened 3'6" in '59 and converted to a self-unloading cement barge in '91 by Kingston Shipbuilding & Dry Dock Co., Kingston, ON								
EXPLORERS CHARTERERS, CASEVILLE, MI (explorercharters.com)								
Lady of the Lake		ES	1946	D	39*	52' 00"	14' 00"	8' 00"
(Namaycush '46-'59, Manitou Isle '59-'18)								

F-G

Fleet Name / Vessel Name	Vessel IMO #	Vessel Type	Year Built	Engine Type	Cargo Cap. or Gross*	Overall Length	Vessel Breadth	Vessel Depth
FAMOUS SOO LOCKS BOAT TOURS, SAULT STE. MARIE, MI (famoussoolocks.com)								
Le Voyageur		ES	1959	D	70*	65' 00"	25' 00"	7' 00"
Built: Sturgeon Bay Shipbuilding & Dry Dock Co., Sturgeon Bay, WI								
Nokomis		ES	1959	D	70*	65' 00"	25' 00"	7' 00"
Built: Sturgeon Bay Shipbuilding & Dry Dock Co., Sturgeon Bay, WI								
FITZ SUSTAINABLE FORESTRY MANAGEMENT LTD., MANITOWANING, ON								
Wyn Cooper		TB	1973	D	25*	48' 00"	13' 00"	4' 00"
FIVE LAKES MARINE TOWING, STURGEON BAY, WI								
Cheyenne	6515851	TB	1965	D	146*	84' 05"	25' 03"	12' 06"
Built: Ira S. Bushey and Sons Inc., Brooklyn, NY (Glenwood '65-'70)								
FRASER SHIPYARDS INC., SUPERIOR, WI (frasershipyards.com)								
FSY III		TB	1959	D	30*	47' 04"	13' 00"	6' 06"
Built: Fraser-Nelson Shipyard & Drydock Co., Superior, WI (Susan A. Fraser '59-'78, Maxine Thompson '78-'14)								
FRIENDS OF PLUM AND PILOT ISLANDS, WASHINGTON ISLAND, WI (plumandpilot.org)								
Shoreline (The)		ES	1973	D	12*	33' 00"	11' 4"	3' 00"
GAELIC TUGBOAT CO., DETROIT, MI (gaelictugboat.com)								
Patricia Hoey {2}		TB	1949	D	146*	88' 06"	25' 06"	11' 00"
Built: Alexander Shipyard Inc., New Orleans, LA (Propeller '49-'82, Bantry Bay '82-'91)								
William Hoey {3}	5029946	TB	1951	D	149*	88' 06"	25' 06"	11' 00"
Built: Alexander Shipyard Inc., New Orleans, LA (Atlas '51-'84, Susan Hoey {1} '84-'85, Atlas '85-'87, Carolyn Hoey '87-'13)								
GALCON MARINE LTD., TORONTO, ON (galconmarine.com)								
Barney Drake (The)		TB	1954	D	10*	31' 02"	9' 05"	3' 04"
Built: Toronto Drydock Co. Ltd., Toronto ON (T.T.&S. No. 9)								
Hope G		TB	2018	D	38*	48' 00"	14' 76"	8' 00"
Built: Progressive Industrial Inc., Palmetto, FL								

French-flagged passenger ship Le Bellot meets laker Edwin H. Gott on the St. Marys River. (Roger LeLievre)

Fleet Name Vessel Name	Vessel IMO #	Vessel Type	Year Built	Engine Type	Cargo Cap. or Gross*	Overall Length	Vessel Breadth	Vessel Depth
Kenteau		TB	1937	D	15*	54' 07"	16' 04"	4' 02"
Built: George Gamble, Port Dover, ON								
Patricia D		TB	1958	D	12*	38' 08"	12' 00"	3' 08"
Built: Toronto Drydock Co. Ltd., Toronto, ON (Big Chief III)								
William Rest		TB	1961	D	62*	65' 00"	18' 06"	10' 06"
Built: Erieau Shipbuilding & Drydock Co. Ltd., Erieau, ON								

GANANOQUE BOAT LINE BY HORNBLOWER, GANANOQUE, ON *(ganboatline.com)*

Fleet Name Vessel Name	Vessel IMO #	Vessel Type	Year Built	Engine Type	Cargo Cap. or Gross*	Overall Length	Vessel Breadth	Vessel Depth
Thousand Islander	7227346	ES	1972	D	200*	96' 11"	22' 01"	5' 05"
Thousand Islander II	7329936	ES	1973	D	200*	99' 00"	22' 01"	5' 00"
Thousand Islander III	8744963	ES	1975	D	376*	118' 00"	28' 00"	6' 00"
Thousand Islander IV	7947984	ES	1976	D	347*	110' 09"	28' 04"	10' 08"
Thousand Islander V	8745187	ES	1979	D	246*	88' 00"	24' 00"	5' 00"

GANNON UNIVERSITY, ERIE, PA *(gannon.edu)*

Fleet Name Vessel Name	Vessel IMO #	Vessel Type	Year Built	Engine Type	Cargo Cap. or Gross*	Overall Length	Vessel Breadth	Vessel Depth
Environaut		RV	1950	D	18*	48' 00"	13' 00"	4' 05"

GEO. GRADEL CO., TOLEDO, OH *(geogradelco.com)*

Fleet Name Vessel Name	Vessel IMO #	Vessel Type	Year Built	Engine Type	Cargo Cap. or Gross*	Overall Length	Vessel Breadth	Vessel Depth
Bessie B		TB	1947	D	30*	52' 03"	13' 09"	5' 05"
Built: Fred Socie, Toledo, OH								
George Gradel		TB	1956	D	128*	84' 00"	26' 00"	9' 02"
Built: Parker Brothers & Co. Inc., Houston, TX (Harbor Queen '56-'76, St. John '76-'16)								
John Francis		TB	1965	D	99*	75' 00"	22' 00"	9' 00"
Built: Bollinger Shipbuilding Inc., Lockport, LA (Dad '65-'98, Creole Eagle '98-'03)								
Josephine		TB	1957	D		86' 09"	20' 00"	7' 06"
Built: Willemsoord Naval Yard, Den Helder, Netherlands; recreational tug								
Mighty Jake		TB	1969	D	15*	36' 00"	12' 03"	7' 03"
Built: Lone Star Marine Salvage, Houston, TX								
Mighty John III		TB	1962	D	24*	45' 00"	15' 00"	5' 10"
Built: Toronto Drydock Co., Toronto, ON (Niagara Queen '62-'99)								
Norman G		DB	2016	B	578*	141' 01"	54' 00"	10' 00"
Pioneerland		TB	1943	D	53*	58' 00"	16' 08"	8' 00"
Built: Maritime Oil Transport Co., Houston, TX								
Prairieland		TB	1955	D	35*	49' 02"	15' 02"	6' 00"
Built: Main Iron Works, Houma, LA								
Timberland		TB	1946	D	20*	41' 03"	13' 01"	7' 00"

GEORGIAN SPIRIT CRUISES, MIDLAND, ON *(georgianspiritcruises.com)*

Fleet Name Vessel Name	Vessel IMO #	Vessel Type	Year Built	Engine Type	Cargo Cap. or Gross*	Overall Length	Vessel Breadth	Vessel Depth
Georgian Spirit		ES	1968	D	112*	85' 00"	23' 04"	7' 03"
Built: Hike Metal Products, Wheatley, ON (Peche Island V '68-'71, Papoose V '71-'82, Friendship '82-'19, Spirit of the Kawarthas '19-'21)								

GILLEN MARINE CONSTRUCTION LLC, MEQUON, WI *(gillenmarine.com)*

Fleet Name Vessel Name	Vessel IMO #	Vessel Type	Year Built	Engine Type	Cargo Cap. or Gross*	Overall Length	Vessel Breadth	Vessel Depth
Kristin J.		TB	1963	D	60*	52' 06"	19' 01"	7' 04"
Built: St. Charles Steel Works, Thibodaux, LA (Milly Lee, Jason A. Kadinger '63-'06)								

Kaministiqua and a herd of deer share the ice near Sault Ste. Marie, ON. (Graham Grattan)

Fleet Name Vessel Name	Vessel IMO #	Vessel Type	Year Built	Engine Type	Cargo Cap. or Gross*	Overall Length	Vessel Breadth	Vessel Depth
GOODTIME CRUISE LINE INC., CLEVELAND, OH *(goodtimeiii.com)*								
Goodtime III		ES	1990	D	95*	161'00"	40'00"	11'00"
Built: Leevac Shipyards Inc., Jennings, LA								
GORDON'S SHORELINE MARINE, SARNIA, ON *(gordonsm.com)*								
Sandra-E		TB	1954	D	34*	40'10"	12'02"	4'05"
Built: Russel Brothers Ltd., Owen Sound, ON (Sandra-E, Marion B.)								
GRAND PORTAGE / ISLE ROYALE TRANSPORTATION LINES, GRAND PORTAGE, MN *(isleroyaleboats.com)*								
Sea Hunter III		ES	1985	D	47*	65'00"	16'00"	7'05"
Voyageur II		ES	1970	D	40*	63'00"	18'00"	5'00"
GRAND RIVER NAVIGATION CO. – SEE RAND LOGISITCS INC.								
GRAND VALLEY STATE UNIVERSITY, ROBERT B. ANNIS WATER RESOURCES, MUSKEGON, MI *(gvsu.edu/wri)*								
D.J. Angus		RV	1986	D	16*	45'00"	14'00"	4'00"
W.G. Jackson		RV	1996	D	80*	64'10"	20'00"	5'00"
GRAYFOX ASSOCIATION, PORT HURON, MI								
Grayfox		TV	1985	D	213*	120'00"	25'00"	12'00"
Built: Marinette Marine Corp., Marinette, WI; at press time it was learned this vessel had been sold to MCM Marine Inc., Sault Ste. Marie, MI (USS TWR-825 '85-'97)								
GREAT LAKES DOCK & MATERIALS LLC, MUSKEGON, MI *(greatlakesdock.com)*								
Defiance		TB	1965	D	39*	48'00"	18'00"	6'03"
Built: Harrison Bros. Drydock, Mobile, AL								
Duluth		TB	1954	D	87*	70'01"	19'05"	9'08"
Built: Missouri Valley Bridge & Iron Works, Leavenworth, KS (U. S. Army ST-2015 '54-'62)								
Ethan George		TB	1940	D	27*	42'05"	12'08"	6'06"
Built: Sturgeon Bay Shipbuilding, Sturgeon Bay, WI (Holland, Captain Roy)								
Fischer Hayden		TB	1967	D	64*	54'00"	22'01"	7'01"
Built: Main Iron Works Inc., Houma, LA (Gloria G. Cheramie, Joyce P. Crosby)								
George F. Bailey	8951487	TB	1981	D	127*	68'08"	26'01"	9'04"
Built: Service Marine Group Inc., Amelia, LA (Alpha, Specialist, The Rock '12-'16, Meredith Ashton {1} '16-'20)								
Hannah Avery		DB	2001	B	423*	140'00"	45'00	16'00"
Sarah B.		TB	1953	D	23*	45'00"	13'00"	7'00"
Built: Nashville Bridge Co., Nashville, TN (ST-2161 '53-'63, Tawas Bay '63-'03)								
GREAT LAKES FLEET INC., DULUTH, MN (KEY LAKES INC., MANAGER)								
Arthur M. Anderson	5025691	SU	1952	T	25,300	767'00"	70'00"	36'00"
Built: American Shipbuilding Co., Lorain, OH; lengthened 120' in '75 and converted to a self-unloader in '82 at Fraser Shipyards, Superior, WI								

Netherlands-flagged Humbergracht takes on a rare load of ore at Two Harbors, MN. (David Schauer)

Fleet Name Vessel Name	Vessel IMO #	Vessel Type	Year Built	Engine Type	Cargo Cap. or Gross*	Overall Length	Vessel Breadth	Vessel Depth
Cason J. Callaway	5065392	SU	1952	T	25,300	767' 00"	70' 00"	36' 00"

Built: Great Lakes Engineering Works, River Rouge, MI; lengthened 120' in '74 and converted to a self-unloader in '82 at Fraser Shipyards, Superior, WI; entered long-term lay-up at Sturgeon Bay, WI, Jan. 16, 2021

Edgar B. Speer	7625952	SU	1980	D	73,700	1,004' 00"	105' 00"	56' 00"

Built: American Shipbuilding Co., Lorain, OH

Edwin H. Gott	7606061	SU	1979	D	74,100	1,004' 00"	105' 00"	56' 00"

Built: Bay Shipbuilding Co., Sturgeon Bay, WI; converted from shuttle self-unloader to deck-mounted self-unloader in '96 at Bay Shipbuilding Co., Sturgeon Bay, WI

Great Republic	7914236	SU	1981	D	25,600	634' 10"	68' 00"	39' 07"

Built: Bay Shipbuilding Co., Sturgeon Bay, WI (American Republic '81-'11)

John G. Munson {2}	5173670	SU	1952	D	25,550	768' 03"	72' 00"	36' 00"

Built: Manitowoc Shipbuilding Co., Manitowoc, WI; lengthened 102' in '76 at Fraser Shipyards, Superior, WI; repowered in '16

Philip R. Clarke	5277062	SU	1952	T	25,300	767' 00"	70' 00"	36' 00"

Built: American Shipbuilding Co., Lorain, OH; lengthened 120' in '74 and converted to a self-unloader in '82 at Fraser Shipyards, Superior, WI

Presque Isle {2}	7303877	IT	1973	D	1,578*	153' 03"	54' 00"	31' 03"

Built: Halter Marine, New Orleans, LA; paired with the self-unloading barge Presque Isle

Presque Isle {2}		SU	1973	B	57,500	974' 06"	104' 07"	46' 06"
Tug/barge dimensions together:						1,000' 00"	104' 07"	46' 06"

Bow section built at DeFoe Shipbuilding Co., Bay City, MI, cargo section built at Erie Marine Inc., Erie, PA

Roger Blough	7222138	SU	1972	D	43,900	858' 00"	105' 00"	41' 06"

Built: American Shipbuilding Co., Lorain, OH; damaged by fire on Feb. 1, 2021, at Sturgeon Bay, WI, and laid up there; in Nov. '22 towed to Conneaut, OH, for continued lay up/eventual scrapping at Port Colborne, ON

GREAT LAKES GROUP, CLEVELAND, OH (thegreatlakesgroup.com)

THE GREAT LAKES TOWING CO., CLEVELAND, OH – DIVISION OF THE GREAT LAKES GROUP

Alaska		TB	1914	D	98*	81' 00"	20' 00"	12' 05"

Built: Great Lakes Towing Co., Cleveland, OH (Illinois {2} '14-'21)

Arizona		TB	1931	D	98*	84' 04"	19' 09"	11' 06"

Built: Great Lakes Towing Co., Cleveland, OH

Arkansas {2}		TB	1909	D	97*	81' 00"	20' 00"	12' 06"

Built: Great Lakes Towing Co., Cleveland, OH; oldest of the State class of tugs (Yale '09-'48)

Cameron O		TB	1955	D	26*	50' 00"	15' 00"	7' 03"

Built: Peterson Builders Inc., Sturgeon Bay, WI (Escort II '55-'06)

Cleveland		TB	2017	D	100*	63' 05"	24' 02"	11' 00"

Built: Great Lakes Shipyard, Cleveland, OH

Colorado		TB	1928	D	98*	84' 04"	20' 00"	12' 04"

Built: Great Lakes Towing Co., Cleveland, OH

USS Minneapolis-St. Paul departing Duluth, MN, after christening, May 2022, escorted by Heritage Marine tugs Edward H, Helen H and the U.S. Coast Guard. (David Schauer)

Fleet Name / Vessel Name	Vessel IMO #	Vessel Type	Year Built	Engine Type	Cargo Cap. or Gross*	Overall Length	Vessel Breadth	Vessel Depth
Donald J. Sarter		TB	1964	D	186*	87'06"	20'06"	11'02"
Built: Main Iron Works, Houma, LA (Point Comfort '64-'04, Horace '04-'14, Nancy J '14-'20)								
Erie		TB	1971	D	243*	102'03"	29'00"	16'03"
Built: Peterson Builders, Sturgeon Bay, WI (YTB 810 {Anoka} '71-'01, Missy McAllister '01-'15)								
Favorite		FD	1983		300 ton cap	90'00"	50'00"	5'00"
Florida		TB	1926	D	99*	81'00"	20'02"	11'02"
Built: Great Lakes Towing Co., Cleveland, OH (Florida '26-'83, Pinellas '83-'84)								
Georgia {3}		TB	1897	D	105*	90'03"	21'02"	9'06"
Built: Union Dry Dock Co., Buffalo, NY; oldest active tug on the Great Lakes (America {3} 1897-1982, Midway '82-'83, Wisconsin {4} '83-'21)								
Hawaii		TB	1911	DE	97*	81'00"	19'09"	11'06"
Built: Great Lakes Towing Co., Cleveland, OH (Indiana '11-'21)								
Illinois		TB	2021	D	100*	63'05"	24'02"	11'00"
Built: Great Lakes Shipyard, Cleveland, OH								
Indiana		TB	2022	D	100*	63'05"	24'02"	11'00"
Built: Great Lakes Shipyard, Cleveland, OH								
Iowa		TB	1915	D	97*	81'00"	19'09"	11'06"
Built: Great Lakes Towing Co., Cleveland, OH								
Jacquelyn Yvonne		TB	1943	D	29*	45'02"	12'10"	7'08"
Built: Sturgeon Bay Shipbuilding Co., Sturgeon Bay, WI (ST-173 '43-'55, Manistee '55-'87, Robert W. Purcell '87-'17)								
Jimmy L		TB	1939	D	148*	110'00"	25'00"	13'00"
Built: Defoe Shipbuilding Co., Bay City, MI (WYTM 92-Naugatuck '39-'80, Timmy B. '80-'84, '84-'94)								
Kansas		TB	1927	D	97*	81'00"	19'09"	11'06"
Built: Great Lakes Towing Co., Cleveland, OH								
Kentucky {2}		TB	1929	D	98*	84'04"	20'00"	12'04"
Built: Great Lakes Towing Co., Cleveland, OH								
Louisiana		TB	1917	D	97*	81'00"	19'09"	11'06"
Built: Great Lakes Towing Co., Cleveland, OH								
Massachusetts		TB	1928	D	98*	84'04"	20'00"	12'04"
Built: Great Lakes Towing Co., Cleveland, OH								
Michigan {12}		TB	2019	D	100*	63'05"	24'02"	11'00"
Built: Great Lakes Shipyard, Cleveland, OH								

Fleet Name Vessel Name	Vessel IMO #	Vessel Type	Year Built	Engine Type	Cargo Cap. or Gross*	Overall Length	Vessel Breadth	Vessel Depth
Mississippi		TB	1916	DE	97*	81' 00"	19' 09"	11' 06"
Built: Great Lakes Towing Co., Cleveland, OH								
Missouri {2}		TB	1927	D	149*	88' 04"	24' 06"	12' 03"
Built: American Shipbuilding Co., Lorain, OH (Rogers City {1} '27-'56, Dolomite {1} '56-'81, Chippewa {7} '81-'90)								
Nebraska		TB	1929	D	98*	84' 04"	20' 00"	12' 05"
Built: Great Lakes Towing Co., Cleveland, OH								
New Jersey		TB	1924	D	98*	81' 00"	20' 00"	12' 04"
Built: Great Lakes Towing Co., Cleveland, OH (New Jersey '24-'52, Petco-21 '52-'53)								
New York		TB	1913	D	98*	81' 00"	20' 00"	12' 04"
Built: Great Lakes Towing Co., Cleveland, OH								
North Carolina {2}		TB	1952	DE	145*	81' 00"	24' 01"	10' 07"
Built: DeFoe Shipbuilding Co., Bay City, MI (Limestone '52-'83, Wicklow '83-'90)								
North Dakota		TB	1910	D	97*	81' 00"	19' 09"	11' 06"
Built: Great Lakes Towing Co., Cleveland, OH (John M. Truby '10-'38)								
Ohio {3}		TB	2018	D	100*	63' 05"	24' 02"	11' 00"
Built: Great Lakes Shipyard, Cleveland, OH								
Oklahoma		TB	1913	DE	97*	81' 00"	19' 09"	11' 06"
Built: Great Lakes Towing Co., Cleveland, OH (T. C. Lutz {2} '13-'34)								
Ontario		TB	1964	D	243*	102' 03"	29' 00"	16' 03"
Built: Mobile Ship Repair, Mobile, AL (YTB 770 {Dahlonega} '64-'01, Jeffrey K. McAllister '01-'15)								
Pennsylvania {2}		TB	2020	D	100*	63' 05"	24' 02"	11' 00"
Built: Great Lakes Shipyard, Cleveland, OH								
Rhode Island		TB	1930	D	98*	84' 04"	20' 00"	12' 04"
Built: Great Lakes Towing Co., Cleveland, OH								
Superior {3}		TB	1912	D	147*	82' 00"	22' 00"	10' 07"
Built: Manitowoc Shipbuilding Co., Manitowoc, WI (Richard Fitzgerald '12-'46)								
Tennessee {2}		TB	1911	D	98*	81' 00"	20' 00"	12' 04"
Built: Great Lakes Towing Co., Cleveland, OH; (Minnesota '27-'21)								
Texas		TB	1916	DE	97*	81' 00"	19' 09"	11' 06"
Built: Great Lakes Towing Co., Cleveland, OH								
Vermont		TB	1914	D	98*	81' 00"	20' 00"	12' 05"
Built: Great Lakes Towing Co., Cleveland, OH								

Philip R. Clarke unloading ore at Conneaut, OH. (John Puda)

Fleet Name Vessel Name	Vessel IMO #	Vessel Type	Year Built	Engine Type	Cargo Cap. or Gross*	Overall Length	Vessel Breadth	Vessel Depth
Virginia {2}		TB	1914	DE	97*	81'00"	19'09"	11'06"
Built: Great Lakes Towing Co., Cleveland, OH								
Washington		TB	1925	DE	97*	81'00"	19'09"	11'06"
Built: Great Lakes Towing Co., Cleveland, OH								
William C. Gaynor	8423818	TB	1956	D	187*	94'00"	27'00"	11'09"
Built: Defoe Shipbuilding Co., Bay City, MI (William C. Gaynor '56-'88, Captain Barnaby '88-'02)								
William C. Selvick	5322623	TB	1944	D	142*	85'00"	23'00"	9'07"
Built: Platzer Boat Works, Houston, TX (U. S. Army ST-500 '44-'49, Sherman H. Serre '49-'77)								
Wisconsin {5}		TB	2020	D	100*	63'05"	24'02"	11'00"
Built: Great Lakes Shipyard, Cleveland, OH								
Wyoming		TB	1929	D	104*	84'04"	20'00"	12'04
Built: Great Lakes Towing Co., Cleveland, OH								

GREAT LAKES MARITIME ACADEMY, TRAVERSE CITY, MI *(nmc.edu/maritime)*

Anchor Bay		TV	1953	D	23*	45'00"	13'00"	7'00"
Built: Roamer Boat Co., Holland, MI (ST-2158 '53-'62)								
State of Michigan	8835451	TV	1985	D	1,914*	224'00"	43'00"	20'00"
Built: Tacoma Boatbuilding Co., Tacoma, WA (USNS Persistent '85-'98, USCG Persistent '98-'02)								

GREAT LAKES OFFSHORE SERVICES INC., PORT DOVER, ON

H.H. Misner		TB	1946	D	28*	66'09"	16'04"	4'05"
Built: George Gamble, Port Dover, ON								

GREAT LAKES SCIENCE CENTER – U.S. GEOLOGICAL SURVEY, ANN ARBOR, MI *(glsc.usgs.gov)*

Arcticus		RV	2014	D	148*	77'03"	26'11"	11'00"
Kaho		RV	2011	D	55*	70'02"	18'00"	5'00"
Kiyi		RV	1999	D	290*	107'00"	27'00"	12'02"
Muskie		RV	2011	D	55*	70'02"	18'00"	7'09"
Sturgeon		RV	1977	D	325*	100'00"	25'05"	10'00"

GREAT LAKES SHIPWRECK HISTORICAL SOCIETY, SAULT STE. MARIE, MI *(shipwreckmuseum.com)*

David Boyd		RV	1982	D	26*	47'00"	17'00"	3'00"

CCGS Griffon breaking ice in the Mackinac Straits. *(Scott Tomlinson)*

Herbert C. Jackson making the Port Fisher-Bay Aggregates dock in Bay City, MI. Across the Saginaw River, barge Innovation (with tug Samuel de Champlain) unloads at the Holcim Cement Dock in Essexville, MI. *(Gordy Garris)*

53

GREAT LAKES WATER STUDIES INSTITUTE, TRAVERSE CITY, MI *(nmc.edu/resources/water-studies)*

Northwestern {2}		RV	1969	D	12*	55' 00"	15' 00"	6' 06"

Built: Paasch Marine Services Inc., Erie, PA (USCOE North Central '69-'98)

GROUPE DESGAGNÉS INC., QUEBEC CITY, QC *(groupedesgagnes.com)*

OPERATED BY SUBSIDIARY TRANSPORT DESGAGNÉS

Acadia Desgagnés	9651541	GC	2013	D	7,875	393' 04"	59' 07"	34' 05"

Built: Shandong Baibuting Shipbuilding Co. Ltd., Shandong, China (BBT Ocean '12-'13, Sider Tis '13-'17)

Argentia Desgagnés	9409895	GC	2007	D	6,369	390' 08"	60' 03"	32' 08"

Built: Ustaoglu Shipyard, Zonguldak, Turkey (Ofmar '07-'17)

Claude A. Desgagnés	9488059	GC	2011	D	9,627	454' 05"	69' 11"	36' 01"

Built: Sanfu Ship Engineering, Taizhou Jiangsu, China (Elsborg '11-'12)

Miena Desgagnés	9700380	GC	2017	D	11,492	482' 04"	74' 10"	37' 01

Built: Jiangzhou Union Shipbuilding Co. Ltd., Ruichang, China (Jan '17-'18)

Nordika Desgagnés	9508316	GC	2010	D	12,936	469' 05"	74' 08"	43' 06"

Built: Xingang Shipbuilding Heavy Industry, Tianjin, China (BBC Oder '10-'17)

Rosaire A. Desgagnés	9363534	GC	2007	D	9,611	453' 00"	68' 11"	36' 01"

Built: Quingshan/Jiangdong/Jiangzhou Shipyards, Jiangzhou, China (Beluga Fortification '07-'07)

Sedna Desgagnés	9402093	GC	2009	D	9,611	456' 00"	68' 11"	36' 01"

Built: Quingshan/Jiangdong/Jiangzhou Shipyards, Jiangzhou, China (Beluga Festivity '09-'09)

Taiga Desgagnés	9303302	GC	2007	D	12,936	469' 07"	74' 08"	43' 06"

Built: Tianjin Xingang Shipyard, Tianjin, China (BBC Amazon '07-'17)

Zélada Desgagnés	9402081	GC	2008	D	9,611	455' 10"	68' 11"	36' 01"

Built: Quingshan/Jiangdong/Jiangzhou Shipyards, Jiangzhou, China (Beluga Freedom '09-'09)

THE FOLLOWING VESSELS CHARTERED TO PETRO-NAV INC., MONTREAL, QC,
A SUBSIDIARY OF GROUPE DESGAGNÉS INC.

Damia Desgagnés	9766437	TK	2016	D	12,061	442' 11"	77' 01"	37' 01"

Built: Besiktas Gemi Insa A.S., Istanbul, Turkey

Gaia Desgagnés	9739800	TK	2018	D	12,770	491' 08"	74' 08"	39' 70"

Built: Avic Dingheng Shipbuilding Co. Ltd., Shanghai, China (Fure Vinga '18-'19)

Mia Desgagnés	9772278	TK	2017	D	12,061	442' 11"	77' 01"	37' 01"

Built: Besiktas Gemi Insa A.S., Istanbul, Turkey

Paul A. Desgagnés	9804423	TK	2018	D	12,061	442' 11"	77' 01"	37' 01"

Built: Besiktas Gemi Insa A.S., Istanbul, Turkey

Rossi A. Desgagnés	9804435	TK	2018	D	12,061	442' 11"	77' 01"	37' 01"

Built: Besiktas Gemi Insa A.S., Istanbul, Turkey

Sarah Desgagnés	9352171	TK	2007	D	11,711	483' 11"	73' 06"	41' 04"

Built: Gisan Shipyard, Tuzla, Turkey (Besiktas Greenland '07-'08)

THE FOLLOWING VESSEL CHARTERED TO RELAIS NORDIK INC., RIMOUSKI, QC *(relaisnordik.com)*
A SUBSIDIARY OF GROUPE DESGAGNÉS INC.

Bella Desgagnés	9511519	PF/RR	2012	D	6,655	312' 00"	63' 06"	22' 08"

Built: Brodogradil Kraljevica d.d., Kraljevica, Croatia

TRANSPORT MARITIME ST-LAURENT INC., A SUBSIDIARY OF GROUPE DESGAGNÉS INC.

Espada Desgagnés	9334698	TK	2006	D	42,810	750' 00"	105' 08"	67' 01"

Built: Brodosplit, Split, Croatia (Stena Poseidon '06-'14)

Laurentia Desgagnés	9334703	TK	2007	D	42,810	750' 00"	105' 08"	67' 01"

Built: Brodosplit, Split, Croatia (laid down as Neste Polaris, Palva '07-'14)

GROUPE OCÉAN INC., QUEBEC CITY, QC *(groupocean.com)*

Duga	7530030	TB	1977	D	382*	114' 02"	32' 10"	16' 05"

Built: Langsten Slip & Båtbyggeri A/S, Lansten, Norway

Josee H.		PB	1961	D	66*	63' 50"	16' 02"	9' 50"

Built: Ferguson Industries Ltd., Pictou, NS (Le Bic '61-'98)

Kim R.D.		TB	1954	D	36*	48' 08"	14' 01"	5' 01"

Built: Port Dalhousie Shipyard Co., Port Dalhousie, ON (Constructor '54-'86)

La Prairie	7393585	TB	1975	D	110*	73' 09"	25' 09"	11' 08"

Built: Georgetown Shipyard, Georgetown, PEI

Le Phil D.		TB	1961	D	38*	56' 01"	16' 00"	5' 08"

Built: Russel Brothers Ltd., Owen Sound, ON (Expanse)

Océan Abys	8644644	DB	1948	B	1,000	140' 00"	40' 00"	9' 00"

Built: Marine Industries Ltd., Sorel, QC (Omni No. 1 '48-'94)

Ocean Aqua		TB	2003	D	130*	65' 00"	26' 00"	9' 8 "

Built: Damen Shipyards, Gorichem, Netherlands

Océan Arctique	9261607	TB	2005	D	512*	102' 08"	39' 05"	17' 00"

Built: Industries Ocean Inc., Ile-Aux-Coudres, QC (Stevns Arctic '05-'13)

Océan A. Gauthier	7305904	TT	1973	D	390*	98' 11"	36' 00"	12' 04"

Built: Star Shipyards Ltd., New Westminster, BC (Vachon '73-'17)

Fleet Name / Vessel Name	Vessel IMO #	Vessel Type	Year Built	Engine Type	Cargo Cap. or Gross*	Overall Length	Vessel Breadth	Vessel Depth
Océan A. Simard	8000056	TT	1980	D	286*	92' 00"	34' 00"	13' 07"
Built: Georgetown Shipyards Ltd., Georgetown, PEI (Alexis-Simard '80-'11)								
Océan Bertrand Jeansonne	9521526	TB	2008	D	402*	94' 05"	36' 05"	17' 02"
Built: East Isle Shipyard, Georgetown, PEI								
Océan Bravo	7025279	TB	1970	D	320*	110' 00"	28' 06"	17' 00"
Built: Davie Shipbuilding Co., Lauzon, QC (Takis V. '70-'80, Donald P '80-'80, Nimue '80-'83, Donald P. '83-'98)								
Océan Borromée Verreault		DR	1952		647*	131' 04"	44' 00"	9' 02"
Built: Saint John Dry Dock Co. Ltd., Saint John, NB (Rosaire)								
Océan Catatug 1		TW	2016	D	55*	52' 00"	30' 00"	8' 07"
Built: Industries Ocean Inc., Ile-Aux-Coudres, QC								
Océan Catatug 2		TW	2016	D	52*	52' 00"	30' 00"	8' 07"
Built: Industries Ocean Inc., Ile-Aux-Coudres, QC								
Ocean Champlain II		PB	1994	D	30*	48' 55"	14' 00"	7 '01"
Built: F.R. Fassmer & Co., Weser, Germany								
Océan Charlie	7312024	TB	1973	D	448*	123' 02"	31' 07"	16' 01"
Built: Davie Shipbuilding Co., Lauzon, QC (Leonard W. '73-'98)								
Océan Clovis T.	9533036	TB	2009	D	381*	94' 60"	36' 50"	17' 10"
Built: East Isle Shipyard, Georgetown, PEI (Stevns Icequeen, Svitzer Njal '09-'17)								
Océan Comeau	7520322	TB	1976	D	391*	99' 09"	36' 01"	12' 01"
Built: Marystown Shipyard Ltd., Marystown, NL (Pointe Comeau '76-'17)								
Océan Cote-Nord		PB	2001	D	79*	75' 01"	18' 00"	10' 06"
Built: Industries Ocean Inc., Ile-Aux-Coudres, QC (Cote-Nord '01-'14)								
Océan Express		PB	1999	D	29*	47' 02"	14' 00"	7' 05"
Built: Industries Ocean Inc.. Charlevoix, QC (H-2000 '99-'00)								
Océan Golf	5146354	TB	1959	D	159*	103' 00"	25' 10"	11' 09"
Built: P.K. Harris & Sons, Appledore, England (launched as Stranton; Helen M. McAllister '59-'97)								
Océan Guide		PB	2001	D	29*	47' 02"	14' 00"	7' 05"
Built: Industries Ocean Inc., Charlevoix, QC								
Océan Henry Bain	9420916	TT	2006	D	402*	94' 08"	30' 01"	14' 09"
Built: East Isle Shipyard, Georgetown, PEI								
Océan Intrepide	9203423	TT	1998	D	302*	80' 00"	30' 01"	14' 09"
Built: Industries Ocean Inc., Ile-Aux-Coudres, QC								
Océan Iroquois		WB	1974	D	20*	37' 09"	10' 00"	6' 06"
Built: Sigama Ltd., Cap-de-la-Madeline, QC (SLS Iroquois '74-??, S/VM Iroquis ??-'09)								
Océan Jupiter	9220160	TT	1998	D	302*	80' 00"	30' 01"	14' 09"
Built: Industries Ocean Inc., Ile-Aux-Coudres, QC								
Océan K. Rusby	9345556	TT	2005	D	402*	94' 08"	30' 01"	14' 09"
Built: East Isle Shipyard, Georgetown, PEI								
Océan Lima		TB	1977	D	15*	34' 02"	11' 08"	4' 00"
(VM/S St. Louis III '77-'10)								
Océan Maisonneuve II		PB	1994	D	30*	48' 55"	14' 00"	7 '01"
Built: F.R. Fassmer & Co., Weser, Germany								
Océan Nigiq		TT	2008	D	12*	31' 05"	13' 05"	6' 00"
Built: Industries Océan Inc., Ile-aux-Coudres, QC								
Océan Pierre Julien	9688142	TT	2013	D	204*	75' 01"	30' 01"	12' 09"
Built: Industries Ocean Inc., Ile-Aux-Coudres, QC								
Océan Raymond Lemay	9420904	TT	2006	D	402*	94' 08"	30' 01"	14' 09"
Built: East Isle Shipyard, Georgetown, PEI								
Océan Raynald T.	9533048	TT	2009	D	381*	94' 60"	36' 50"	17' 10"
Built: East Isle Shipyard, Georgetown, PEI (Stevns Iceflower '09-'09, Svitzer Nerthus '09-'17)								
Océan Ross Gaudreault	9542221	TT	2011	D	402*	94' 04"	36' 05"	17' 00"
Built: East Isle Shipyard, Georgetown, PEI								
Océan Sept-Iles	7901162	TB	1980	D	427*	98' 04"	36' 01"	13' 01"
Built: Canadian Shipbuilding & Engineering Co., Collingwood, ON (Pointe Sept-Iles '80-'13)								
Océan Serge Genois	9553907	TT	2010	D	204*	75' 01"	30' 01"	12' 09"
Built: Industries Ocean Inc., Ile-Aux-Coudres, QC								
Océan Taiga	9679488	TT	2016	D	719*	118' 01"	42' 08"	22' 06"
Built: Industries Ocean Inc., Ile-Aux-Coudres, QC								
Océan Traverse Nord	9666534	DR	2012	B	1,165*	210' 00"	42' 06"	14' 07"
Built: Industries Ocean Inc., Ile-Aux-Coudres, QC								
Océan Tundra	9645504	TT	2013	D	710*	118' 01"	42' 03"	22' 09"
Built: Industries Ocean Inc., Ile-Aux-Coudres, QC								
Océan Uannaq		TB	2008	D	N/A	31' 06"	13' 06"	6' 00"
Built: Industries Ocean Inc., Ile-Aux-Coudres, QC								
Océan Yvan Desgagnés	9542207	TT	2010	D	402*	94' 04"	36' 05"	17' 00"
Built: East Isle Shipyard, Georgetown, PEI								

Fleet Name / Vessel Name	Vessel IMO #	Vessel Type	Year Built	Engine Type	Cargo Cap. or Gross*	Overall Length	Vessel Breadth	Vessel Depth
Omni-Atlas	8644668	CS	1913	B	479*	133'00"	42'00"	10'00"
Built: Sir William Arrol & Co. Ltd., Glasgow, Scotland								
Service Boat No. 2		TB	1934	D	78*	65'02"	17'00"	8'01"
Built: Canadian Vickers Ltd., Montreal, QC (Weymontachingue '34-'72)								
Service Boat No. 4		PB	1959	D	26*	39'01"	14'02"	6'03"
Built: Three Rivers Boatmen Ltd., St. Antione de Tilly, QC								

H

H2O LIMOS, HARRISON TOWNSHIP, MI *(h2olimos.com)*

Captain Paul II		ES	1960	D	14*	63'08"	15'04"	4'09"
Built: J.W. Nolan & Sons Inc., Erie, PA (Laurie Gene, Treasure Islander, Chee Maun Nes)								

HAMILTON PORT AUTHORITY, HAMILTON, ON *(hamiltonport.ca)*

Judge McCombs		TB	1948	D	10*	33'01"	10'03"	4'00"
Built: Northern Shipbuilding & Repair Co. Ltd., Bronte, ON (Bronte Sue '48-'50)								

HAMILTON HARBOUR QUEEN CRUISES, HAMILTON, ON

Hamilton Harbour Queen		ES	1956	D	252*	100'00"	40'00"	4'05"
Built: Russel-Hipwell Engines, Owen Sound, ON (Johnny B. '56-'89, Garden City '89-'00, Harbour Princess '00-'05)								

HARBOR BOAT CRUISE CO., TORONTO, ON *(rivergambler.ca)*

River Gambler		ES	1992	D	332*	100'06"	16'00"	4'07"
Built: Jacques Beauchamp, Windsor, ON								

HARBOR COUNTRY ADVENTURES, MICHIGAN CITY, IN *(harborcountryadventures.com)*

Emita II		ES	1953	D	13*	63'00"	23'03"	6'05"

HEDDLE MARINE SERVICE INC., HAMILTON, ON *(heddlemarine.com)*

Burch Nash		TB	1944	D	51*	64'00"	16'07"	7'10"
Built: Central Bridge Co., Trenton, ON (Tanac 75 '44-'52, Manitoba '52-'57, Lac Manitoba '57-'21)								
King Fish 1		TB	1955	D	24*	47'09"	13'00"	5'03"
Built: Russel Hipwell Engines Ltd., Owen Sound, ON (Anglo Duchess '55-'84, Duchess V '84-'??)								

HERBERT F. DARLING INC., TONAWANDA, NY

Marcey		TB	1966	D	22*	42'00"	12'00"	7'00"

HERCULES INDUSTRIES INC., GLADSTONE, MI

Jen Anne		TB	1905	D	32*	57'09"	15'00"	7'00"
Built: Benjamin F. Cowles, Buffalo, NY (Theodore E. Cowles '05-'55, Joe Van '55-'17)								

HERITAGE MARINE, KNIFE RIVER, MN *(heritagemarinetug.com)*

Edward H. {2}	8990471	TB	1970	D	196*	102'08"	29'00"	16'03"
Built: Peterson Builders Inc., Sturgeon Bay, WI (YTB-809-Agawam '70-'02, Fort Point '02-'17)								

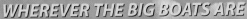

WHEREVER THE BIG BOATS ARE

The busy tugs of the Great Lakes Towing Co. can be found in almost every Great Lakes port. Sometimes they even start the season in one port and end in another. On this page, the 1929-built Nebraska is helping Algoma Niagara at South Chicago, IL, February 2022. (Lou Gerard)

Fleet Name / Vessel Name	Vessel IMO #	Vessel Type	Year Built	Engine Type	Cargo Cap. or Gross*	Overall Length	Vessel Breadth	Vessel Depth
Helen H.	8624670	TB	1967	D	138*	82′ 03″	26′ 08″	10′ 05″

Built: Bludworth Shipyard, Corpus Christi, TX *(W. Douglas Masterson '67-'11)*

Nels J. {2}		TB	1952	D	197*	101′ 00″	26′ 07″	12′ 06″

Built: National Steel and Shipbuilding Co., San Diego, CA *(LT-2078 '52-'64, YTM-748-Yuma '64-'80, Delaware '80-'89, Mobile Point '89-'95, Delaware '95-'08, Mobile Point '08-'09, Lesli M '09-'12, Taurus '12-'17)*

HOLCIM U.S., CHICAGO, IL *(holcim.com)*

J.A.W. Iglehart	5139179	CC	1936	T	12,500	501′ 06″	68′ 03″	37′ 00″

Built: Sun Shipbuilding and Drydock Co., Chester, PA; converted from a saltwater tanker to a self-unloading cement carrier in '65 at American Shipbuilding Co., South Chicago, IL; last operated Oct. 29, 2006; in use as a cement storage/transfer vessel at Superior, WI *(Pan Amoco '36-'55, Amoco '55-'60, H. R. Schemm '60-'65)*

HORNBLOWER CRUISES AND EVENTS CANADA LTD., TORONTO, ON *(cityexperiences.com/city-cruises)*

Northern Spirit I	8870073	ES	1983	D	489*	136′ 00″	31′ 00″	9′ 00″

Built: Blount Marine Corp., Warren, RI *(New Spirit '83-'89, Pride of Toronto '89-'92)*

Odyssey Toronto		ES	1989	D	99*	149′ 00″	33′ 06″	7′ 08″

Built: Aluminum Boats Inc., Jean Lafitte, LA

Oriole	8800054	ES	1987	D	200*	75′ 00″	23′ 00″	9′ 00″
Rosemary		ES	1960	D	52*	68′ 00″	15′ 06″	6′ 08″
Showboat Royal Grace		ES	1988	D	135*	74′ 00″	21′ 00″	4′ 00″
Toronto Elite		ES	2003	D	176*	82′ 03″	20′ 01″	6′ 00″

HORNE TRANSPORTATION LTD., WOLFE ISLAND, ON *(wolfeisland.com/ferry.php)*

William Darrell		CF	1952	D	66*	66′ 00″	28′ 00″	6′ 00″

HOTTE MARINE CONTRACTING LTD., LASALLE, ON *(hottemarine.com)*

Joan V		TB	1956	D	12*	39′ 07″	13′ 00″	3′ 11″

Built: Mathieson Boat Works, Goderich, ON

Marvin O.		TB	1957	D	21*	44′ 06″	14′ 11″	4′ 01″

HUFFMAN EQUIPMENT RENTAL INC., EASTLAKE, OH

Benjamin Ridgway		TW	1969	D	51*	53′ 00″	18′ 05″	7′ 00″
Bert Huffman		TW	1979	D	34*	38′ 00″	13′ 06″	5′ 02″
Paddy Miles		TB	1934	D	16*	45′ 04″	12′ 04″	4′ 07″

HURON DISTRICT CONTRACTING LTD., GODERICH, ON

Chuckie Joe		TB	1951	D	11*	39′ 06″	13′ 00″	4′ 00″

Built: Mathieson Boat Works, Goderich, ON

Debbie Lyn		TB	1950	D	10*	45′ 00″	14′ 00″	10′ 00″

Built: Mathieson Boat Works, Goderich, ON *(Skipper '50-'60)*

HURON LADY CRUISES, PORT HURON, MI *(huronlady.com)*

Huron Lady II		ES	1993	D	82*	65′ 00″	19′ 00″	10′ 00″

(Lady Lumina '93-'99)

CHANCES ARE THERE'S A G-TUG STANDING BY

Nebraska ended her season at Toledo, OH. She's shown passing the 1943-built Cuyahoga. GLT repositions its tugs multiple times a season. *(Joe Cioletti)*

HYDRO-QUEBEC, MONTREAL, QC

Des Chenaux		TB	1953	D	46*	51'08"	16'00"	7'08"
Desprairies		TB	1998	D	14*	41'09"	11'08"	5'04"

I

ILLINOIS & MICHIGAN OIL LLC, JOLIET, IL
Vessels active on the Illinois River system as well as the Calumet River in Chicago and other southern Lake Michigan ports

Derek E.		TW	1968	D	98*	78'00"	26'00"	9'06"

Built: Jeffboat Inc., Jeffersonville, IN (National Star, Ellen C, Ann G., Dale White)

Lisa E		TB	1963	D	75*	65'06"	20'00"	8'06"

Built: Main Iron Works Inc., Houma, LA (Dixie Scout '63-'90)

INFINITY AND OVATION YACHT CHARTERS LLC, ST. CLAIR SHORES, MI *(infinityandovation.com)*

Infinity		PA	2001	D	82*	117'00"	22'00"	6'00"
Ovation		PA	2005	D	97*	138'00"	27'00"	7'00"

INLAND LAKES MANAGEMENT INC., MUSKEGON, MI

Alpena {2}		CC	1942	T	13,900	519'06"	67'00"	35'00"

Built: Great Lakes Engineering Works, River Rouge, MI; shortened by 120' and converted to a self-unloading cement carrier in '91 at Fraser Shipyards, Superior, WI (Leon Fraser '42-'91)

INLAND SEAS EDUCATION ASSOCIATION, SUTTONS BAY, MI *(schoolship.org)*

Alliance		RV	1995	W	51*	77'06'	19'70"	9'00"

Built: Treworgy Yachts, Palm Coast, FL (Kathryn B. '95'-05)

Inland Seas		RV	1994	W	41*	61'06"	17'00"	7'00"

Built: Treworgy Yachts, Palm Coast, FL

Utopia		RV	1946	W	49*	65'0"	18'00"	6'08"

INTERLAKE LOGISTICS SOLUTIONS
MANAGED BY INTERLAKE MARITIME SERVICES, MIDDLEBURG HEIGHTS, OH *(interlake-steamship.com)*

Pere Marquette 41	5073894	SU	1941	B	3,413*	403'00"	58'00"	23'05"

Built: Manitowoc Shipbuilding Co., Manitowoc, WI; converted from a powered train/carferry to a self-unloading barge in '97; paired with tug Undaunted, length together 494'00" (City of Midland 41 '41-'97)

Alpena in spring ice off Muskegon, MI. The veteran cement carrier is marking her 81st anniversary in 2023.
(Brian Caswell)

Fleet Name Vessel Name	Vessel IMO #	Vessel Type	Year Built	Engine Type	Cargo Cap. or Gross*	Overall Length	Vessel Breadth	Vessel Depth
Undaunted	8963210	AT	1943	DE	569*	143' 00"	38' 00"	18' 00"

Built: Gulfport Boiler/Welding, Port Arthur, TX; paired with barge Pere Marquette 41
(USS Undaunted [ATR-126, ATA-199] '44-'63, USMA Kings Pointer '63-'93, Krystal K. '93-'97)

LT-805 (Winfield Scott)		TB	1993	D	N/A	128' 00"	36' 00"	N/A

Built: Moss Point Marine, Moss Point, MS; purchased in 2021 and laid up at Ludington, MI

INTERLAKE STEAMSHIP CO. (interlake-steamship.com)
MANAGED BY INTERLAKE MARITIME SERVICES, MIDDLEBURG HEIGHTS, OH

Dorothy Ann	8955732	AT/TT	1999	D	1,090*	124' 03"	44' 00"	24' 00"

Built: Bay Shipbuilding Co., Sturgeon Bay, WI; paired with self-unloading barge Pathfinder; overall length for Dorothy Ann / Pathfinder is 700' 02"

Herbert C. Jackson	5148417	SU	1959	D	24,800	690' 00"	75' 00"	37' 06"

Built: Great Lakes Engineering Works, River Rouge, MI; converted to a self-unloader in '75 at Defoe Shipbuilding Co., Bay City, MI; repowered in '16

Hon. James L. Oberstar	5322518	SU	1959	D	31,000	806' 00"	75' 00"	37' 06"

Built: American Shipbuilding Co., Toledo, OH; lengthened 96' in '72; converted to a self-unloader in '81 at Fraser Shipyards, Superior, WI; repowered in '09 (Shenango II '59-'67, Charles M. Beeghly '67-'11)

James R. Barker	7390260	SU	1976	D	63,300	1,004' 00"	105' 00"	50' 00"

Built: American Shipbuilding Co., Lorain, OH

John Sherwin {2}	5174428	BC	1958	B	31,500	806' 00"	75' 00"	37' 06"

Built: American Shipbuilding Co., Toledo, OH; lengthened 96' in '73 at Fraser Shipyards, Superior, WI; last operated Nov. 16, 1981; in long-term lay-up at DeTour, MI

Kaye E. Barker	5097450	SU	1952	D	25,900	767' 00"	70' 00"	36' 00"

Built: American Shipbuilding Co., Toledo, OH; lengthened 120' at Fraser Shipyards, Superior, WI, in '76; converted to a self-unloader in '81 at American Shipbuilding Co., Toledo, OH; repowered in '12 (Edward B. Greene '52-'85, Benson Ford {3} '85-'89)

Lee A. Tregurtha	5385625	SU	1942	D	29,360	826' 00"	75' 00"	39' 00"

Built: Bethlehem Shipbuilding and Drydock Co., Sparrows Point, MD; converted from a saltwater tanker to a Great Lakes bulk carrier in '61; lengthened 96' in '76 and converted to a self-unloader in '78, all at American Shipbuilding Co., Lorain, OH; repowered in '06 (laid down as Mobiloil; launched as Samoset;
USS Chiwawa [AO-68] '42-'46, Chiwawa '46-'61, Walter A. Sterling '61-'85, William Clay Ford {2} '85-'89)

Mark W. Barker	9962445	SU	2022	D	28,000	639' 00"	78' 00"	45' 00"

Built: Fincantieri Bay Shipbuilding Corp., Sturgeon Bay, WI

Fleet Name / Vessel Name	Vessel IMO #	Vessel Type	Year Built	Engine Type	Cargo Cap. or Gross*	Overall Length	Vessel Breadth	Vessel Depth
Mesabi Miner	7390272	SU	1977	D	63,300	1,004' 00"	105' 00"	50' 00"
Built: American Shipbuilding Co., Lorain, OH								
Pathfinder {3}	5166768	SU	1953	B	26,700	629' 03"	70' 03"	36' 03"
Built: Great Lakes Engineering Works, River Rouge, MI; converted to a self-unloading barge in '98 at Bay Shipbuilding Co., Sturgeon Bay, WI; paired with articulated tug Dorothy Ann (J. L. Mauthe '53-'98)								
Paul R. Tregurtha	7729057	SU	1981	D	68,000	1,013' 06"	105' 00"	56' 00"
Built: American Shipbuilding Co., Lorain, OH; largest vessel on the lakes (William J. DeLancey '81-'90)								
Stewart J. Cort	7105495	SU	1972	D	58,000	1,000' 00"	105' 00"	49' 00"
Built: Erie Marine Inc., Erie, PA; built for Bethlehem Steel Corp.; first 1,000-footer on the Great Lakes								

IRON WORKS CONSTRUCTION, BAILEYS HARBOR, WI
Kevin C. Kane		TB	1992	D	45*	52' 00"	15' 05"	8' 00"
Built: Gladding-Hearn Shipbuilding, Somerset, MA; converted from a New York City fireboat around 2017								

ISLAND FERRY SERVICES CORP., CHEBOYGAN, MI
Polaris		CF	1952	D	99*	60' 02"	36' 00"	8' 06"

ISLE ROYALE LINE INC., COPPER HARBOR, MI *(isleroyale.com)*
Isle Royale Queen IV		PA/PK	1980	D	93*	98' 09"	22' 01"	7' 00"
Built: Neuville Boat Works Inc., New Iberia, LA (American Freedom, John Jay, Shuttle V, Danielle G, Harbor Commuter V)								

J-K

J & J MARINE LTD., LASALLE, ON *(jjmarine.com)*
John D.		TB	1949	D		42' 00"	13' 03"	4' 00"
J.W. Hudson		TB	1965	D	55*	57' 10"	16' 01"	7' 07"
Built: Three Rivers Boatmen Ltd., St. Antoine de Tilly, QC (Service Boat No. 1 '65-'20)								
Sea Horse		TB	1945	D		45' 00"	13' 00"	4' 05"
(Dona Gay, C.E. Park)								

J & K STEAMBOAT CO., GRAND LEDGE, MI *(michiganprincess.com)*
Harbor Princess		ES	1955	D	82*	72' 00"	25' 00"	7' 03"
Built: Christy Corp., Sturgeon Bay, WI (Emerald Isle {1} '55-'91, Diamond Jack '91-'22); operating out of Petoskey, MI								

J & M CRUISE LINES, TOLEDO, OHIO *(jmcruiselines.com)*
Glass City Pearl		ES	2006	D	51*	65' 00"	20' 00"	6' 00"
Sandpiper		ES	1984	D	37*	65' 00"	16' 00"	3' 00"

J.W. WESTCOTT CO., DETROIT, MI *(jwwestcott.com)*
Joseph J. Hogan		MB	1957	D	16*	40' 00"	12' 05"	5' 00"
(USCOE Ottawa '57-'95)								
J.W. Westcott II		MB	1949	D	14*	46' 01"	13' 03"	4' 05"
Built: Paasch Marine Service, Erie, PA; floating post office has its own U.S. ZIP code, 48222								
M.S. Westcott		PB	1977	D	26*	46' 00"	12' 05"	3' 05"
Built: Hans Hansen Welding Co., Toledo, OH; pilot service at Detroit, MI (Huron Maid '77-'21)								

JEFF FOSTER, SUPERIOR, WI
Sundew		IB	1944	DE	1,025*	180' 00"	37' 05"	17' 04"
Built: Marine Ironworks and Shipbuilding Corp., Duluth, MN; former U.S. Coast Guard cutter WLB-404 was decommissioned in '04 and turned into a marine museum; returned to private ownership in '09								

JUBILEE QUEEN CRUISE LINES, TORONTO, ON *(jubileequeencruises.ca)*
Jubilee Queen		ES	1986	D	269*	122' 00"	23' 09"	5' 05"
(Pioneer Princess III '86-'89)								

KEHOE MARINE CONSTRUCTION CO., LANSDOWNE, ON *(kehoemarine.com)*
Bulldog		TB	1949	D		42' 07"	12' 05"	6' 01"
Built: Russel Bros. Ltd., Owen Sound, ON (Long Sault '49-'19)								
Halton		TB	1942	D	15*	42' 08"	14' 00"	5' 08"
Built: Muir Bros. Dry Dock Co. Ltd., Port Dalhousie, ON (Workboat No. 8)								
Houghton		TB	1944	D	15*	45' 00"	13' 00"	6' 00"
Built: Port Houston Iron Works, Houston, TX (ST-573 '44-'48)								
Katanni		TB	1991	D	19*	34' 08"	14' 05"	5' 05"
Built: Duratug Shipyard & Fabricating Ltd., Port Dover, ON								
Sawyer 1		TB	1946	D	11*	35' 02"	10' 02"	4' 04"
Built: Russel Bros. Ltd., Owen Sound, ON (Coulonge, Compass Rose VI)								
Steelhead		TB	1944	D	36*	56' 00"	20' 00"	5' 03"
Built: W.F. Kolbe & Co. Ltd., Port Dover, ON								

KELLEYS ISLAND BOAT LINES, MARBLEHEAD, OH (kelleysislandferry.com)

Carlee Emily		PA/CF	1987	D	98*	101' 00"	34' 06"	10' 00"
Built: Blount Marine Corp., Warren, RI (Endeavor '87-'02)								
Carmen Lee		PA/CF	2022	D	N/A	168' 00"	45 ' 00"	N/A
Built: Thoma-Sea Marine Constructors LLC, Houma, LA								
Juliet Alicia		PA/CF	1969	D	95*	88' 03"	33' 00"	6' 08"
Built: Blount Marine Corp., Warren, RI (Kelley Islander)								
Kayla Marie		PA/CF	1970	D	93*	113' 60"	34' 00"	8' 00"
Built: New Bern Shipyard Inc., New Bern, NC								
Shirley Irene		PA/CF	1991	D	68*	160' 00"	46' 00"	9' 00"
Built: Ocean Group Shipyard, Bayou La Batre, AL								

KING CO. (THE), HOLLAND, MI (kingco.us)

Buxton II		DR	1976	B	147*	130' 02"	28' 01"	7' 00"
Built: Barbour Boat Works Inc., Holland, MI								
Carol Ann		TB	1981	D	86*	61' 05"	24' 00"	8' 07"
Built: Rodriguez Boat Builders, Bayou La Batre, AL								
Dorena		TW	1966	D	27*	40' 00"	13' 50"	6' 00"
Built: Progressive Industrial Inc., Palmetto, FL								
Jessica Joy		TW	1995	D	20*	36' 07"	13' 06"	5' 00"
Built: Master Marine Inc., Bayou La Batre, AL								
John Henry		TB	1954	D	66*	65' 04"	19' 04"	9' 06"
Built: Missouri Valley Steel, Leavenworth, KS (U. S. Army ST-2013 '54-'80)								
Julie Dee		TB	1937	D	64*	68' 08"	18' 01"	7' 06"
Built: Pennsylvania, Beaumont, TX (Dernier, Jerry O'Day, Cindy B)								
Matt Allen		TB	1961	D	146*	80' 04"	24' 00"	11' 03"
Built: Nolty Theriot Inc., Golden Meadow, LA (Gladys Bea '61-'73, American Viking '73-'83, Maribeth Andrie '83-'05)								

KINGSTON 1,000 ISLANDS CRUISES, KINGSTON, ON (1000islandscruises.ca)

Island Belle I		ES	1988	D	150*	65' 00"	22' 00"	8' 00"
Built: Kettle Creek Boat Works, Port Stanley, ON (Spirit of Brockville '88-'91)								
Island Queen III		ES	1975	D	300*	96' 00"	26' 00"	11' 00"
Built: Marlin Yacht Co., Summerstown, ON								
Le Bateau-Mouche II		ES	1994	D	318*	97' 01"	29' 05"	11' 03"
Built: Bateau Mouche Au Vieux Port Inc., Montreal, QC								

KOKOSING INDUSTRIAL INC., GREAT LAKES MARINE DIVISION, CHEBOYGAN, MI (kokosing.biz)

Champion {3}		TB	1974	D	125*	75' 00"	23' 05"	9' 05"
Built: Service Machine & Shipbuilding Co., Amelia, LA								
General {2}		TB	1954	D	119*	71' 00"	19' 06"	10' 00"
Built: Missouri Valley Bridge & Iron Works, Leavenworth, KS (U. S. Army ST-1999 '54-'61, USCOE Au Sable '61-'84, Challenger {3} '84-'87)								
Nancy Anne		TB	1969	D	73*	60' 00"	20' 00"	8' 00"
Built: Houma Shipbuilding Co., Houma, LA								
Ray Durocher		TB	1943	D	20*	45' 06"	12' 05"	7' 06"
Built: Port Houston Iron Works, Houston, TX (U.S. Army ST-550 '43-'61)								
Valerie B.		TB	1981	D	101*	65' 00"	25' 06"	10' 00"
Built: Rayco Shipbuilders & Repairers, Bourg, LA (Mr. Joshua, Michael Van)								

L

LAGASGO INC., LONDON, ON
Vessels engaged in oil and gas exploration on Lake Erie

Dr. Bob	8771992	DV	1973	B	1,022*	160' 01"	54' 01"	11' 01"
Built: Cenac Shipyard Co. Inc., Houma, LA (Mr. Chris '73-'03)								
J.R. Rouble	8767020	DV	1958	D	562*	123' 06"	49' 08"	16' 00"
Built: American Marine Machinery Co., Nashville, TN (Mr. Neil)								
Miss Libby		DV	1972	B	924*	160' 01"	54' 01"	11' 01"
Built: Service Machine & Shipbuilding Corp., Morgan City, LA								
Sarah No. 1		WB	1969	D	43*	72' 01"	17' 03"	6' 08"
Built: Halter Marine, New Orleans, LA (Auries)								
Susan Michelle		TB	1995	D	89*	79' 10"	20' 11"	6' 02"
Built: Vic Powell Welding Ltd., Dunnville, ON								

LAKE ERIE ISLAND CRUISES LLC, SANDUSKY, OH (goodtimeboat.com)

Goodtime I		ES	1960	D	81*	111' 00"	29' 08"	9' 05"
Built: Blount Marine Corp., Warren, RI								

Fleet Name Vessel Name	Vessel IMO #	Vessel Type	Year Built	Engine Type	Cargo Cap. or Gross*	Overall Length	Vessel Breadth	Vessel Depth

LAKE EXPRESS LLC, MILWAUKEE, WI *(lake-express.com)*

Lake Express — 9329253 — PA/CF — 2004 — D — 96* — 179' 02" — 57' 07" — 16' 00"
Built: Austal USA, Mobile, AL; high-speed ferry service from Milwaukee, WI, to Muskegon, MI; capacity is 250 passengers, 46 autos

LAKEHEAD TUGBOATS INC., THUNDER BAY, ON *(lakeheadtugs.com)*

Florence M — 5118797 — TB — 1961 — D — 236* — 90' 00" — 28' 08" — 11' 04"
Built: P.K. Harris, Appledore, England (Foundation Vibert '61-'73, Point Vibert '73-'06)

George N. Carleton — — TB — 1943 — D — 97* — 82' 00" — 21' 00" — 11' 00"
Built: Russel Brothers Ltd., Owen Sound, ON (HMCS Glenlea [W-25] '43-'45, Bansaga '45-'64)

Teclutsa — — TB — 1973 — D — 235* — 102' 10" — 30' 00" — 15' 00"
Built: Marinette Marine Ltd., Marinette, WI (YTB-822 – USS Pawhuska '73-'95)

Wolf River — — BC — 1956 — D — 5,880 — 349' 02" — 43' 07" — 25' 04"
Built: Port Weller Dry Docks, Port Weller, ON; last operated in 1998; in long-term lay-up at Thunder Bay, ON (Tecumseh {2} '56-'67, New York News {3} '67-'86, Stella Desgagnés '86-'93, Beam Beginner '93-'95)

LAKE MICHIGAN CARFERRY, LUDINGTON, MI *(ssbadger.com)*
MANAGED BY INTERLAKE MARITIME SERVICES, MIDDLEBURG HEIGHTS, OH

Badger — 5033583 — PA/CF — 1953 — S — 4,244* — 410' 06" — 59' 06" — 24' 00"
Built: Christy Corp., Sturgeon Bay, WI; traditional ferry service from Ludington, MI, to Manitowoc, WI; capacity is 520 passengers, 180 autos; last coal-fired steamship on the Great Lakes; listed on the National Register of Historic Places in 2016; last vessel in Great Lakes service powered by Skinner Unaflow steam engines

Spartan — — PA/CF — 1952 — S — 4,244* — 410' 06" — 59' 06" — 24' 00"
Built: Christy Corp., Sturgeon Bay, WI; last operated Jan. 20, 1979; in long-term lay-up at Ludington, MI

LAKES PILOTS ASSOCIATION, PORT HURON, MI *(lakespilots.com)*

Huron Belle — — PB — 1979 — D — 38* — 50' 00" — 15' 07" — 7' 09"
Built: Gladding-Hearn Shipbuilding, Somerset, MA; pilot service at Detroit, MI

Huron Pride — — PB — 2022 — D — N/A — 40' 00" — 14' 00" — 5' 00"
Built: Gladding-Hearn Shipbuilding, Somerset, MA; pilot service at Port Huron, MI

Huron Spirit — — PB — 2016 — D — 47* — 52' 05" — 16' 07" — 8' 01"
Built: Gladding Hearn Shipbuilding, Somerset, MA; pilot service at Port Huron, MI

Michipicoten downbound with Port Huron, MI, in the background. (Eric Treece)

Fleet Name / Vessel Name	Vessel IMO #	Vessel Type	Year Built	Engine Type	Cargo Cap. or Gross*	Overall Length	Vessel Breadth	Vessel Depth
LAMBTON MARINE LTD., PORT LAMBTON, ON								
Mary Ellen I		TB	2008	D	18*	41'08"	14'02"	7'0"
LAURENTIAN PILOTAGE AUTHORITY, MONTREAL, QC (pilotagestlaurent.gc.ca)								
Vessels offer pilot service at Les Escoumins, QC, on the St. Lawrence River								
Grandes Eaux		PB	2008	D	63*	62'06"	17'02"	9'05"
Taukamaim		PB	2012	D	82*	72'01"	19'05"	10'05"
LES BARGES DE MATANE INC., MATANE, QC (bargesmatane.com)								
Denis M		TB	1942	D	21*	46'07"	12'08"	4'01"
Built: Russel Brothers Ltd., Owen Sound, ON (Lac Kenogami, Marcel D.)								
Point Vim	5118852	TB	1962	D	207*	98'06"	26'18"	12'02"
Built: Davie Shipbuilding Co., Lauzon, QC (Foundation Vim '62-'74)								
LITTLE TRAVERSE BAY FERRY, TRAVERSE CITY, MI (littletraversebayferry.org)								
Miss Lauren		PA	1986	D	32*	42'00"	14'05"	8'00"
LOWER LAKES TOWING LTD. – SEE RAND LOGISTICS INC.								
LUEDTKE ENGINEERING CO., FRANKFORT, MI (luedtke-eng.com)								
Alan K. Luedtke		TB	1944	D	149*	86'04"	23'00"	10'03"
Built: Allen Boat Co., Harvey, LA; inactive at Frankfort, MI (U. S. Army ST-527 '44-'55, USCOE Two Rivers '55-'90)								
Ann Marie		TB	1954	D	81*	71'00"	19'05"	9'06"
Built: Smith Basin & Drydock, Pensacola, FL (U-26-1449 and TG-26-1449 '54- '80, Lewis Castle '80-'98, Apache '98-'01)								
Chris E. Luedtke		TB	1936	D	18*	42'05"	11'09"	5'00"
Built: Manitowoc Shipbuilding, Manitowoc, WI (Manshipco '36-'80)								
Erich R. Luedtke		TB	1939	D	18*	42'05"	11'09"	5'00"
Built: Manitowoc Shipbuilding Co., Manitowoc, WI								
Gretchen B		TB	1943	D	18*	41'09"	12'05"	6'00"
Built: Sturgeon Bay Shipbuilding, Sturgeon Bay, WI (ST-175 '43-'46, Jane T '46-'70)								
Karl E. Luedtke		TB	1928	D	32*	55'02"	14'09"	6'00"
Built: Leathem D. Smith Dock Co., Sturgeon Bay, WI (Betty D. '28-'32, Killarney '32-'35)								
Kurt R. Luedtke		TB	1956	D	95*	72'00"	22'06"	7'06"
Built: Lockport Shipyard, Lockport, LA (Miss Lana, Jere C.)								

Tug Laura L. VanEnkevort and barge Joseph H. Thompson heading up the Cuyahoga River at Cleveland. (Roger Durfee)

Fleet Name / Vessel Name	Vessel IMO #	Vessel Type	Year Built	Engine Type	Cargo Cap. or Gross*	Overall Length	Vessel Breadth	Vessel Depth
Paul L. Luedtke		TB	1988	D	97*	75' 00"	26' 00"	9' 06"
Built: Terrebonne Fabricators Inc., Houma, LA (Edward E. Gillen III '88-'13)								

M

Fleet Name / Vessel Name	Vessel IMO #	Vessel Type	Year Built	Engine Type	Cargo Cap. or Gross*	Overall Length	Vessel Breadth	Vessel Depth
MCM MARINE INC., SAULT STE. MARIE, MI (mcmmarine.com)								
Drummond Islander II		TB	1961	D	97*	65' 00"	36' 00"	9' 00"
Built: Marinette Marine Corp., Marinette, WI; former carferry was built to serve DeTour / Drummond Island, MI								
Madison		TB	1975	D	17*	33' 08"	13' 05"	4' 07"
Mohawk		TB	1945	D	46*	65' 00"	19' 00"	10' 06"
Built: Robert Jacob Shipyard, City Island, NY (YTL-440 '45-'75)								
Paul Bunyan		DB	1945	B		150' 00"	65' 00"	12' 06"
Built: Wiley Equipment Co., Port Deposit, MD								
(The company also operates two small pushboats, Kelli Anne and Tammy)								
MacDONALD MARINE LTD., GODERICH, ON (www.mactug.com)								
Dover		TB	1931	D	70*	84' 00"	17' 00"	6' 00"
Built: Canadian Mead-Morrison Co. Ltd., Welland, ON; inactive at Goderich, ON (Earleejune, Iveyrose)								
MACKINAC ISLAND STATE PARK COMMISSION, MACKINAC ISLAND, MI								
LCM 6			1952	D	N/A	56' 00"	14' 01"	3 10"
(U.S. Army LCM 6050)								
MADELINE ISLAND FERRY LINE INC., LA POINTE, WI (madferry.com)								
Bayfield {2}		PA/CF	1952	D	83*	120' 00"	43' 00"	10' 00"
Built: Chesapeake Marine Railway, Deltaville, VA (Charlotte '52-'99)								
Island Queen {2}		PA/CF	1966	D	90*	75' 00"	34' 09"	10' 00"
La Pointe		PA/CF	1987	D	95*	95' 00"	43' 40"	11' 70"
Built: Halter Marine, Lockport, LA (B.L. DeBerry '87-'19)								
Madeline		PA/CF	1984	D	94*	90' 00"	35' 00"	8' 00"
Nichevo II		PA/CF	1962	D	89*	65' 00"	32' 00"	8' 09"
MALCOLM MARINE, ST. CLAIR, MI (malcolmmarine.com)								
Capt. Keith		TB	1955	D	39*	53' 03"	15' 06"	6' 04"
Built: Diamond Manufacturing, Savannah GA (Richard Merritt '55-'13)								
Debbie Lee		TB	1955	D	13*	32' 00"	11' 00"	4' 04"
Built: U.S. Coast Guard, Baltimore, MD (CG-40397, Hooligan, Shy Poke)								
Manitou {2}	8971695	TB	1942	D	199*	110' 00"	26' 02"	15' 06"
Built: U.S. Coast Guard, Curtis Bay, MD (USCGC Manitou [WYT-60] '43-'84)								
MANISTEE HARBOR TOURS, MANISTEE, MI (manisteeharbortours.com)								
Princess		ES	1973	D	63*	65' 07"	20' 05"	7' 03"
(Island Princess {2} '73-'20, Princess of Ludington '20-'21)								

Great Lakes Towing tug Cleveland, with Capt. Paul C. LaMarre III at the helm. (Drone Selfie)

Fleet Name / Vessel Name	Vessel IMO #	Vessel Type	Year Built	Engine Type	Cargo Cap. or Gross*	Overall Length	Vessel Breadth	Vessel Depth
MANITOU ISLAND TRANSIT, LELAND, MI *(manitoutransit.com)*								
Mishe Mokwa		PA/CF	1966	D	49*	65' 00"	17' 06"	8' 00"
Built: J.W. Nolan & Sons, Erie, PA (Patricia '63-'74, Sunshine City '74-'79, LaSalle '79-'82)								
MARINE NAVIGATION AND TRAINING ASSOCIATION INC., CHICAGO, IL *(manatra.org)*								
Manatra [YP-671]		TV	1974	D	67*	80' 05"	17' 09"	5' 04"
Name stands for MArine NAvigation and TRaining Association (USS YP-671 '74-'89)								
MARINE RECYCLING CORP., PORT COLBORNE & PORT MAITLAND, ON *(marinerecycling.ca)*								
Charlie E.		TB	1943	D	32*	63' 00"	16' 06"	7' 06"
Built: W.F. Kolbe & Co. Ltd., Port Dover, ON (Kolbe '43-'86, Lois T. '86-'02)								
MARINE SERVICES INC., OAK PARK, MI								
Sean Patrick		WB	1944	D	25*	44' 00"	15' 00"	5' 00"
Built: Chrysler Corp., Detroit MI (J. Hawkley, Push Hog)								
Tenacious	5238004	TB	1960	D	149*	79' 01"	25' 06"	12' 06"
Built: Ingalls Shipbuilding Corp., Pascagoula, MS (Mobil 8 '60-'91, Tatarrax '91-'93, Nan McKay '93-'95)								
Titan		TB	1940	D	31*	56' 03"	15' 08"	7' 00"
(Gotham '40-'10)								
MARTIN GAS & OIL INC., BEAVER ISLAND, MI								
Mary M.		TB	1954	D	76*	71' 00"	22' 00"	8' 04"
Built: Missouri Valley Steel Inc., Leavenworth, KS (ST-1991, Oriskany, Hot Dog, Bowditch)								
Petroqueen		TK	2015	B	112*	70' 00"	24' 00"	8' 00"
Built: Basic Marine Inc., Escanaba, MI								
McASPHALT MARINE TRANSPORTATION LTD., HAMILTON, ON *(mcasphalt.com)*								
Everlast	7527332	AT	1976	D	1,361*	143' 04"	44' 04"	21' 04"
Built: Hakodate Dock Co., Hakodate, Japan; paired with barge Norman McLeod (Bilibino '77-'96)								
John J. Carrick	9473444	TK	2008	B	11,613	407' 06"	71' 07"	30' 00"
Built: Penglai Bohai Shipyard Co. Ltd., Penglai, China								
Leo A. McArthur	9473262	AT	2009	D	1,299	122' 00"	44' 03"	26' 02
Built: Penglai Bohai Shipyard Co. Ltd., Penglai, China; paired with barge John J. Carrick (Victorious '09-'17)								
McAsphalt Advantage		TK	2023	LNG		459' 31"	77' 91"	38' 38"
Built: Wuhu Shipyard Co. Ltd., Wuhu, China								
Norman McLeod	8636219	TK	2001	B	6,809*	379' 02"	71' 06"	30' 02"
Built: Jinling Shipyard, Nanjing, China								
McKEIL MARINE LTD., BURLINGTON, ON *(mckeil.com)*								
McKEIL INTERNATIONAL, BURLINGTON, ON								
Atlantic Spirit	9580974	TK	2011	D	13,239	530' 05"	75' 06"	40' 08"
(Osttank Denmark '11-'11, Osttank Sweden '11-'11, Adfines Star '11-'20)								

Great Lakes Trader near Big Point on the upper St. Marys River. (Matt Miner)

Fleet Name Vessel Name	Vessel IMO #	Vessel Type	Year Built	Engine Type	Cargo Cap. or Gross*	Overall Length	Vessel Breadth	Vessel Depth
Northern Spirit	9580962	TK	2011	D	13,239	530' 05"	75' 06"	40' 08"
Built: Yangfan Group Co., Zhoushan, China (Osttank Denmar '11-'11, Osttank Sweden '11-'11, Adfines Sea '11-'20)								
McKEIL WORK BOATS GP INC., BURLINGTON, ON								
Alouette Spirit	8641537	DB	1969	B	10,087*	425' 01"	74' 02"	29' 05"
Built: Gulfport Shipbuilding Co., Port Arthur, TX (KTC 135 '69-'04, Lambert's Spirit '04-'05)								
Arctic Dock 400		DB	1970	B	4,285*	382' 07"	76' 00"	20' 01"
Built: Bethlehem Steel Corp., San Francisco, CA (Labrador Spirit)								
Beverly M I	9084047	TT	1994	D	450*	114' 06"	34' 04"	17' 04"
Built: Imamura Shipbuilding, Kure, Japan (Shek O, Hunter, Pacific Typhoon)								
Blain M	7907099	RV	1981	D	925*	165' 05"	36' 00"	19' 09"
Built: Ferguson Industries, Picton, ON (Wilfred Templeman '81-'11)								
Blair McKeil	9546045	GC	2010	D	9,286	459' 02"	68' 11	34' 09"
Built: Tuzla Shipbuilding Industry, Istanbul, Turkey (Gagliarda '10-'18, Sider Gagliarda '18-'19, Gagliarda '19-'19)								
Dover Spirit	9662174	TB	1998	D	83*	65' 00"	22' 00"	8' 00"
Built: Dovercraft Marine, Nanticoke, ON (Kaliutik '98-'18)								
Evans Spirit	9327774	GC	2007	D	14,650	459' 02"	68' 11"	34' 09"
Built: Royal Niestern Sander, Delfzijl, Netherlands (Spavalda '07-'16)								
Florence Spirit	9314600	BC	2004	D	13,988	447' 07"	69' 07"	37' 01"
Built: Kyokuyo Shipyard Corp., Shimonoseki, Japan (Arklow Willow '04-'16)								
Glovertown Spirit	9662174	DB	2012	B	2,073*	243' 07"	77' 02"	14' 09"
Built: Damen Shipyards, Gorichem, Netherlands								
Harvest Spirit	9655951	BC	2012	D	11,953	500' 04"	73' 10"	35' 05"
Built: Sefine Shipyard, Altinova, Turkey (Zealand Juliana '12-'15, Juliana '15-'20, Julian '20-'20)								
Huron Spirit	8646642	SU	1995	D	4,542*	328' 01"	81' 11"	23' 06"
Built: Jiangsu Shipyard, Tiangsu Province, China (Mulege '95-'14)								
Jarrett M	5030086	TB	1945	D	96*	82' 00"	20' 00"	10' 00"
Built: Russel Brothers Ltd., Owen Sound, ON (Atomic '45-'06)								
John D.		TB	1954	D	37*	55' 00"	19' 10"	5' 00"
Built: Harry Gamble, Port Dover, ON								
Lambert Spirit	8641525	DB	1968	B	9,645	400' 01"	70' 02"	27' 06"
Built: Avondale Shipyards Inc., Avondale, LA (KTC 115 '68-'06)								
Leonard M.	8519215	TB	1986	D	457*	103' 07"	36' 01"	19' 02"
Built: McTay Marine, Bromborough, England (Point Halifax '86-'12)								
Lois M.	9017616	TT	1991	D	453*	107' 09"	34' 05"	17' 05"
Built: Matsuura Tekko Zosen, Higashino, Japan (Lambert '91-'14)								
McKeil Spirit	9347023	CC	2007	D	14,650	459' 02"	68' 11"	34' 00"
Built: Royal Niestern Sander, Delfzijl, Netherlands; converted to a self-discharging cement carrier in '17 (Ardita '07-'18)								
MM Newfoundland		DB	2011	B	2,165*	260' 00"	72' 00"	16' 01"
Built: Signal International, Pascagoula, MS								

McKeil Marine's Huron Spirit meets fleetmate Harvest Spirit at Marine City, MI. (Adam Hagan)

Fleet Name / Vessel Name	Vessel IMO #	Vessel Type	Year Built	Engine Type	Cargo Cap. or Gross*	Overall Length	Vessel Breadth	Vessel Depth
Molly M I	5118838	TB	1962	D	207*	98'06"	27'10"	12'02"

Built: Davie Shipbuilding Co., Lauzon, QC (Foundation Vigour '62-'74, Point Vigour '74-'07)

Niagara Spirit	8736021	DB	1984	D	9,164*	340'01"	78'02"	19'06"

Built: FMC Corp., Portland, OR (Alaska Trader '84-'99, Timberjack '99-'08)

Northern Venture	9167681	SU	1981	D	12,475*	508'05"	72'02	41'34"

Built: Shin Kurushima Hiroshima Dockyard, Hiroshima, Japan (Asia Cement No. 7 '09-'13); at press time being rebuilt in China for Canadian Great Lakes and Seaway service (Da Shen '81-'23)

Nunavut Spirit	8636673	DB	1983	B	6,076*	400'00"	105'00"	20'06"

Built: FMC Corp., Portland, OR (Barge 5001)

Sharon M I	9084059	TT	1993	D	450*	114'06"	34'04"	17'03"

Built: Inamura Shipbuilding, Kure, Japan (Mai Po, Pacific Tempest)

Stormont	8959893	TB	1953	D	108*	80'00"	20'00"	15'00"

Built: Canadian Dredge & Dock Co., Kingston, ON

S/VM 86		DB	1958	B	487*	168'01"	40'00"	10'00"

Built: Canadian Shipbuilding & Engineering Ltd., Collingwood, ON (S.L.S. 86)

Tim McKeil	9017604	TT	1991	D	453*	107'07"	34'04"	17'03"

Built: Matsuura Tekko Zosen, Higashino, Japan (Pannawonica 1 '91-'14)

Viateur's Spirit		DB	2004	D	253*	141'01"	52'03"	5'01"

Built: Port Weller Dry Dock, Port Weller, ON (Traverse René Lavasseur '04-'06)

Wilf Seymour	5215789	AT	1961	D	442*	122'00"	31'00"	17'00"

Built: Gulfport Shipbuilding, Port Arthur, TX (M. Moran '61-'70, Port Arthur '70-'72, M. Moran '72-'00, Salvager '00-'04)

Wyatt M.	8974178	TB	1948	D	123*	85'00"	20'00"	10'00"

Built: Russel Brothers Ltd., Owen Sound, ON (P. J. Murer '48-'81, Michael D. Misner '81-'93, Thomas A. Payette '93-'96, Progress '96-'06)

McKEIL-MALASPINA LTD., BURLINGTON, ON – A SUBSIDIARY OF McKEIL MARINE LTD.

Tobias	9642253	DB	2012	B	8,870*	377'11"	105'08"	26'07

Built: Damien Shipyards, Gorinchem, Netherlands

McKEIL TANKERS LTD., BURLINGTON, ON – A SUBSIDIARY OF McKEIL MARINE LTD.

Hinch Spirit	9508940	TK	2009	D	8,638	448'09"	65'06"	35'09"

Built: Selah Shipyard, Istanbul, Turkey (Topaz-T '09-'19)

Wicky Spirit	9404388	TK	2008	D	8,638	448'09"	65'06"	35'09"

Built: Gisan Shipbuilding & Shipping, Istanbul, Turkey (Turquoise-T '09-'19)

NADRO MARINE SERVICES LTD., PORT DOVER, ON – A SUBSIDIARY OF McKEIL MARINE LTD.

Ecosse	8624682	TB	1979	D	142*	91'00"	26'00"	8'06"

Built: Hike Metal Products Ltd., Wheatley, ON (R & L No. 1 '79-'96)

Seahound		TB	1941	D	57*	65'00"	18'00"	8'00"

Built: Equitable Equipment Co., New Orleans, LA ([Unnamed] '41-'56, Sea Hound '56-'80, Carolyn Jo '80-'00)

Vac		TB	1942	D	36*	65'00"	20'04"	4'03"

Built: George Gamble, Port Dover, ON

Stewart J. Cort at the blue hour, St. Marys River. (Stephen Sostaric)

Fleet Name Vessel Name	Vessel IMO #	Vessel Type	Year Built	Engine Type	Cargo Cap. or Gross*	Overall Length	Vessel Breadth	Vessel Depth
Vigilant I	8994178	TB	1944	D	111*	79'06"	20'11"	10'02"

Built: Russell Brothers Ltd., Owen Sound, ON (HMCS Glenlivet [W-43] '44-'75, Glenlivet II '75-'77, Canadian Franko '77-'82, Glenlivet II '82-'00)

McNALLY CONSTRUCTION INC., HAMILTON, ON (mcnallycorp.com)
A SUBSIDIARY OF WEEKS MARINE INC., CRANFORD, NJ

Beaver Delta II		TB	1959	D	14*	35'08"	12'00"	4'04"

Built: Allied Builders Ltd., Vancouver, BC (Halcyon Bay)

Beaver Gamma		TB	1960	D	17*	37'01"	12'09"	6'00"

Built: Diesel Sales & Service Ltd., Burlington, ON (Burlington Bertie)

Carl M.		TB	1957	D	21*	47'00"	14'06"	6'00"
D.L. Stanyer		TB	2014	D	14*	40'03"	11'08"	6'02"
Jamie L.		TB	1988	D	25*	36'04"	14'07"	5'09"

(Baie Ste-Anne '88-'96, T-1 '96-'98, Baie Ste-Anne II '98-'05)

J.F. Whalen		TB	2014	D	14*	40'03"	11'08"	6'02"
Lac Como		TB	1944	D	63*	65'00"	16'10"	7'10"

Built: Canadian Bridge Co., Walkerville, ON (Tanac 74 '44-'64)

Lac Vancouver		TB	1943	D	65*	60'09"	16'10"	7'08"

Built: Central Bridge Co., Trenton, ON (Vancouver '43-'74)

Mister Joe		TB	1964	D	70*	61'00"	19'00"	7'02"

Built: Russel Brothers Ltd., Owen Sound, ON (Churchill River '64-'01)

Oshawa		TB	1969	D	24*	42'09"	13'08"	5'04"
Paula M.		TB	1959	D	12*	48'02"	10'05"	3'01"
Sandra Mary		TB	1962	D	97*	80'00"	21'00"	10'09"

Built: Russel Brothers Ltd., Owen Sound, ON (Flo Cooper '62-'00)

Whitby		TB	1978	D	24*	42'19"	13'08"	6'05"
Willmac		TB	1959	D	16*	40'00"	13'00"	3'07"

MICHELS CORP., BROWNSVILLE, WI (michels.us)

Edith J.		TB	1962	D	18*	43'02"	13'00"	5'04"
Leona B.		TB	1972	D	99*	59'08"	24'01"	10'03"

(Kings Squire '72-'89, Juanita D. '78-'89, Peggy Ann '89-'93, Mary Page Hannah {2} '93-'04)

Ruth Lucille		TB	1966	D	N/A	59'05"	22'00"	9'06"

Built: St. Charles Steel Works, Thibodaux, LA (Capt. John Chappelle, Ocean Endeavor)

MICHIGAN CROSSROADS COUNCIL, BOY SCOUTS OF AMERICA, MACKINAW CITY, MI

Retriever		TV	1980	D/S	24*	51'08"	13'05"	7'00"

MICHIGAN DEPARTMENT OF NATURAL RESOURCES, LANSING, MI (michigan.gov/dnr)

Channel Cat		RV	1968	D	24*	46'00"	13'06"	4'00"
Lake Char		RV	2006	D	26*	56'00"	16'00"	4'05"
Steelhead		RV	1967	D	70*	63'00"	16'04"	6'06"
Tanner		RV	2016	D	26*	57'00"	16'00"	4'05"

MICHIGAN TECHNOLOGICAL UNIVERSITY, HOUGHTON, MI (mtu.edu/greatlakes/fleet/agassiz)

Agassiz		RV	2002	D	14*	36'00"	13'00"	4'00"

MIDDLE RIVER MARINE, MOKENA, IL (gomiddleriver.com)

Buckley		TB	1958	D	94*	95'00"	26'00"	11'00"

Built: Parker Bros. Shipyard, Houston, TX (Linda Brooks '58-'67, Eddie B. {2} '67-'95)

Ellie		TW	1970	D	29*	39'07"	16'00"	4'06"

Built: Big River Shipbuilding Inc., Vicksburg, MS; laid up at Chicago, IL (Miss Bissy '09)

Gwyneth Anne		TB	2017	D	103*	65'00"	28'00"	8'06"

Built: Marine Builders Inc., Utica, IN

Koolcat		TW	1982	D		66'08"	24'00"	8'06"

Built: Superior Boat Works Inc., Greenville, MS (Sean L, Ray Eckstein)

Morgan		TW	1974	D	134*	90'00"	30'00"	10'06"

Built: Peterson Builders Inc., Sturgeon Bay, WI (Donald O' Toole '74-'86, Bonesey B. '86-'95)

Sydney Reese		TW	1965	D	103*	75'03"	19'04"	8'00"

Built: Twin City Shipyard Inc., St. Paul, MN (Paul H. Lambert '65-'80, Minneapolis '80-??)

Tanner		TW	1977	D	62*	56'06"	22'03"	6'00"

Built: Thrift Shipbuilding Inc., Sulphur, LA; (J.H. Tanner '76-'00)

MILLER FERRIES, PUT-IN-BAY, OH (millerferry.com)

Islander {3}		PA/CF	1983	D	92*	90'03"	38'00"	8'03"

Built: G & W Industries Inc., Cleveland, OH

Mary Ann Market		PA/CF	2021	D	TBA	140'00"	38'05"	N/A

Built: Fraser Shipyards, Superior, WI

Put-in-Bay {3}		PA/CF	1997	D	97*	136'00"	38'06"	9'06"

Built: Sturgeon Bay Shipbuilding Co., Sturgeon Bay, WI; lengthened 40' in '09 at Cleveland, OH

Fleet Name / Vessel Name	Vessel IMO #	Vessel Type	Year Built	Engine Type	Cargo Cap. or Gross*	Overall Length	Vessel Breadth	Vessel Depth
South Bass		PA/CF	1989	D	95*	96′ 00″	38′ 06″	9′ 06″
Built: G & W Industries Inc., Cleveland, OH								
Wm. Market		PA/CF	1993	D	95*	96′ 00″	38′ 06″	8′ 09″
Built: Peterson Builders Inc., Sturgeon Bay, WI								

MILWAUKEE BOAT LINE LLC, MILWAUKEE, WI *(mkeboat.com)*

Fleet Name / Vessel Name	Vessel IMO #	Vessel Type	Year Built	Engine Type	Cargo Cap. or Gross*	Overall Length	Vessel Breadth	Vessel Depth
Iroquois		PA	1922	D	91*	61′ 09″	21′ 00″	6′ 04″
Vista King		ES	1978	D	60*	78′ 00″	23′ 00″	5′ 02″
Voyageur		PA	1988	D	94*	67′ 02″	21′ 00″	7′ 04″

MILWAUKEE HARBOR COMMISSION, MILWAUKEE, WI *(city.milwaukee.gov/port)*

Fleet Name / Vessel Name	Vessel IMO #	Vessel Type	Year Built	Engine Type	Cargo Cap. or Gross*	Overall Length	Vessel Breadth	Vessel Depth
Harbor Seagull		TB	1961	D	23*	44′ 05″	16′ 04″	5′ 00″
Built: T.D. Vinette Co., Escanaba, MI								
Joey D.		TB	2011	D	65*	60′ 00″	20′ 06″	6′ 06″
Built: Great Lakes Shipyard, Cleveland, OH								

MILWAUKEE METROPOLITAN SEWERAGE DISTRICT, MILWAUKEE, WI

Fleet Name / Vessel Name	Vessel IMO #	Vessel Type	Year Built	Engine Type	Cargo Cap. or Gross*	Overall Length	Vessel Breadth	Vessel Depth
Pelagos		RV	1989	D	32*	42′ 09″	13′ 08″	6′ 06″

MILWAUKEE RIVER CRUISE LINE, MILWAUKEE, WI *(edelweissboats.com)*

Fleet Name / Vessel Name	Vessel IMO #	Vessel Type	Year Built	Engine Type	Cargo Cap. or Gross*	Overall Length	Vessel Breadth	Vessel Depth
Edelweiss II		ES	1989	D	95*	73′ 08″	20′ 00″	2′ 08″
Harbor Lady		ES	1996	D	76*	80′ 08″	20′ 00″	6′ 00″
Lakeside Spirit		ES	1992	D	25*	63′ 00″	15′ 00″	4′ 00″
Miss Wisconsin		ES	1994	D	51*	72′ 06″	20′ 00″	5′ 04″

MINISTRY OF TRANSPORTATION, TORONTO, ON *(www.mto.gov.on.ca)*

Fleet Name / Vessel Name	Vessel IMO #	Vessel Type	Year Built	Engine Type	Cargo Cap. or Gross*	Overall Length	Vessel Breadth	Vessel Depth
Amherst Islander II	N/A	PC/CF	2020	E	N/A	236′ 06″	N/A	N/A
Built: Damen Shipyards, Galati, Romania; ferry runs from Millhaven, ON, to Amherst Island, ON								
Frontenac Howe Islander		PF/CF	2004	D	130*	100′ 00″	32′ 03″	5′ 05″
Built: Heddle Marine Service Inc., Hamilton, ON; 15-car cable ferry to Howe Island, east of Kingston, ON								
Frontenac II	5068875	PA/CF	1962	D	666*	181′ 00″	45′ 00″	10′ 00″
Built: Chantier Maritime de St-Laurent, St-Laurent, QC; ferry from Millhaven, ON, to Amherst Island, ON (Charlevoix {2} '62-'92)								
Glenora	5358074	PA/CF	1952	D	189*	127′ 00″	33′ 00″	9′ 00″
Built: Port Arthur Shipbuilding Co., Port Arthur, ON; ferry from Adolphustown, ON, to Glenora, ON (St. Joseph Islander '52-'74)								
Jiimaan	9034298	PA/CF	1992	D	2,807*	176′ 09″	42′ 03″	13′ 06″
Built: Port Weller Dry Docks, Port Weller, ON; ferry from Leamington/Kingsville, ON, to Pelee Island, ON; towed to Sarnia, ON, August '21 for lay-up and evaluation for future service								
Pelee Islander	5273274	PA/CF	1960	D	334*	145′ 00″	32′ 00″	10′ 00″
Built: Erieau Shipbuilding & Drydock Co. Ltd., Erieau, ON; ferry from Leamington/Kingsville, ON, to Pelee Island, ON								
Pelee Islander II		PA/CF	2018	D	3,147*	222′ 00″	48′ 06″	15′ 09″
Built: Asenav, Santiago, Chile; service from Leamington, ON, to Pelee Island, ON								
Quinte Loyalist	5358062	PA/CF	1954	D	204*	127′ 00″	32′ 00″	8′ 00″
Built: Erieau Shipbuilding & Drydock Co. Ltd., Erieau, ON; service to Wolfe Island/Kingston, ON, and Glenora/Adolphustown, ON								
Wolfe Islander III	7423079	PA/CF	1975	D	985*	205′ 00″	68′ 00″	6′ 00″
Built: Port Arthur Shipbuilding Co., Port Arthur, ON; ferry from Kingston, ON, to Wolfe Island, ON								
Wolfe Islander IV	N/A	PA/CF	2021	E	N/A	321′ 06″	65′ 00″	15′ 00′
Built: Damen Shipyards, Galati, Romania; ferry from Kingston, ON, to Wolfe Island, ON								

MJO CONTRACTING INC., HANCOCK, MI *(mjocontracting.com)*

Fleet Name / Vessel Name	Vessel IMO #	Vessel Type	Year Built	Engine Type	Cargo Cap. or Gross*	Overall Length	Vessel Breadth	Vessel Depth
Lily North		TB	1986	D	85*	60′ 00″	16′ 00″	10′ 02″

MONTREAL BOATMEN LTD., TROIS-RIVIÈRES, QC

Fleet Name / Vessel Name	Vessel IMO #	Vessel Type	Year Built	Engine Type	Cargo Cap. or Gross*	Overall Length	Vessel Breadth	Vessel Depth
Aldo H.		PB	1979	D	37*	56′ 04″	15′ 04″	6′ 02″
Boatman No. 6		TB	1977	D	39*	56′ 07″	18′ 07″	6′ 03″
Primrose *In use as a floating office/dock*		DR	1915	B	916*	136′ 06″	42′ 00″	10′ 02

MONTREAL PORT AUTHORITY, MONTREAL, QC *(port-montreal.com)*

Fleet Name / Vessel Name	Vessel IMO #	Vessel Type	Year Built	Engine Type	Cargo Cap. or Gross*	Overall Length	Vessel Breadth	Vessel Depth
Maisonneuve	7397749	PA	1972	D	84*	63′ 10″	20′ 07″	9′ 03″
Built: Fercraft Marine Inc., Ste. Catherine D'Alexandrie, QC								
Turbulent		TB	2016	D	38*	48′ 06″	19′ 00″	9′ 02″
Built: Besiktas Tersane A.S., Istanbul, Turkey								

MUNISING BAY SHIPWRECK TOURS INC., MUNISING, MI *(shipwrecktours.com)*

Fleet Name / Vessel Name	Vessel IMO #	Vessel Type	Year Built	Engine Type	Cargo Cap. or Gross*	Overall Length	Vessel Breadth	Vessel Depth
Miss Munising		ES	1967	D	50*	60′ 00″	14′ 00″	4′ 04″
Shipwreck Express		ES	2019	D	94*	63′ 08″	31′ 04″	7′ 01″

MUSIQUE AQUATIQUE CRUISE LINES INC., TORONTO, ON *(citysightseeingtoronto.com)*

Fleet Name / Vessel Name	Vessel IMO #	Vessel Type	Year Built	Engine Type	Cargo Cap. or Gross*	Overall Length	Vessel Breadth	Vessel Depth
Harbour Star		ES	1978	D	45*	63′ 06″	15′ 09″	3′ 09″

MUSKOKA STEAMSHIPS & DISCOVERY CENTRE, GRAVENHURST, ON *(realmuskoka.com)*

Fleet Name / Vessel Name	Vessel IMO #	Vessel Type	Year Built	Engine Type	Cargo Cap. or Gross*	Overall Length	Vessel Breadth	Vessel Depth
Segwun		PA	1887	R	308*	128′ 00″	24′ 00″	7′ 06″
Built: Melancthon Simpson, Toronto, ON (Nipissing {2} 1887-'1925)								

Wanda III		PA	1915	E	59.82*	94' 00"	12' 00"	0' 04"
Built: Polson Iron Works Ltd., Toronto, ON								
Wenonah II	8972003	PA	2001	D	447*	127' 00"	28' 00"	6' 00"
Built: McNally Construction Inc., Belleville, ON								

N

NAUTICA QUEEN CRUISE DINING, CLEVELAND, OH *(nauticaqueen.com)*

Nautica Queen		ES	1981	D	95*	124' 00"	31' 02"	8' 09"
Built: Blount Marine Corp., Warren, RI (Bay Queen '81-'85, Arawanna Queen '85-'88, Star of Nautica '88-'92)								

NAUTICAL ADVENTURES, TORONTO, ON *(nauticaladventure.com)*

Empire Sandy	5071561	ES/3S	1943	D/W	338*	140' 00"	32' 08"	14' 00"
Built: Clellands Ltd., Wellington Quay-on-Tyne, England (Empire Sandy '43-'48, Ashford '48-'52, Chris M. '52-'79)								

NEAS (NUNAVUT EASTERN ARCTIC SHIPPING), MONTREAL, QC *(neas.ca)*

Vessels offer service between St. Lawrence River ports and the Canadian Arctic between July and November

Aujaq	9081320	HL	1994	D	8,448	446' 02"	65' 00"	38' 03"
Built: Scheepswerf en Machinefabriek, Hardinxveld, Netherlands (Egmondgracht '94-'19)								
Mitiq	9081306	HL	1995	D	12,754	447' 04"	62' 00"	38' 03"
Built: Frisian Shipbuilding Welgelegen B.V., Harlingen, Netherlands; operated by Spliethoff's, Amsterdam, Netherlands (Emmagracht '95-'19)								
Nunalik	9466996	HL	2009	D	12,837	453' 00"	68' 11"	36' 01"
Built: Jiandong Shipyard, Wuhu, China; operated by Spliethoff's, Amsterdam, Netherlands (Beluga Fairy '09-'11, HHL Amazon '11-'16, Hemgracht '16-'17)								
Qamutik	9081289	HL	1995	D	12,760	446' 00"	62' 00"	38' 02"
Built: Frisian Shipbuilding Welgelegen B.V., Harlingen, Netherlands; operated by Spliethoff's, Amsterdam, Netherlands (Edisongracht)								
Sinaa	9081318	HL	1994	D	8,448	446' 02"	65' 00"	38' 03""
Built: Van Der Giessen-D Noord B.V., Krimper, Netherlands (Egelantiersgracht '94-'19)								

Fleet Name / Vessel Name	Vessel IMO #	Vessel Type	Year Built	Engine Type	Cargo Cap. or Gross*	Overall Length	Vessel Breadth	Vessel Depth

NELSON CONSTRUCTION, LA POINTE, WI

Eclipse		TB	1937	D	23*	45' 00"	12' 00"	4' 03"
Built: Marine Iron & Shipbuilding, Duluth, MN								

NEW YORK POWER AUTHORITY, LEWISTON, NY *(nypa.gov)*

Breaker		IB/TB	1962	D	29*	43' 03"	14' 03"	5' 00"
Built: Toronto Drydock Co., Toronto, ON								
Breaker II		IB/TB	2020	D	46*	56' 00"	18' 05"	6' 09
Built: Blount Boats, Warren, RI								
Daniel Joncaire II		IB/TB	2015	D	47*	45' 00"	19' 07"	6' 01"
Built: Great Lakes Shipyard, Cleveland, OH								

NEW YORK DEPARTMENT OF ENVIRONMENTAL CONSERVATION, LAKE ONTARIO UNIT, ALBANY, NY

Seth Green		RV	1984	D	50*	47' 00"	17' 00"	8' 00"

NICHEVO CONSTRUCTION CO., BAYFIELD, WI

Robert H.		TB	1910	D	51*	64' 03"	16' 09"	8' 06"
Built: American Shipbuilding Co., Lorain, OH (Chattanooga '10-'79, Howard T. Hagen '79-'94, Nancy Ann '94-'01, Callie M '01-'18)								

NOAA GREAT LAKES ENVIRONMENTAL RESEARCH LABORATORY, ANN ARBOR, MI *(glerl.noaa.gov)*

Huron Explorer		RV	1979	D	15*	41' 00"	14' 08"	4' 08"
Laurentian		RV	1974	D	129*	80' 00"	21' 06"	11' 00"
Shenehon		SV	1953	D	90*	65' 00"	17' 00"	6' 00"
Storm		RV	1992	D		50' 00"	17' 00"	6' 00"

NORTH CHANNEL TRANSPORT LLC, ALGONAC, MI

Islander (2)		PA/CF	1967	D	38*	41' 00"	15' 00"	3' 06"

NORTH SHORE MARINE TERMINAL & LOGISTICS, ESCANABA, MI *(northshoremarineterminal.com)*

Erika Kobasic	8654235	TB	1939	DE	226*	110' 00"	25' 01"	14' 03"
Built: Gulfport Shipbuilding, Port Arthur, TX (USCGC Arundel [WYT / WYTM-90] '39-'84, Karen Andrie '84-'90)								
Escort		TB	1969	D	26*	50' 00"	14' 00"	6' 03"
Built: Jakobson Shipyard, Oyster Bay, NY								

John G. Munson heads for the Rock Cut in the lower St. Marys River, January 2023. (Logan Vasicek)

Fleet Name / Vessel Name	Vessel IMO #	Vessel Type	Year Built	Engine Type	Cargo Cap. or Gross*	Overall Length	Vessel Breadth	Vessel Depth
Krystal		TB	1954	D	23*	45' 02"	12' 08"	6' 00"
Built: Roamer Boat Co., Holland, MI (ST-2168 '54-'62, Thunder Bay '62-'02)								
Nickelena	8654247	TB	1973	D	240*	109' 00"	30' 07"	15' 08"
Built: Marinette Marine Corp., Marinette, WI (USS Chetek [YTB-827] '73-'96, Chetek '96-'00, Koziol '00-'08)								

NOVAALGOMA CEMENT CARRIERS LTD., ST. CATHARINES, ON *(novaalgomacc.com)*
A PARTNERSHIP BETWEEN ALGOMA CENTRAL CORP. AND NOVA MARINE HOLDINGS SA

NACC Alicudi	9586435	CC	2011	D	5,566*	370' 70"	55' 11"	26' 90"
Built Ningbo Xinle Shipbuilding Group Co. Ltd., Zhejiang, China								
NACC Argonaut	9287302	CC	2003	D	9,255	447' 07"	69' 07"	37' 01
Built: Kyokuyo Shipyard Corp., Shimonoseki, Japan; converted to a cement carrier in '18 (Arklow Wave '03-'16, NACC Toronto '16-'18)								
NACC Quebec	9546057	CC	2011	D	10,246	459' 02"	68' 11"	34' 09
Built: Tuzla Gemi Endustrisi A.S., Tulza, Turkey; converted to a cement carrier in '16; vessel chartered to McInnis Cement, Montreal, QC (Tenace '11-'16)								

O-P

OAK GROVE & MARINE TRANSPORTATION INC., CLAYTON, NY

Maple Grove		PK	1954	D	55*	73' 07"	20' 00"	9' 00"
(LCM 8168)								

OHIO DEPARTMENT OF NATURAL RESOURCES, COLUMBUS, OH *(dnr.state.oh.us)*

Explorer II		RV	1999	D		53' 00"	15' 05"	4' 05"
Grandon		RV	1990	D	47*	47' 00"	16' 00"	5' 05"

OLYMPIA CRUISE LINE INC., THORNHILL, ON *(torontocruises.com)*

Enterprise 2000		ES	1998	D	370*	121' 06"	35' 00"	6' 00"

ONTARIO MINISTRY OF NATURAL RESOURCES, PETERBOROUGH, ON *(mnr.gov.on.ca)*

Erie Explorer		RV	1981	D	72*	53' 05"	20' 01"	4' 08"
Built: Hopper Fisheries Ltd., Port Stanley, ON (Janice H.X. '81-'97)								
Huron Explorer I		RV	2010	D	112*	62' 00"	21' 03"	6' 00"
Built: Hike Metal Products Ltd., Wheatley, ON								
Keenosay		RV	1957	D	68*	51' 04"	20' 07"	2' 07"
Built: S.G. Powell Shipyard Ltd., Dunnville, ON								
Nipigon Osprey		RV	1990	D	33*	42' 04"	14' 09"	6' 08"
Built: Kanter Yachts Corp., St. Thomas, ON								
Ontario Explorer		RV	2009	D	84*	64' 09"	21' 03"	6' 00"
Built: Hike Metal Products Ltd., Wheatley, ON								
Superior Explorer		RV	1954	D	82*	42' 03"	20' 02"	5' 08"
Built: Mathieson Boat Works, Goderich, ON (Atigamayg)								

ONTARIO POWER GENERATION INC., TORONTO, ON

Niagara Queen II		IB	1992	D	58*	56' 01"	18' 00"	6' 08"
Built: Hike Metal Products Ltd., Wheatley, ON								

ORIGINAL SOO LOCKS BOAT TOURS, SAULT STE. MARIE, MI *(originalsoolocktours.com)*
MANAGED BY INTERLAKE MARITIME SERVICES, MIDDLEBURG HEIGHTS, OH

Bide-A-Wee {3}		ES	1955	D	99*	64' 07"	23' 00"	7' 11"
Built: Blount Marine Corp., Warren, RI								
Hiawatha {2}		ES	1959	D	99*	64' 07"	23' 00"	7' 11"
Built: Blount Marine Corp., Warren, RI								
Holiday		ES	1957	D	99*	64' 07"	23' 00"	7' 11"
Built: Blount Marine Corp., Warren, RI								

OWEN SOUND TRANSPORTATION CO., OWEN SOUND, ON *(ontarioferries.com)*

Chi-Cheemaun	7343607	PA/CF	1974	D	6,991*	365' 05"	61' 00"	21' 00"
Built: Canadian Shipbuilding and Engineering Ltd., Collingwood, ON								

PARKS CANADA AGENCY, GATINEAU, QC *(pc.gc.ca)*

David Thompson	9065778	RV	1991	D	228*	89' 07"	29' 05"	12' 09"
(CCGS Arrow Post '91-'19)								

PARTY TIME CRUISE LINES, ST. JOSEPH, MI *(partytimecruiselines.com)*

Par-Te-Tyme		ES	1985	D	84*	58' 06"	21' 08"	7' 01"

PEARL BEACH CONSTRUCTION, WASHBURN, WI *(pearlbeachonline.com)*

Courtney Danielle		TB	1922	D	67*	65' 00"	14' 01"	10' 00"
Built: Glove Shipyard, Buffalo, NY (E.W. Sutton '22-'52, Venture '52-'98, Amber Mae '98-??)								

PICTURED ROCKS CRUISES INC., MUNISING, MI *(picturedrocks.com)*

Chapel Rock		ES	2019	D	55*	65' 00"	25' 00"	N/A
Grand Island {2}		ES	1989	D	52*	68' 00"	16' 01"	7' 01"

Algoma Discovery turns the BNSF ore dock in Superior, WI, over to the Stewart J. Cort, while American Spirit waits in the background.
(David Schauer)

Great Republic drydocked at Ironhead Marine in Toledo, OH. (Mike Mishler)

GREAT REPUBLIC

Fleet Name / Vessel Name	Vessel IMO #	Vessel Type	Year Built	Engine Type	Cargo Cap. or Gross*	Overall Length	Vessel Breadth	Vessel Depth
Grand Portal		ES	2004	D	76*	64' 08"	20' 00"	8' 04"
Miners Castle		ES	1974	D	82*	68' 00"	16' 06"	6' 04"
Miss Superior		ES	1984	D	83*	68' 00"	16' 09"	10' 04"
Pictured Rocks		ES	1972	D	53*	55' 07"	13' 07"	4' 04"
Pictured Rocks Express		ES	1988	D	90*	82' 07"	28' 06"	4' 04"

Built: Gladding-Hearn Shipbuilding, Somerset, MA (Island Express '88-'15)

PICTURED ROCKS KAYAKING, MUNISING, MI (paddlepicturedrocks.com)

Great Lakes Paddler		ES	2021	D	35*	50' 00"	20' 00"	5' 03"
Kayak Express		ES	2019	D	71*	64' 00"	19' 00"	N/A
Lieutenant Dan		ES	2021	D	35*	50' 00"	20' 00"	5' 03"
Pictured Rocks Paddler		ES	2021	D	35*	50' 00"	20' 00"	5' 03"

PLAUNT TRANSPORTATION CO. INC., CHEBOYGAN, MI (bbiferry.com)

Kristen D		CF	1987	D	83*	94' 11"	36' 00"	4' 06"

POMERLEAU INC., SAINT-GEORGES, QC (pomerleau.ca)

Fervent		WB	2014	D	47*	56' 01"	26' 16"	6' 08"

Built: Boats Ltd., Wallasea Island, England

Herve (The)		TB	2018	D	10*	34' 03"	13' 01"	5' 01"

Built: Chantier Naval Forillon Inc., Gaspe, QC

Intense		TB	2016	D	21*	41' 00"	14' 04"	7' 08"

Built: Besiktas Tersane A.S., Istanbul, Turkey

Saint-Georges		TB	2015	D	21*	38' 05"	16' 27"	7' 05"

Built: Damen Shipyards, Gorinchem, The Netherlands

PORT CITY CRUISE LINES LLC, MUSKEGON, MI (aquastarcruises.com)

Aquastar		ES	1966	D	79*	64' 09"	27' 00"	5' 06"

Built: Blount Marine Corp., Warren, RI (Island Queen {1} '66-'87, Port City Princess '87-'18)

PORT OF CLEVELAND, CLEVELAND, OH (portofcleveland.com)
Vessels capture and remove plastic and organic floating debris from Cleveland harbor

Flotsam		EV	2012	D	7*	26' 00"	8' 03"	5' 02"
Jetsam		EV	2012	D	7*	26' 00"	8' 03"	5' 02"

PORTS TORONTO, TORONTO, ON (portstoronto.com)

Brutus I		TB	1992	D	10*	36' 01"	11' 09"	4' 04"

Built: Harry Gamble Shipyard, Port Dover, ON (Angela F.)

David Hornell VC		PA/CF	2006	D	219*	95' 10"	37' 07"	7' 05"

Built: Hike Metal Products, Wheatley, ON (TCCA 1 '06-'10)

Iron Guppy		TB	2016	D	65*	64' 96"	20' 99"	11' 87"

Built: Hike Metal Products, Wheatley, ON

Marilyn Bell I		PA/CF	2009	E	270*	95' 10"	37' 07"	7' 05"

Built: Hike Metal Products, Wheatley, ON (TCCA 2 '09-'10)

Windmill Point		PA/CF	1954	D	118*	65' 00"	36' 00"	10' 00"

Built: Kingston Shipyards Ltd., Kingston, ON; in long-term lay-up

PORTOFINO ON THE RIVER, WYANDOTTE, MI (portofinoontheriver.com)

Portofino		ES	1997	D	76*	80' 08"	20' 00"	6' 00"

Built: Skipper Liner, La Crosse, WI (Island Girl X, Naples Royal Princess, Romantics, Infinity, The Jude Thaddeus, Infinity, Jacksonville Princess II, Miami Magic)

PRESQUE ISLE BOAT TOURS, ERIE, PA (piboattours.com)

Lady Kate {2}		ES	1952	D	11*	59' 03"	15' 00"	3' 09"

Built: J.W. Nolan & Sons, Erie, PA (G.A. Boeckling II '52-'69, Cedar Point III '69-'88, Island Trader '88-'98)

PRO-TECH MARINE INC., GRAND HAVEN, MI (pro-techmarineinc.com)

Jacob Sam		TB	1972	D	31*	43' 08"	14' 03"	7' 05"

PURVIS MARINE LTD., SAULT STE. MARIE, ON (purvismarine.com)

Adanac III		TB	1913	D	108*	80' 03"	19' 03"	9' 10"

Built: Western Drydock & Shipbuilding Co., Port Arthur, ON (Edward C. Whalen '13-'66, John McLean '66-'95)

Anglian Lady	5141483	TB	1953	D	398*	132' 00"	31' 00"	14' 00"

Built: John I. Thornecroft & Co., Southampton, England (Hamtun '53-'72, Nathalie Letzer '72-'88)

Avenger IV	5401297	TB	1962	D	291*	120' 00"	30' 00"	19' 00"

Built: Cochrane & Sons Ltd., Selby, England (Avenger '62-'85)

G.L.B. No. 2		DB	1953	B	3,215	240' 00"	50' 00"	12' 00"

Built: Ingalls Shipbuilding Corp., Birmingham, AL (Jane Newfield '53-'66, ORG 6502 '66-'75)

Malden		DB	1946	B	1,075	150' 00"	41' 09"	10' 03"

Built: Russel Brothers Ltd., Owen Sound, ON

Martin E. Johnson		TB	1959	D	26*	47' 00"	16' 00"	7' 00"

Built: Russel Hipworth Engines Ltd., Owen Sound, ON

Fleet Name Vessel Name	Vessel IMO #	Vessel Type	Year Built	Engine Type	Cargo Cap. or Gross*	Overall Length	Vessel Breadth	Vessel Depth
Osprey		TB	1944	D	36*	45' 00"	13' 06"	7' 00"
Built: Kewaunee Shipbuilding and Engineering Corp., Kewaunee, WI (ST-606 '43-'46)								
PML 2501		TK	1980	B	1,954*	302' 00"	52' 00"	17' 00"
Built: Cenac Shipyard, Houma, LA (CTCO 2505 '80-'96)								
PML 9000		DB	1968	B	4,285*	400' 00"	76' 00"	20' 00"
Built: Bethlehem Steel – Shipbuilding Division, San Francisco, CA (Palmer '68-'00)								
PML Alton		DB	1933	B	150	93' 00"	30' 00"	8' 00"
Built: McClintic- Marshall, Sturgeon Bay, WI								
PML Ironmaster		DB	1962	B	7,437*	360' 00"	75' 00"	25' 00"
Built: Yarrows Ltd., Esquimalt, BC (G.T. Steelmaster, Ceres, American Gulf VII, Seaspan 241, G.T. Ironmaster)								
PML Tucci		CS	1958	B	601*	150' 00"	52' 00"	10' 00"
Built: Calumet Shipyard & Drydock Co., Chicago, IL (MCD '58-'73, Minnesota '73-'88, Candace Andrie '88-'08)								
PML Tucker		DS	1971	B	477*	140' 00"	50' 00"	9' 00"
Built: Twin City Shipyard, St. Paul, MN (Illinois '71-'02, Meredith Andrie '02-'08)								
Reliance	7393808	TB	1974	D	708*	148' 03"	35' 07"	21' 07"
Built: Ulstein Hatlo A/S, Ulsteinvik, Norway (Sinni '74-'81, Irving Cedar '81-'96, Atlantic Cedar '96-'02)								
Rocket		TB	1901	D	40*	73' 00"	16' 00"	7' 00"
Built: Buffalo Shipbuilding Co., Buffalo, NY								
Tecumseh II		DB	1976	B	2,500	180' 00"	54' 00"	12' 00"
Built: Bergeron Machine Shop Inc., New Orleans, LA								
Wilfred M. Cohen	7629271	TB	1947	D	284*	102' 06"	28' 00"	15' 00"
Built: Newport News Shipbuilding and Drydock Co., Newport News, VA (A. T. Lowmaster '48-'75)								
W.I. Scott Purvis	5264819	TB	1938	D	203*	96' 00"	26' 00"	10' 00"
Built: Marine Industries, Sorel, QC (Orient Bay '38-'75, Guy M. No. 1 '75-'90)								
W.J. Isaac Purvis		TB	1962	D	71*	72' 00"	19' 00"	12' 00"
Built: McNamara Marine Ltd., Toronto, ON (Angus M. '62-'92, Omni Sorel '92-'02, Joyce B. Gardiner '02-'09)								
W.J. Ivan Purvis	5217218	TB	1938	D	190*	100' 00"	26' 00"	10' 00"
Built: Marine Industries, Sorel, QC (Magpie '38-'66, Dana T. Bowen '66-'75)								
PUT-IN-BAY BOAT LINE CO., PORT CLINTON, OH (jet-express.com)								
Jet Express		PF/CA	1989	D	93*	92' 08"	28' 06"	8' 04"
Jet Express II		PF/CA	1992	D	85*	92' 06"	28' 06"	8' 04"
Jet Express III		PF/CA	2001	D	70*	78' 02"	27' 06"	8' 02"
Jet Express IV		PF/CA	1995	D	71*	77' 02"	28' 05"	7' 07"

Q-R

QUEBEC PORT AUTHORITY, QUEBEC, QC (portquebec.ca)								
Le Cageux		TB	2011	D	24*	42' 06"	16' 01"	7' 07"
Built: Meridien Maritime Reparation Inc., Matane, QC								
QUYON FERRY, QUYON, QC (quyonferry.com)								
Grant Beattie (The)		PF	2013	E	235*	115' 00"	46' 00"	7' 05"
RAND LOGISTICS INC., JERSEY CITY, NJ (randlog.com)								
AMERICAN STEAMSHIP CO., WILLIAMSVILLE, NY (americansteamship.com)								
American Century	7923196	SU	1981	D	80,900	1,000' 00"	105' 00"	56' 00"
Built: Bay Shipbuilding Co., Sturgeon Bay, WI (Columbia Star '81-'06)								
American Integrity	7514696	SU	1978	D	80,900	1,000' 00"	105' 00"	56' 00"
Built: Bay Shipbuilding Co., Sturgeon Bay, WI (Lewis Wilson Foy '78-'91, Oglebay Norton '91-'06)								
American Spirit	7423392	SU	1978	D	62,400	1,004' 00"	105' 00"	50' 00"
Built: American Shipbuilding Co., Lorain, OH (George A. Stinson '78-'04)								
Burns Harbor	7514713	SU	1980	D	80,900	1,000' 00"	105' 00"	56' 00"
Built: Bay Shipbuilding Co., Sturgeon Bay, WI								
Indiana Harbor	7514701	SU	1979	D	80,900	1,000' 00"	105' 00"	56' 00"
Built: Bay Shipbuilding Co., Sturgeon Bay, WI								
Walter J. McCarthy Jr.	7514684	SU	1977	D	80,500	1,000' 00"	105' 00"	56' 00"
Built: Bay Shipbuilding Co., Sturgeon Bay, WI (Belle River '77-'90)								
GRAND RIVER NAVIGATION CO., TRAVERSE CITY, MI (randlog.com/grn)								
American Courage	7634226	SU	1979	D	24,300	636' 00"	68' 00"	40' 00"
Built: Bay Shipbuilding Co., Sturgeon Bay, WI; (Fred R. White Jr. '79-'06)								
American Mariner	7812567	SU	1980	D	37,300	730' 00"	78' 00"	42' 00"
Built: Bay Shipbuilding Co., Sturgeon Bay, WI (Laid down as Chicago {3})								
Ashtabula	8637495	SU	1982	B	17,982	610' 01"	78' 01"	49' 08"
Built: Bay Shipbuilding Co., Sturgeon Bay, WI; Ashtabula / tug Defiance length together 705' 00" (Erol Y. Beker '82-'87, Mary Turner '82-'12)								

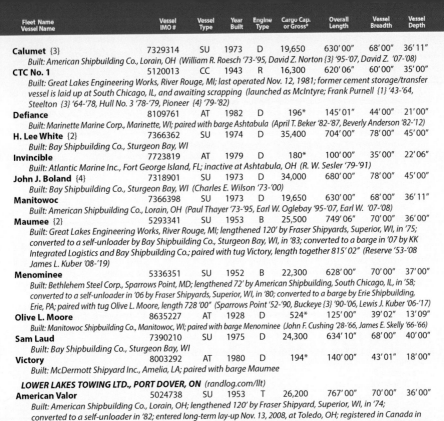

Fleet Name / Vessel Name	Vessel IMO #	Vessel Type	Year Built	Engine Type	Cargo Cap. or Gross*	Overall Length	Vessel Breadth	Vessel Depth
Calumet {3}	7329314	SU	1973	D	19,650	630' 00"	68' 00"	36' 11"

Built: American Shipbuilding Co., Lorain, OH (William R. Roesch '73-'95, David Z. Norton {3} '95-'07, David Z. '07-'08)

| **CTC No. 1** | 5120013 | CC | 1943 | R | 16,300 | 620' 06" | 60' 00" | 35' 00" |

Built: Great Lakes Engineering Works, River Rouge, MI; last operated Nov. 12, 1981; former cement storage/transfer vessel is laid up at South Chicago, IL, and awaiting scrapping (launched as McIntyre; Frank Purnell {1} '43-'64, Steelton {3} '64-'78, Hull No. 3 '78-'79, Pioneer {4} '79-'82)

| **Defiance** | 8109761 | AT | 1982 | D | 196* | 145' 01" | 44' 00" | 21' 00" |

Built: Marinette Marine Corp., Marinette, WI; paired with barge Ashtabula (April T. Beker '82-'87, Beverly Anderson '82-'12)

| **H. Lee White** {2} | 7366362 | SU | 1974 | D | 35,400 | 704' 00" | 78' 00" | 45' 00" |

Built: Bay Shipbuilding Co., Sturgeon Bay, WI

| **Invincible** | 7723819 | AT | 1979 | D | 180* | 100' 00" | 35' 00" | 22' 06" |

Built: Atlantic Marine Inc., Fort George Island, FL; inactive at Ashtabula, OH (R. W. Sesler '79-'91)

| **John J. Boland** {4} | 7318901 | SU | 1973 | D | 34,000 | 680' 00" | 78' 00" | 45' 00" |

Built: Bay Shipbuilding Co., Sturgeon Bay, WI (Charles E. Wilson '73-'00)

| **Manitowoc** | 7366398 | SU | 1973 | D | 19,650 | 630' 00" | 68' 00" | 36' 11" |

Built: American Shipbuilding Co., Lorain, OH (Paul Thayer '73-'95, Earl W. Oglebay '95-'07, Earl W. '07-'08)

| **Maumee** {2} | 5293341 | SU | 1953 | B | 25,500 | 749' 06" | 70' 00" | 36' 00" |

Built: Great Lakes Engineering Works, River Rouge, MI; lengthened 120' by Fraser Shipyards, Superior, WI, in '75; converted to a self-unloader by Bay Shipbuilding Co., Sturgeon Bay, WI, in '83; converted to a barge in '07 by KK Integrated Logistics and Bay Shipbuilding Co.; paired with tug Victory, length together 815' 02" (Reserve '53-'08 James L. Kuber '08-'19)

| **Menominee** | 5336351 | SU | 1952 | B | 22,300 | 628' 00" | 70' 00" | 37' 00" |

Built: Bethlehem Steel Corp., Sparrows Point, MD; lengthened 72' by American Shipbuilding, South Chicago, IL, in '58; converted to a self-unloader in '06 by Fraser Shipyards, Superior, WI, in '80; converted to a barge by Erie Shipbuilding, Erie, PA; paired with tug Olive L. Moore, length 728' 00" (Sparrows Point '52-'90, Buckeye {3} '90-'06, Lewis J. Kuber '06-'17)

| **Olive L. Moore** | 8635227 | AT | 1928 | D | 524* | 125' 00" | 39' 02" | 13' 09" |

Built: Manitowoc Shipbuilding Co., Manitowoc, WI; paired with barge Menominee (John F. Cushing '28-'66, James E. Skelly '66-'66)

| **Sam Laud** | 7390210 | SU | 1975 | D | 24,300 | 634' 10" | 68' 00" | 40' 00" |

Built: Bay Shipbuilding Co., Sturgeon Bay, WI

| **Victory** | 8003292 | AT | 1980 | D | 194* | 140' 00" | 43' 01" | 18' 00" |

Built: McDermott Shipyard Inc., Amelia, LA; paired with barge Maumee

LOWER LAKES TOWING LTD., PORT DOVER, ON (randlog.com/llt)

| **American Valor** | 5024738 | SU | 1953 | T | 26,200 | 767' 00" | 70' 00" | 36' 00" |

Built: American Shipbuilding Co., Lorain, OH; lengthened 120' by Fraser Shipyard, Superior, WI, in '74; converted to a self-unloader in '82; entered long-term lay-up Nov. 13, 2008, at Toledo, OH; registered in Canada in 2018 as Valo but name not put on vessel; may eventually be repowered and returned to service (Armco '53-'06)

Lake Michigan sunset from the Lake Express ferry. (Danny Hecko)

Fleet Name Vessel Name	Vessel IMO #	Vessel Type	Year Built	Engine Type	Cargo Cap. or Gross*	Overall Length	Vessel Breadth	Vessel Depth
Cuyahoga	5166392	SU	1943	D	15,675	620' 00"	60' 00"	35' 00"

Built: American Shipbuilding Co., Lorain, OH; converted to a self-unloader in '74 by Manitowoc Shipbuilding Co., Manitowoc, WI; repowered in '01 (J. Burton Ayers '43-'95)

Kaministiqua	8119285	BC	1983	D	34,500	730' 01"	75' 09"	48' 00"

Built: Govan Shipyards, Glasgow, Scotland (Saskatchewan Pioneer '83-'95, Lady Hamilton '95-'06, Voyageur Pioneer '06-'08)

Manitoulin {6}	8810918	SU	1991	D	25,000	662' 09"	77' 09"	44' 11"

Former saltwater tanker rebuilt for Great Lakes service in 2015 with a new self-unloading bow section; **bow section** built 2014-15 at Chengxi Shipyards, Jiangyin, China; **stern section** built in 1991 at Uljanik Shipyard, Pula, Croatia (Trelsi '91-'01, Euro Swan '01-'11, Lalandia Swan '11-'15)

Michipicoten {2}	5102865	SU	1952	D	22,300	698' 00"	70' 00"	37' 00"

Built: Bethlehem Shipbuilding & Drydock Co., Sparrows Point, MD; lengthened 72' by American Shipbuilding Co., South Chicago, IL, in '57; converted to a self-unloader by American Shipbuilding Co., Toledo, OH, in '80; repowered in '11 (Elton Hoyt 2nd '52-'03)

Robert S. Pierson {2}	7366403	SU	1974	D	19,650	630' 00"	68' 00"	36' 11"

Built: American Shipbuilding Co., Lorain, OH (Wolverine {2} '74-'08)

Saginaw {3}	5173876	SU	1953	D	20,200	639' 03"	72' 00"	36' 00"

Built: Manitowoc Shipbuilding Co., Manitowoc, WI, repowered in '08 (John J. Boland {3} '53-'99)

Tecumseh {2}	7225855	BC	1973	D	29,510	641' 00"	78' 00"	45' 03"

Built: Lockheed Shipbuilding & Construction Co., Seattle, WA; engine room damaged in a December 2019 fire; remains laid up at Ashtabula, OH (Sugar Islander '73-'96, Islander '96-'96, Judy Litrico '96-'06, Tina Litrico '06-'11)

RIO TINTO-ALCAN INC., LA BAIE, QC (riotintoalcan.com)

Fjord Éternité	9364348	TT	2006	D	381*	94' 00"	36' 05"	16' 04"

Built: East Isle Shipyard, Georgetown, PEI (Stevns Icecap '06-'07, Svitzer Nanna '07-'11, Stevns Icecap '10-'11)

Fjord Saguenay	9351012	TT	2006	D	381*	94' 00"	36' 05"	16' 04"

Built: East Isle Shipyard, Georgetown, PEI (Stevns Iceflower '06-'07, Svitzer Njord '07-'09, Stevns Iceflower '09-'09)

ROCKPORT CRUISES, ROCKPORT, ON (rockportcruises.com)

Canada Spirit		ES	1976	D	325*	92' 00"	26' 00"	10' 00"
Chief Shingwauk		ES	1965	D	109*	70' 00"	24' 00"	4' 06"
Ida M.		ES	1970	D	29*	55' 00"	14' 00"	3' 00"
Ida M. II		ES	1973	D	121*	63' 02"	22' 02"	5' 00"
Sea Prince II		ES	1978	D	172*	83' 00"	24' 02"	6' 08"

ROBERT DANIEL WELSH, OWEN SOUND, ON

Dawn Light		ES	1891	D	41*	75' 00"	17' 06"	9' 06"

Built: Craig Shipbuilding Co., Toledo, OH; rebuilt as a tug in '54 (Leroy Brooks '91-'25, Henry Stokes '25-'54, Aburg '54-'81)

Homecoming for the Saginaw at Manitowoc, WI. In 2022, the 1953-vintage laker returned to the port in which she was built to unload barley at the Briess Malting Co.'s marine tower. The company has shifted its inbound cargo from rail to ship, so there may be increased vessel calls in the future. (Tim Keefe)

Fleet Name Vessel Name	Vessel IMO #	Vessel Type	Year Built	Engine Type	Cargo Cap. or Gross*	Overall Length	Vessel Breadth	Vessel Depth
ROEN SALVAGE CO., STURGEON BAY, WI (roensalvage.com)								
Chas. Asher		TB	1967	D	39*	49' 02"	17' 06"	6' 10"
Built: Sturgeon Bay Shipbuilding Co., Sturgeon Bay, WI								
David R. Schanock		TB	1978	D	147*	69' 00"	26' 00"	9' 06"
Built: Main Iron Works, Houma, LA (Itco XVI '78–'78, H.A. Walker '78–'94, Trevor '94–'21)								
John R. Asher		TB	1943	D	93*	68' 09"	20' 00"	8' 00"
Built: Platzer Boat Works, Houston, TX (U. S. Army ST-71 '43–'46, Russell 8 '46–'64, Reid McAllister '64–'67, Donegal '67–'85)								
Louie S.		TB	1956	D	10*	37' 00"	12' 00"	4' 05"
Built: Roen Salvage Co., Sturgeon Bay, WI								
Spuds		TB	1944	D	19*	42' 00"	12' 05"	5' 04"
Built: Roen Salvage Co., Sturgeon Bay, WI								
Stephan M. Asher		TB	1954	D	60*	65' 00"	19' 01"	5' 04"
Built: Burton Shipyard Inc., Port Arthur, TX (Captain Bennie '54–'82, Dumar Scout '82–'87)								
Timmy A.		TB	1953	D	12*	33' 06"	10' 08"	5' 02"
Built: M.D. Moody & Sons, Jacksonville, FL (Calhoun '53–'64)								
RYBA MARINE CONSTRUCTION CO., CHEBOYGAN, MI (rybamarine.com)								
Kathy Lynn	8034887	TB	1944	D	140*	85' 00"	24' 00"	9' 06"
Built: Decatur Iron & Steel Co., Decatur, AL (U. S. Army ST-693 '44–'79, Sea Islander '79–'91)								
Kristin Joelle	6604016	TB	1965	D	148*	75' 05"	24' 00"	8' 06"
Built: Equitable Equipment Co., Madisonville, LA (Vincent J. Robin IV, Betty Smith, Seaco Enterprise '91–'97, Leo '97–'98, Ybor '98–'99, Capt. Sweet '99–'01, Susan McAllister '01–'15, Michigan '15–'17)								
Rochelle Kaye		TB	1963	D	52*	51' 06"	19' 04"	7' 00"
Built: St. Charles Steel Works Inc., Thibodeaux, LA (Jaye Anne '63–?, Katanni ?–'97)								
Thomas R. Morrish		TB	1980	D	88*	64' 00"	14' 05"	8' 06"
Built: Houma Shipbuilding Co., Houma, LA (Lady Ora '80–'99, Island Eagle '99–'04, Captain Zeke '01–'14)								

S

Fleet Name Vessel Name	Vessel IMO #	Vessel Type	Year Built	Engine Type	Cargo Cap. or Gross*	Overall Length	Vessel Breadth	Vessel Depth
SAIL DOOR COUNTY, SISTER BAY, WI (saildoorcounty.com)								
Edith M. Becker		PA	1984	D/W	22*	62' 00"	24' 00"	8' 06"
SAND PRODUCTS CORP., MUSKEGON, MI								
LAKE SERVICE SHIPPING, MUSKEGON, MI								
McKee Sons	5216458	SU	1945	B	19,900	579' 02"	71' 06"	38' 06"
Built: Sun Shipbuilding and Drydock Co., Chester, PA; converted from a saltwater vessel to a self-unloading Great								

Algoma Compass upbound on the St. Clair River. (Eric Treece)

Fleet Name Vessel Name	Vessel IMO #	Vessel Type	Year Built	Engine Type	Cargo Cap. or Gross*	Overall Length	Vessel Breadth	Vessel Depth

Lakes bulk carrier by Maryland Drydock Co., Baltimore, MD, in '52; completed as a self-unloader by Manitowoc Shipbuilding Co., Manitowoc, WI, in '53; converted to a self-unloading barge in '91 by Upper Lakes Towing, Escanaba, MI; laid up at Erie, PA, '12-'14 and Muskegon, MI, since Dec. 20, 2014 (USNS Marine Angel '45-'52)

PORT CITY MARINE SERVICES, MUSKEGON, MI (portcitymarine.com)

Bradshaw McKee 7644312 AT 1977 D 174* 121' 06" 34' 06" 18' 02"
Built: Toche Enterprises Inc., Ocean Springs, MS; (Lady Elda '77-'78, Kings Challenger '78-'78, ITM No. 1 '78-'81, Kings Challenger '81-'86, Susan W. Hannah '86-'11)

Caroline McKee 7303853 AT 1972 D 169* 122' 02" 34' 06" 12' 07"
Built: Main Iron Works Inc., Houma, LA; (David P. Guidry '72-'81, Thunder '81-'90, Sharon DeHart '90-'13, Coastal 303 '13-'18, Southern Dawn '18-'19)

Colleen McAllister 7338872 TB 1967 D 194* 124' 00" 31' 06" 13' 08"
Built: Gulfport Shipbuilding Corp., Port Arthur, TX; laid up at Muskegon, MI (Ellena Hicks '67-'03)

Commander CC 1957 B 13,453 495' 00" 71' 00" 27' 00"
Built: Todd Shipyards Corp., Houston, TX; converted to a self-unloader in '93; converted to a cement carrier in '17-'18 at Bay Shipbuilding Co., Sturgeon Bay, WI, paired with tug Caroline McKee, length together 567' 00" (M-211 '57-'81, Virginia '81-'88, C-11 '88-'93, Kellstone 1 '93-'04, Cleveland Rocks '04-'18)

Katie G. McAllister 7046089 TB 1966 D 194* 124' 00" 31' 06" 13' 08"
Built: Gulfport Shipbuilding Corp., Port Arthur, TX; laid up at Muskegon, MI (Libby Black '67-'03)

Prentiss Brown 7035547 AT 1967 D 197* 123' 05" 31' 06" 19' 00"
Built: Gulfport Shipbuilding Corp., Port Arthur, TX; (Betty Culbreath '67-'03, Michaela McAllister '03-'09)

St. Marys Challenger 5009984 CC 1906 B 10,250 527' 00" 56' 00" 31' 00"
Built: Great Lakes Engineering Works, Ecorse, MI; repowered in '50; converted to a self-unloading cement carrier by Manitowoc Shipbuilding Co., Manitowoc, WI, in '67; converted to a barge over the winter of '13-'14 by Bay Shipbuilding Co., Sturgeon Bay, WI; paired with tug Prentiss Brown, length together 613' 00" (William P. Snyder '06-'26, Elton Hoyt II (1) '26-'52, Alex D. Chisholm '52-'66, Medusa Challenger '66-'99, Southdown Challenger '99-'05)

St. Marys Conquest 5015012 CC 1937 B 8,500 437' 06" 55' 00" 28' 00"
Built: Manitowoc Shipbuilding Co., Manitowoc, WI; converted from a powered tanker to a self-unloading cement barge in '87 by Bay Shipbuilding Co., Sturgeon Bay, WI; paired with tug Bradshaw McKee, length together 498' 00" (Red Crown '37-'62, Amoco Indiana '62-'87, Medusa Conquest '87-'99, Southdown Conquest '99-'03, Cemex Conquest '03-'05)

PORT CITY MARINE SERVICES CANADA INC., BURLINGTON, ON

Petite Forte 6826119 TB 1969 D 368* 127' 00" 32' 00" 14' 06"
Built: Cochrane and Sons Ltd., Selby, England; paired with barge St. Marys Cement

H. Lee White making the Mistersky fuel dock in the Detroit River. (Scott Bjorklund)

79

Fleet Name / Vessel Name	Vessel IMO #	Vessel Type	Year Built	Engine Type	Cargo Cap. or Gross*	Overall Length	Vessel Breadth	Vessel Depth

FOLLOWING VESSELS OWNED BY ST. MARYS CEMENT INC.(CANADA), OPERATED BY PORT CITY MARINE SERVICES CANADA INC., BURLINGTON, ON

Fleet Name / Vessel Name	Vessel IMO #	Vessel Type	Year Built	Engine Type	Cargo Cap. or Gross*	Overall Length	Vessel Breadth	Vessel Depth
Sea Eagle II	7631860	AT	1979	D	560*	132' 00"	35' 00"	19' 00"

Built: Modern Marine Power Co., Houma, LA; paired with barge St. Marys Cement II (Sea Eagle '79-'81, Canmar Sea Eagle '81-'91)

St. Marys Cement	8972077	CC	1986	B	9,400	360' 00"	60' 00"	23' 03"

Built: Merce Industries East, Toledo, OH

St. Marys Cement II	8879914	CC	1978	B	19,513	496' 06"	76' 00"	35' 00"

Built: Galveston Shipbuilding Co., Galveston, TX (Velasco '78-'81, Canmar Shuttle '81-'90)

SAULT LOCKS TOURS INC., SAULT STE. MARIE, ON *(saultlocktours.ca)*

Miss Marie		ES	1988	D	51*	65' 00"	18' 50"	3' 50"

Built: Three Buoys Houseboat Builders Ltd., Temagami, ON

SEA SERVICE LLC, SUPERIOR, WI *(seaservicellc.com)*

Sea Bear		PB	1959	D	28*	45' 08"	13' 08"	7' 00"

Provides pilot service at Duluth, MN

SEAWAY MARINE GROUP LLC, CLAYTON, NY *(seawaymarinegroup.com)*

Seaway Joan		TB	1965	D	9*	45' 00"	13' 00"	7' 00"
(Portsmouth Lady '65-'21)								
Seaway Maid		TW	2004	D	14*	45' 05"	12' 05"	5' 00"
Seaway Supplier		GC	1952	D	97*	73' 06"	21' 00"	9' 04"
(LCM-8010)								

SHELL CANADA LIMITED, CALGARY, AB

Juno Marie	9301641	RT	2004	D	2,191	262' 05"	45' 04"	22' 00"

Built: Miura Shipbuilding, Saiki, Japan; stationed at Montreal, QC (Alios Apollo '04-'10, Elin Apollo '10-'12, Milo '12-'16)

SHEPLER'S MACKINAC ISLAND FERRY, MACKINAW CITY, MI *(sheplersferry.com)*

Capt. Shepler		PF	1986	D	71*	84' 00"	21' 00"	7' 10"

Built: Camcraft Inc., Jean Laffite, LA; lengthened in '02; capacity is 265 passengers

Felicity		PF	1972	D	65*	65' 00"	18' 01"	8' 03"

Built: Camcraft Inc., Jean Laffite, LA; capacity is 150 passengers

Hope (The)		PF	1975	D	87*	77' 00"	20' 00"	8' 03"

Built: Camcraft Inc., Jean Laffite, LA; lengthened in '10; capacity is 150 passengers

Miss Margy		PF	2015	D	70*	85' 00"	22' 00"	8' 00"

Built: Moran Iron Works, Onaway, MI; capacity is 281 passengers

Welcome (The)		PF	1969	D	66*	60' 06"	16' 08"	8' 02"

Built: Camcraft Inc., Jean Laffite, LA; capacity is 97 passengers

William Richard		PF	2020	D	N/A	84' 00"	21' 00"	8' 00"

Built: Moran Iron Works, Onaway, MI; capacity is 210 passengers

Wyandot		PF	1979	D	83*	77' 00"	20' 00"	8' 00"

Built: Burgeron Shipyards, Crown Point, LA; lengthened in '01; capacity is 265 passengers

SHORELINE CONTRACTORS INC., AMHERST, OH *(shorelinecontractors.com)*

Eagle		TB	1943	D	31*	57' 07"	35' 09"	6' 08"

Built: Defoe Shipbuilding Co., Bay City, MI (Jack Boyce '43-'78, Jan B. '78-'79, Sea Search II '79-'86)

Putzfrau		TB	1930	D	20*	56' 00"	13' 09"	4' 05"

SIP N' SAIL CRUISES, MACKINAC ISLAND, MI *(puremichiganboatcruises.com)*

Isle Royale Queen III		PA	1959	D	88*	74' 03"	18' 04"	6' 05"

Built: T.D. Vinette Co., Escanaba, MI (Isle Royale Queen II)

SIXTH GREAT LAKE MARINE SERVICES, PENETANGUISHENE, ON *(georgianbaysalvage.ca)*

Mink Isle		TB	1947	D	27*	47' 08"	12' 11"	6' 06"

Built: Russel Brothers Ltd., Owen Sound, ON (Brompton Duchess)

SOCIÉTÉ DES TRAVERSIERS DU QUEBEC CITY, QUÉBEC, QC *(traversiers.com)*

Alexandrina-Chalifoux	7902271	PA/CF	1980	D	1,287*	203' 07"	72' 00"	18' 04"

Built: Marine Industries Ltd., Sorel, QC (Jos-Deschenes '80-'22)

Alphonse-Desjardins	7109233	PA/CF	1971	D	1,741*	214' 00"	71' 06"	20' 00"

Built: Davie Shipbuilding Co., Lauzon, QC

Armand-Imbeau II	9703215	PA/CF	2018	D	5,000*	301' 08"		

Built: Davie Shipbuilding Co., Lauzon, QC

Catherine-Legardeur	8409355	PA/CF	1985	D	1,348*	205' 09"	71' 10"	18' 10"

Built: Davie Shipbuilding Co., Lauzon, QC

Fleet Name / Vessel Name	Vessel IMO #	Vessel Type	Year Built	Engine Type	Cargo Cap. or Gross*	Overall Length	Vessel Breadth	Vessel Depth
Didace-Guévremont	7902269	PA/CF	1980	D	1,285*	203' 07"	72' 00"	18' 04"
Built: Marine Industries Ltd., Sorel, QC (Armand-Imbeau '80-'22)								
F.-A.-Gauthier	9669861	PA/CF	2015	DE	15,901*	436' 03"	73' 05"	26' 02"
Built: Fincantieri Castellammare di Stabia, Naples, Italy								
Felix-Antoine-Savard	9144706	PA/CF	1997	D	2,489*	272' 00"	70' 00"	21' 09"
Built: Davie Shipbuilding Co., Lauzon, QC (fueled by liquid natural gas)								
Grue-des-Iles	8011732	PA/CF	1981	D	447*	155' 10"	41' 01"	12' 06"
Built: Bateaux Tur-Bec Ltd., Ste-Catherine, QC								
Ivan-Quinn	9554028	PA/CF	2008	D	241*	83' 07"	26' 09"	11' 03"
Built: Meridien Maritime Reparation Inc., Matane, QC								
Jos-Deschenes II	9703227	PA/CF	2018	D	2.903*	286' 04"	85' 03"	22' 09""
Built: Davie Shipbuilding Co., Lauzon, QC								
Joseph-Savard	8409343	PA/CF	1985	D	1,445*	206' 00"	71' 10"	18' 10"
Built: Davie Shipbuilding Co., Lauzon, QC								
Lomer-Gouin	7109221	PA/CF	1971	D	1,741*	214' 00"	71' 06"	20' 00"
Built: Davie Shipbuilding Co., Lauzon, QC								
Peter-Fraser	8674778	PA/CF	2012	DE	292*	110' 02"	39' 03"	7' 03"
Built: Chantier Naval Forillon, Gaspé, QC								
Radisson {1}	8647115	PA/CF	1954	D	1,037*	164' 03"	72' 00"	10' 06"
Built: Davie Shipbuilding Co., Lauzon, QC								
Saaremaa 1	9474072	PA/CF	2010	D	5,233*	437' 03"	59' 00"	18' 07"
Built: Fiskerstrand Verft AS, Fiskerstrand, Norway (Saaremaa '10-'19)								

SOO MARINE SUPPLY INC., SAULT STE. MARIE, MI *(soomarine.com)*

Ojibway		SB	1945	D	53*	53' 00"	28' 00"	7' 00"
Built: Great Lakes Engineering Works, Ashtabula, OH; supplies vessels with groceries and other items								

SPIRIT OF THE SOUND SCHOONER CO. LTD., PARRY SOUND, ON *(mvchippewa.com)*

Chippewa III		PA	1954	D	47*	65' 00"	16' 00"	6' 06"
Built: Russel-Hipwell Engines Ltd., Owen Sound, ON (Maid of the Mist III '54-'56, Maid of the Mist '56-'92)								

ST. JAMES MARINE CO. & FOGG TOWING & MARINE, BEAVER ISLAND, MI *(stjamesmarine.com)*

Clyde W. Fogg		TB	1944	D	133*	86' 00"	23' 00"	10' 04"
Built: Equitable Equipment Co., New Orleans, LA (U. S. Army ST-709 '44-'47, USCOE Stanley '47-'99, Susan L '99-'22)								
Wendy Anne		TB	1955	D	89*	71' 00"	20' 00"	8' 05"
Built: Smith Basin Drydock, Port Everglades, FL (ST-2199)								

ST. LAWRENCE CRUISE LINES INC., KINGSTON, ON *(stlawrencecruiselines.com)*

Canadian Empress		PA	1981	D	463*	108' 00"	30' 00"	8' 00"

ST. LAWRENCE SEAWAY DEVELOPMENT CORP., MASSENA, NY *(www.seaway.dot.gov)*

Grasse River		GL	1958	GL		150' 00"	65' 08"	5' 06"
Performance		TB	1997	D		50' 00"	16' 06"	7' 05"
Built: Marine Builders Inc., Utica, IN								
Robinson Bay		TB	1958	DE	213*	103' 00"	26' 10"	14' 06"
Built: Christy Corp., Sturgeon Bay, WI								
Seaway Guardian	9883039	TB	2019		N/A	118' 11"	45' 00"	16' 01"
Built: Gulf Island Fabrication, Jennings, LA								
Seaway Trident		TB	2022		N/A	60' 00"	28' 00"	N/A
Built: Washburn & Doughty Associates Inc., East Boothbay, ME								

ST. LAWRENCE SEAWAY MANAGEMENT CORP., CORNWALL, ON *(greatlakes-seaway.com)*

VM/S Hercules		GL	1962	D	2,107*	200' 00"	75' 00"	18' 08"
VM/S St. Lambert		TB	1974	D	20*	30' 08"	13' 01"	6' 05"

STAR LINE MACKINAC ISLAND FERRY, ST. IGNACE, MI *(mackinacferry.com)*

Algomah		PF/PK	1961	D	81*	93' 00"	29' 08"	5' 02"
Built: Paasch Marine Services Inc., Erie, PA; laid up at St. Ignace, MI								
Anna May		PK	1947	D	94*	64' 10"	30' 00"	7' 03"
Built: Sturgeon Bay Shipbuilding & Dry Dock, Sturgeon Bay, WI (West Shore '47-'12)								
Cadillac {5}		PF	1990	D	73*	64' 07"	20' 00"	7' 07"
Chippewa {6}		PF/PK	1962	D	81*	93' 00"	29' 08"	5' 02"
Built: Paasch Marine Services Inc., Erie, PA								
Good Fortune		PA	2015	D	57*	64' 09"	19' 00"	7' 00"
Huron {5}		PF/PK	1955	D	99*	91' 06"	25' 00"	7' 00"
Built: Paasch Marine Services Inc., Erie, PA								
Joliet {3}		PF	1993	D	83*	64' 08"	22' 00"	8' 03"
LaSalle {4}		PF	1983	D	55*	65' 00"	20' 00"	7' 05"
Mackinac Express		PF/CA	1987	D	90*	82' 07"	28' 04"	8' 04"
Built: Gladding-Hearn Shipbuilding, Somerset, MA								

Fleet Name / Vessel Name	Vessel IMO #	Vessel Type	Year Built	Engine Type	Cargo Cap. or Gross*	Overall Length	Vessel Breadth	Vessel Depth
Marquette II {2}		PF	2005	D	65*	74' 00"	23' 06"	8' 00"
Ottawa {2}		PF/PK	1959	D	81*	93' 00"	29' 08"	5' 02"
Built: Paasch Marine Services Inc., Erie, PA								
Radisson {2}		PF	1988	D	97*	80' 00"	23' 06"	7' 00"
Straits of Mackinac II		PF/PK	1969	D	89*	90' 00"	27' 06"	8' 08"
Built: Blount Marine Corp., Warren, RI								

STERLING FUELS LTD., HAMILTON, ON (sterlingfuels.ca)

Sterling Energy	9277058	RT	2002	D	749*	226' 03"	32' 10"	14' 09"

Built: Selahattin Aslan Shipyard, Istanbul, Turkey; refueling tanker serves vessels in the vicinity of Hamilton and Toronto, ON, and the Welland Canal (Melisa D '02-'13)

STRAITS AREA TOUR CO., CHEBOYGAN, MI (mackinawtour.com)

Ugly Anne		PA	1976	D	20*	39' 00"	13' 10"	5' 05"

T

TALL SHIP WINDY, CHICAGO, IL (tallshipwindy.com)

Windy		ES/4S	1996	W	75*	148' 00"	25' 00"	8' 00"

TALL SHIP RED WITCH LLC, KENOSHA, WI (redwitch.com)

Red Witch		ES/2S	1986	W	41*	77' 00"	17' 06"	6' 05"

Built: Nathaniel Zirlott, Bayou La Batre, AL

THEODORE TUGBOAT, BURLINGTON, ON (theodoretugboat.ca)

Theodore Too			2000	D	81*	60' 37"	20' 01"	8' 08"

Built: Snyder's Shipyard, Dayspring, NS; replica tug of CBC TV fame is on a new mission – to be a champion for the marine industry and the beautiful waterways of the Great Lakes

THOUSAND ISLANDS & SEAWAY CRUISES, BROCKVILLE, ON (1000islandscruises.com)

General Brock III		ES	1977	D	56*	56' 05"	15' 04"	5' 02"
Lady of the Isles		ES	1986	D	105*	65' 00"	20' 00"	6' 08"
Sea Fox II		ES	1988	D	55*	39' 08"	20' 00"	2' 00"

THUNDER BAY TUG SERVICES LTD., THUNDER BAY, ON

Glenada		TB	1943	D	107*	80' 06"	25' 00"	10' 01"

Built: Russel Brothers Ltd., Owen Sound, ON (HMCS Glenada [W-30] '43-'45)

Kaye E. Barker arriving at Grand Haven, MI.
(Jason Bhaskaran)

Fleet Name Vessel Name	Vessel IMO #	Vessel Type	Year Built	Engine Type	Cargo Cap. or Gross*	Overall Length	Vessel Breadth	Vessel Depth
Miseford		TB	1915	D	116*	85' 00"	20' 00"	9' 06"
Built: M. Beatty & Sons Ltd., Welland, ON								
Point Valour		TB	1958	D	246*	97' 08"	28' 02"	13' 10"
Built: Davie Shipbuilding Co., Lauzon, QC (Foundation Valour '58-'83)								
Robert W.		TB	1949	D	48*	60' 00"	16' 00"	8' 06"
Built: Russel Brothers Ltd., Owen Sound, ON								
Rosalee D.		TB	1943	D	22*	55' 00"	12' 07"	4' 11"
Built: Northern Shipbuilding & Repair Co., Bronte, ON								
TORONTO FIRE SERVICES, TORONTO, ON *(toronto.ca/fire)*								
William Thornton		FB	1982	D	55*	70' 10"	18' 00"	8' 09"
Built: Breton Industrial & Marine Ltd., Port Hawkesbury, NS (CCGS Cape Hurd '82-'14)								
Wm. Lyon Mackenzie	6400575	FB	1964	D	102*	81' 01"	20' 00"	10' 00"
Built: Russel Brothers Ltd., Owen Sound, ON								
TOBERMORY CRUISE LINE INC., OWEN SOUND, ON *(tobermorycruiseline.com)*								
Georgian Legacy	7426667	ES	1974	D	106*	68' 07"	19' 04"	6' 04"
Built: Marlin Yachts Co. Ltd., Gananoque, ON (Miss Midland '74-'21, Tobermory Legacy '21-'22)								
TORONTO HARBOUR TOURS INC., TORONTO, ON *(harbourtourstoronto.ca)*								
Miss Kim Simpson		ES	1960	D	33*	90' 02"	13' 04"	3' 09"
New Beginnings		ES	1961	D	28*	41' 09"	13' 01"	4' 09"
Shipsands		ES	1972	D	23*	58' 03"	12' 01"	4' 07"
TORONTO PADDLEWHEEL CRUISES LTD., MISSISSAUGA, ON								
Pioneer Aurora Borealis		ES	1983	D	276*	95' 01"	23' 03"	11' 11"
(Aurora Borealis '83-'20)								
Pioneer Princess		ES	1984	D	96*	56' 00"	17' 01"	3' 09"
Pioneer Queen		ES	1968	D	110*	85' 00"	30' 06"	7' 03"
(Peche Island III '68-'71, Papoose IV '71-'96)								
TORONTO TUG & TRANSPORT LTD., TORONTO, ON *(torontotugandtransport.com)*								
Coastal Titan	7700477	HL	1978	B	3,000*	300' 00"	55' 00"	27' 00"
Built: Peterson Builders Inc., Sturgeon Bay, WI; converted to a barge in '09 at Port Colborne, ON								
(John Henry '78-'00, Revival '00-'08, Marinelink Explorer '08-'13, Chaulk Lifter '13-'15)								
Menier Consol		FD	1962					
Built: Davie Shipbuilding Co., Lauzon, QC; former pulpwood carrier was converted to a floating drydock in 1984								

Oakglen against a Lake Huron sunset. (Ethan Severson)

Fleet Name / Vessel Name	Vessel IMO #	Vessel Type	Year Built	Engine Type	Cargo Cap. or Gross*	Overall Length	Vessel Breadth	Vessel Depth
M.R. Kane		TB	1945	D	51*	60' 06"	16' 05"	6' 07"
Built: Central Bridge Co. Ltd., Trenton, ON (Tanac V-276 '45-'47)								
Omni Coastal	6923084	TB	1969	D	144*	83' 00"	24' 06"	13' 06"
Built: Pictou Industries Ltd., Pictou, NS (Port Alfred II '69-'82, Omni-Richelieu '82-'20)								
Radium Yellowknife	5288956	TB	1948	D	235*	120' 00"	28' 00"	6' 06"
Built: Yarrows Ltd., Esquimalt, BC								
Salvage Monarch	5308275	TB	1959	D	219*	97' 09"	29' 00"	13' 06"
Built: P.K. Harris Ltd., Appledore, England								

TRAVERSE TALL SHIP CO., TRAVERSE CITY, MI *(tallshipsailing.com)*

Fleet Name / Vessel Name	Vessel IMO #	Vessel Type	Year Built	Engine Type	Cargo Cap. or Gross*	Overall Length	Vessel Breadth	Vessel Depth
Manitou {1}		ES/2S	1983	W	78*	114' 00"	21' 00"	9' 00"

30,000 ISLANDS CRUISE LINES INC., PARRY SOUND, ON *(islandqueencruise.com)*

Fleet Name / Vessel Name	Vessel IMO #	Vessel Type	Year Built	Engine Type	Cargo Cap. or Gross*	Overall Length	Vessel Breadth	Vessel Depth
Island Queen V		ES	1990	D	526*	130' 00"	35' 00"	6' 06"
Built: Herb Fraser & Associates, Port Colborne, ON								

TRIDENT MARINE CORP., CLEVELAND, OH *(holidaycleveland.com)*

Fleet Name / Vessel Name	Vessel IMO #	Vessel Type	Year Built	Engine Type	Cargo Cap. or Gross*	Overall Length	Vessel Breadth	Vessel Depth
Holiday		PA	1964	D	25*	60' 00"	16' 01"	5' 06"

TUCKER MARINE CONSTRUCTION, SAUGATUCK, MI *(tuckermarineconstruction.com)*

Fleet Name / Vessel Name	Vessel IMO #	Vessel Type	Year Built	Engine Type	Cargo Cap. or Gross*	Overall Length	Vessel Breadth	Vessel Depth
Ernest M		TB	1949	D		45' 00"	13' 00"	6' 00"

U

UNCLE SAM BOAT TOURS, ALEXANDRIA BAY, NY *(usboattours.com)*

Fleet Name / Vessel Name	Vessel IMO #	Vessel Type	Year Built	Engine Type	Cargo Cap. or Gross*	Overall Length	Vessel Breadth	Vessel Depth
Alexandria Belle		ES	1988	D	92*	82' 00"	32' 00"	8' 00"
Island Duchess		ES	1988	D	73*	90' 03"	27' 08"	9' 00"
Island Wanderer		ES	1971	D	57*	62' 05"	22' 00"	7' 02"
Uncle Sam 7		ES	1976	D	55*	60' 04"	22' 00"	7' 01"

U.S. ARMY CORPS OF ENGINEERS – GREAT LAKES AND OHIO RIVER DIV., CINCINNATI, OH *(www.lre.usace.army.mil)*

U.S. ARMY CORPS OF ENGINEERS – BUFFALO DISTRICT

Fleet Name / Vessel Name	Vessel IMO #	Vessel Type	Year Built	Engine Type	Cargo Cap. or Gross*	Overall Length	Vessel Breadth	Vessel Depth
Cheraw		TB	1970	D	356*	109' 00"	30' 06"	16' 03"
Built: Southern Shipbuilding Corp., Slidell, LA (USS Cheraw [YTB-802] '70-'96)								
Mike Donlon		TB	1999	TB	64*	53' 00"	19' 02"	7' 07"
Built: Marine Builders Inc., Utica, IN								

U.S. ARMY CORPS OF ENGINEERS – DETROIT DISTRICT, LAKE MICHIGAN AREA OFFICE, KEWAUNEE SUB-OFFICE

Fleet Name / Vessel Name	Vessel IMO #	Vessel Type	Year Built	Engine Type	Cargo Cap. or Gross*	Overall Length	Vessel Breadth	Vessel Depth
Kenosha		TB	1954	D	82*	70' 00"	20' 00"	9' 08"
Built: Missouri Valley Bridge & Iron Works, Leavenworth, KS (U. S. Army ST-2011 '54-'65)								
Manitowoc		CS	1976	B		132' 00"	44' 00"	8' 00"
Racine		TB	1931	D	61*	66' 03"	18' 05"	7' 08"
Built: Marine Iron & Shipbuilding Co., Duluth MN								

Nordika Desgagnés upbound on the St. Marys River in 2022. (Emmett Hawkes)

Fleet Name / Vessel Name	Vessel IMO #	Vessel Type	Year Built	Engine Type	Cargo Cap. or Gross*	Overall Length	Vessel Breadth	Vessel Depth
U.S. ARMY CORPS OF ENGINEERS – DETROIT DISTRICT, DETROIT AREA OFFICE								
Demolen		TB	1974	D	356*	109'00"	30'06"	16'03"
Built: Marinette Marine Corp., Marinette, WI (USS Metacom [YTB-829] '74-'01, Metacom '01-'02)								
Veler		CS	1991	B	613*	150'00"	46'00"	10'06"
U.S. ARMY CORPS OF ENGINEERS – DETROIT DISTRICT, DULUTH AREA OFFICE								
D.L. Billmaier		TB	1968	D	356*	109'00"	30'06"	16'03"
Built: Southern Shipbuilding Corp., Slidell, LA (USS Natchitoches [YTB-799] '68-'95)								
Hammond Bay		TB	1953	D	23*	45'00"	13'00"	7'00"
Built: Roamer Boat Co., Holland, MI (ST-2170 '53-'62)								
H.J. Schwartz		DB	1995	B		150'00"	48'00"	11'00"
U.S. ARMY CORPS OF ENGINEERS – DETROIT DISTRICT, SOO AREA OFFICE								
Harvey		DB	1961	B		120'00"	40'00"	8'00"
Nicolet		DB	1971	B		120'00"	40'00"	8'00"
Owen M. Frederick		TB	1942	D	56*	65'00"	17'00"	7'06"
Built: Sturgeon Bay Shipbuilding Co., Sturgeon Bay, WI								
Whitefish Bay		TB	1953	D	23*	45'00"	13'00"	7'00"
Built: National Steel & Shipbuilding Co., San Diego, CA								
U.S. COAST GUARD 9TH DISTRICT, CLEVELAND, OH (www.uscg.mil/d9)								
Biscayne Bay [WTGB-104]	8635148	IB	1979	D	662*	140'00"	37'06"	12'00"
Built: Tacoma Boatbuilding Co., Tacoma, WA; stationed at St. Ignace, MI								
Bristol Bay [WTGB-102]	8635150	IB	1979	D	662*	140'00"	37'06"	12'00"
Built: Tacoma Boatbuilding Co., Tacoma, WA; stationed at Detroit, MI								
Buckthorn [WLI-642]		BI	1963	D	200*	100'00"	24'00"	4'08"
Built: Mobile Ship Repair Inc., Mobile, AL; stationed at Sault Ste. Marie, MI								
CGB-12001		BT	1991	B	700*	120'00"	50'00"	6'00"
Built: Marinette Marine Corp., Marinette, WI; paired with USCGC Bristol Bay								
CGB-12002		BT	1992	B	700*	120'00"	50'00"	6'00"
Built: Marinette Marine Corp., Marinette, WI; paired with USCGC Mobile Bay								
Hollyhock [WLB-214]	9271133	BT	2003	D	2,000*	225'09"	46'00"	19'08"
Built: Marinette Marine Corp., Marinette, WI; stationed at Port Huron, MI, but scheduled to be replaced by Sequoia in '23								
Katmai Bay [WTGB-101]		IB	1978	D	662*	140'00"	37'06"	12'00"
Built: Tacoma Boatbuilding Co., Tacoma, WA; stationed at Sault Ste. Marie, MI								
Mackinaw [WLBB-30]	9271054	IB	2005	D	3,407*	240'00"	58'00"	15'05"
Built: Marinette Marine Corp., Marinette, WI; stationed at Cheboygan, MI								
Mobile Bay [WTGB-103]	8635162	IB	1979	D	662*	140'00"	37'06"	12'00"
Built: Tacoma Boatbuilding Co., Tacoma, WA; stationed at Sturgeon Bay, WI								
Morro Bay [WTGB-106]	8635215	IB	1980	D	662*	140'00"	37'06"	12'00"
Built: Tacoma Boatbuilding Co., Tacoma, WA; stationed at Cleveland, OH								
Neah Bay [WTGB-105]	8635174	IB	1980	D	662*	140'00"	37'06"	12'00"
Built: Tacoma Boatbuilding Co., Tacoma, WA; stationed at Cleveland, OH								

Detroit pilot boat M.S. Westcott flanking Federal Bering. (Mike Mishler)

Fleet Name / Vessel Name	Vessel IMO #	Vessel Type	Year Built	Engine Type	Cargo Cap. or Gross*	Overall Length	Vessel Breadth	Vessel Depth
Sequoia [WLB-215]	9259989	BT	2003	D	2,000*	225' 09"	46' 00"	19' 08"

Built: Marinette Marine Corp., Marinette, WI; stationed at Guam but was to be relocated to Port Huron, MI, in '23

Spar [WLB-206]	9257838	BT	2001	D	2,000*	225' 09"	46' 00"	19' 08"

Built: Marinette Marine Corp., Marinette, WI; stationed at Duluth, MN; replaced USCGC Alder [WLB-216]

U.S. ENVIRONMENTAL PROTECTION AGENCY, CHICAGO, IL (epa.gov)

Lake Explorer II		RV	1966	D	150*	86' 09"	22' 00"	7' 02"

Built: Jackobson Shipyard, Oyster Bay, NY (NOAA Rude '66-'08)

Lake Guardian	8030609	RV	1981	D	959*	180' 00"	40' 00"	14' 00"

Built: Halter Marine Inc., Moss Point MS (Marsea Fourteen '81-'90)

U.S. FISH & WILDLIFE SERVICE, ALPENA, MI

Spencer F. Baird	9404326	RV	2006	D	256*	95' 00"	30' 00"	9' 05"

Built: Conrad Industries Inc., Morgan City, LA

Stanford H. Smith		RV	2018	D	37*	57' 00"	16' 00"	N/A

Built: Moran Iron Works, Onaway, MI

U.S. NATIONAL PARK SERVICE - ISLE ROYALE NATIONAL PARK, HOUGHTON, MI (nps.gov)

Greenstone II		TK	2003	B	114*	70' 01"	24' 01"	8' 00"
Ranger III	7618234	PK	1958	D	648*	152' 08"	34' 00"	13' 00"

Built: Bay Shipbuilding, Sturgeon Bay, WI

Shelter Bay		TB	1953	D	30*	45' 00"	13' 00"	7' 00

Built: National Steel & Shipbuilding, San Diego, CA; laid up at Houghton, MI

U.S. NAVAL SEA CADET CORPS, GREAT LAKES DIVISION, MOUNT CLEMENS, MI (prideofmichigan.org)

Pride of Michigan [YP-673]		TV	1977	D	70*	80' 06"	17' 08"	5' 03"

Built: Peterson Builders Inc., Sturgeon Bay, WI; based at Mount Clemens, MI (USS YP-673 '77-'89)

UNIVERSITY OF MINNESOTA DULUTH LARGE LAKES OBSERVATORY, DULUTH, MN (scse.d.umn.edu/blue-heron)

Blue Heron		RV	1985	D	175*	87' 00"	23' 00"	11' 00"

Built: Goudy and Stevens, East Boothbay, ME (Fairtry '85-'97)

UNIVERSITY OF WISCONSIN SCHOOL OF FRESHWATER SCIENCES, MILWAUKEE, WI (glwi.uwm.edu)

Neeskay		RV	1952	D	75*	71' 00"	17' 06"	7' 06"

URGENCE MARINE INC., MONTREAL, QC (urgencemarine.com)

Simon Cote		TB	1953	D	14*	38' 02"	11' 05"	4' 00"
Streetsville		TB	1944	D	11*	36' 11"	10' 06"	4' 00"

USS GREAT LAKES LLC, NEW YORK, NY

Robert F. Deegan		TK	1968	B	2,424*	225' 08"	60' 00"	4' 00"

Built: Wyatt Industries, Houston, TX; was paired with tug Candace Elise in '22

V-W

VANE BROTHERS CO., BALTIMORE, MD (vanebrothers.com)

Double Skin 509A		TK	2015	B	4,317*	361' 00"	62' 00"	24' 06"

Built: Conrad Shipyard LLC, Amelia, LA

New York	9820154	TB	2018	D	99*	94' 08"	34' 00"	14' 03"

Built: St. Johns Shipbuilding Inc., Palatka, FL; paired with the barge Double Skin 509A

VanENKEVORT TUG & BARGE INC., ESCANABA MI (vtbarge.com)

Clyde S. VanEnkevort	9618484	AT	2011	D	1,179*	135' 04"	50' 00"	26' 00"

Built: Donjon Shipbuilding & Repair, Erie, PA; paired with the barge Erie Trader (Ken Boothe Sr. '11-'17)

Dirk S. VanEnkevort	5175745	AT	1990	D	841*	147' 00"	49' 07"	33' 00"

Built at Marinette, WI, from steel left over from the conversion of steamer Joseph H. Thompson to a barge in 1990; repowered in '07; rebuilt in '20 at Donjon Shipbuilding and Repair, Erie, PA; (Joseph H. Thompson Jr. '90-'20)

Erie Trader		SU	2012	B	37,600	740' 04"	78' 00"	30' 00"

Built: Donjon Shipbuilding & Repair, Erie, PA; paired with tug Clyde S. VanEnkevort, length together 840' 00"

Great Lakes Trader	8635966	SU	2000	B	39,600	740' 00"	78' 00"	45' 00"

Built: Halter Marine, Pearlington, MS; paired with tug Joyce L. VanEnkevort, length together 840' 00"

Joseph H. Thompson		SU	1944	B	21,200	610' 00"	71' 06"	38' 06"

Built: Sun Shipbuilding & Drydock Co., Chester, PA; converted from a saltwater vessel to a Great Lakes bulk carrier in '52 by Maryland Dry Dock, Baltimore, MD; Ingalls Shipbuilding, Pascagoula, MS; and American Shipbuilding Co., South Chicago, IL; converted to a self-unloading barge by the owners in '90; paired with tug Laura L. VanEnkevort, length together 690' 00" (USNS Marine Robin '44-'52)

Joyce L. VanEnkevort	8973033	AT	1998	D	1,179*	135' 04"	50' 00"	26' 00"

Built: Bay Shipbuilding Co., Sturgeon Bay, WI; paired with barge Great Lakes Trader

Laura L. VanEnkevort	8875310	AT	1994	D	189*	118' 08"	37' 00"	`8' 00"

Built: Halter Marine, Lockport, LA; paired with barge Joseph H. Thompson (Sidney Candies '94-'98, Naida Ramil '98-'19)

Fleet Name / Vessel Name	Vessel IMO #	Type	Year Built	Engine Type	Cargo Cap. or Gross*	Overall Length	Breadth	Depth
Michigan Trader		SU	2020	B	37,512	740'00"	78'00"	45'00"

Built: Bay Shipbuilding Co., Sturgeon Bay, WI; paired with tug Dirk S. VanEnkevort, length together 857'00"

VERREAULT NAVIGATION INC., LES MÉCHINS, QC (verreaultnavigation.com)

Epinette II		TB	1965	D	75*	61'03"	20'01"	8'05"

Built: Russel Brothers Ltd., Owen Sound, ON

Grande Baie		TT	1972	D	194*	86'06"	30'00"	12'00"

Built: Prince Edward Island Lending Authority, Charlottetown, PEI

VICTORIAN PRINCESS CRUISE LINES, ERIE, PA (victorianprincess.com)

Victorian Princess		ES	1985	D	46*	67'00"	24'00"	4'05"

VIKING MARINE CONSTRUCTION CO., HOLLAND, MI (vikingmarineco.com)

Barry J		TB	1954	D	15*	44'03"	12'08"	5'04"

Built: Roamer Boat Co., Holland, MI (W.P. Coppens, Capt. Art Lapish, Heather B.)

VISTA FLEET, DULUTH, MN (vistafleet.com)

Vista Queen		ES	1987	D	97*	64'00"	16'00"	6'02"

Built: Mid-City Steel Fabricating Inc., La Crosse, WI (Queen of Excelsior)

Vista Star		ES	1987	D	95*	91'00"	24'09"	5'02"

Built: Freeport Shipbuilding Inc., Freeport, FL (Island Empress '87-'88)

VOIGHT'S MARINE SERVICES LTD., ELLISON BAY & GILLS ROCK, WI (islandclipper.com)

Island Clipper {2}		PF	1987	D	71*	65'00"	20'00"	8'00"
Yankee Clipper		PF	1971	D	41*	46'06"	17'00"	6'00"

WALPOLE-ALGONAC FERRY LINE, PORT LAMBTON, ON (walpoleislandferry.ca)

City of Algonac		CF	1990	D	82*	62'06"	27'09"	5'09"

Built: Duratug Shipyard & Fabricating Ltd., Port Dover, ON

Walpole Islander		CF	1986	D	72*	54'05"	27'09"	6'03"

Built: Hike Metal Products, Wheatley, ON

WARNER PETROLEUM CORP., CLARE, MI (warnerpetroleum.com)

Coloma L. Warner	7337892	TB	1955	D	134*	86'00"	24'00"	10'00"

Built: Sturgeon Bay Shipbuilding, Sturgeon Bay, WI; (Harbor Ace '55-'61, Gopher State '61-'71, Betty Gale '71-'93, Hannah D. Hannah '93-'10)

Warner Provider	8641185	RT	1962	B	1,698*	264'00"	52'05"	12'00"

Built: Port Houston Iron Works, Houston, TX (Hannah 2903)

Warner Supply		RT	1981	B	1,012*	195'00"	50'00"	9'05"

Built St. Louis Ship, St. Louis, MO; barge is at Detroit being pushed by Gaelic Towing Co. tugs (CBC 196 '81-'14, AGB Ellac '14-'19)

William L. Warner	7322055	RT	1973	D	492*	120'00"	40'00"	14'00"

Built: Halter Marine, New Orleans, LA; laid up at Detroit, MI (Jos. F. Bigane '73-'04)

American Spirit departing Superior, WI. Sea smoke makes it look like she is sailing in the clouds. (David Schauer)

Fleet Name Vessel Name	Vessel IMO #	Vessel Type	Year Built	Engine Type	Cargo Cap. or Gross*	Overall Length	Vessel Breadth	Vessel Depth

WASHINGTON ISLAND FERRY LINE, WASHINGTON ISLAND, WI *(wisferry.com)*

Arni J. Richter		PA/CF	2003	D	92*	104' 00"	38' 06"	10' 11"

Built: Bay Shipbuilding Co., Sturgeon Bay, WI; vessel offers service between Northport, WI, and Washington Island, WI

Eyrarbakki		PA/CF	1970	D	95*	87' 00"	36' 00"	7' 06"

Built: Bay Shipbuilding Co., Sturgeon Bay, WI; vessel offers service between Northport, WI, and Washington Island, WI

Karfi		PA/CF	1967	D	23*	36' 00"	16' 00"	4' 08"

Built: T.D. Vinette Co., Escanaba, MI; vessel offers service between Washington Island, WI, and Rock Island, WI

Madonna		PA/CF	2020	D	N/A	124' 00"	40' 00"	10' 00"

Built: Bay Shipbuilding Co., Sturgeon Bay, WI; vessel offers service between Northport, WI, and Washington Island, WI

Robert Noble		PA/CF	1979	D	97*	90' 04"	36' 00"	8' 03"

Built: Peterson Builders Inc., Sturgeon Bay, WI; vessel offers service between Northport, WI, and Washington Island, WI

Washington {2}		PA/CF	1989	D	97*	100' 00"	37' 00"	9' 00"

Built: Peterson Builders Inc., Sturgeon Bay, WI; vessel offers service between Northport, WI, and Washington Island, WI

WESTERN GREAT LAKES PILOTS LLC, BRIMLEY, MI *(wglpa.com)*

Linda Jean		PB	1950	D	17*	38' 00"	10' 00"	5' 00"

Pilot boat based at DeTour, MI

Soo Pilot		PB	1976	D	21*	40' 08"	13' 05"	4' 00"

Pilot boat based at Brimley, MI

St. Marys Pilot		PB	2004	D		36' 11"	14' 00"	3' 04"

Pilot boat based in DeTour, MI (Red Jacket '04-'22)

Superior Pilot		PB	1968	D	22*	43' 00"	13' 00"	4' 00"

Pilot boat based at Sault Ste. Marie, MI (Hamp Thomas '68-'19)

Waiska Pilot		PB	2021	Gas		38' 00"	12"06"	2' 00"

Pilot boat based at Brimley, MI

Western Pilot		PB	1979	D	21*	40' 08"	13' 05"	4' 00"

Pilot boat based at DeTour, MI

WHITE LAKE DOCK & DREDGE INC., MONTAGUE, MI *(wlddi.com)*

Lauren A		TB	1980	D	68*	51' 05"	21' 00"	6' 00"

Built: Melancon Fabricators Inc., Lockport, LA (Janine Alicia '80-'89)

WILLY'S CONTRACTING CO., SOUTHAMPTON, ON *(willyscontracting.com)*

Pride		TB/IB	1957	D	47*	52' 06"	29' 08"	5' 01"

Built: Peter Mayer, Racine, WI; converted to a tug/icebreaker circa 2005

Ashton Marine's tug
Meredith Ashton
off Monroe, MI.
(Paul C. LaMarre III)

Fleet Name Vessel Name	Vessel IMO #	Vessel Type	Year Built	Engine Type	Cargo Cap. or Gross*	Overall Length	Vessel Breadth	Vessel Depth
Welland		TB	1954	D	94*	86' 00"	20' 00"	8' 00"
Built: Russel-Hipwell Engines, Owen Sound, ON								
WINDSOR PREMIERE CRUISES LTD., WINDSOR, ON (windsorpremiercruises.com)								
Macassa Bay	8624709	ES	1986	D	210*	93' 07"	29' 07"	10' 04"
Built: Boiler Pump & Marine Works Ltd., Hamilton, ON								
WISCONSIN DEPARTMENT OF NATURAL RESOURCES, BAYFIELD & STURGEON BAY, WI (dnr.wi.gov)								
Coregonus		RV	2011	D	37*	60' 00"	16' 00"	5' 09"
Gaylord Nelson		RV	1992	D	12*	45' 09"	16' 00"	5' 05"
Hack Noyes		RV	1947	D	50*	56' 00"	14' 05"	4' 00"
WREN WORKS LLC, POPLAR, WI (wrenworks4u.com)								
Wren I		TW	2013	D	32*	45' 00"	13' 00"	6' 05"
Built: Fraser Shipyards Inc., Superior, WI; (FSY II '13-'22)								

Visitors to Port Weller Dry Docks pose with CSL St-Laurent. (Bill Bird)

Tug Thomas R. Moorish overtakes CSL Welland on the St. Marys River.
(Roger LeLievre)

Tanker Damia Desgagnés passing Detroit. (Andrew Russell)

Algoma Transport looks to a Welland Canal rainbow, perhaps hoping for a pot of gold at the end. This year marks the 1979-built self-unloader's final season, as she is being replaced in the Algoma fleet by a new vessel. (Korey Garceau)

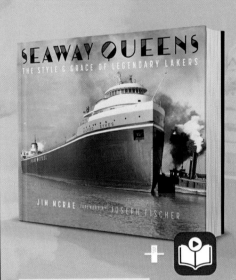

CSL's Majestic Murals

By ROGER LELIEVRE

The unveiling of "The Runners" in March 2022, a massive mural on the aft cabin of Canada Steamship Lines' *CSL Welland* created by four Canadian artists, caught the eye of thousands of shoreline residents last season. Inspired by Greek artistic traditions depicting sport, the colossal 16-by-14-meter mural painted on the ship's accommodation block depicts four runners in motion, striving toward a common goal.

CSL commissioned the mural, created by Bryan Beyung, Emmanuel Jarus, Andrea Wan and K.C. Hall, to celebrate the spirit of the 2022 Canada Summer Games

CSL Welland's "The Runner." (Marc Dease)

taking place throughout the Niagara Region last summer. Each artist painted a runner according to his or her distinct style, vision and tradition. Together, the four runners create, according to CSL, "a collective and harmonious work that reflects the broad mix of people, cultures, backgrounds and abilities in amateur sport today."

The fleet's *CSL St-Laurent* is also adorned with a beautiful mural. Making its debut in 2017, The "Sea Keeper" depicts a Canada goose with its powerful wings spread in flight, its forward motion paying tribute to Canada's 150th birthday, the 375th anniversary of Montreal, and the roles of the St. Lawrence Seaway, marine transport, and CSL in building the nation and the city.

"The Sea Keeper" adorns CSL St-Laurent. (CSL)

Painting an original work of art of this scale on a ship was a first for Montreal urban artist Beyung, a first for CSL and a first for a Canadian commercial vessel. Beyung created it with artists FONKi, Ankh One and Benny Wilding

CSL notched another rare honor in August 2022 when the Canada Games torch was carried on board *CSL St-Laurent* along the St. Lawrence Seaway to Port Colborne, where it disembarked to continue its voyage on land.

A call to CSL revealed there are no immediate plans to similarly adorn another vessel. ◆

LAKER LONGEVITY / 1906-2023

1906: St. Marys Challenger (r '67, '14) **1936:** J.A.W. Iglehart (r '65)* **1937:** St. Marys Conquest (r: '87)

1941: Pere Marquette 41 (r '97) **1942:** Alpena (r '91), Lee A. Tregurtha (r '61) **1943:** Cuyahoga (r '74) **1944:** Joseph H. Thompson (r '52, '91), McKee Sons (r '53, '91**) **1949:** Wilfred Sykes

1952: Arthur M. Anderson (r '75,'82), Kaye E. Barker (r '76, '81), Cason J. Callaway (r '74, '82), Philip R. Clarke (r '74, '82), Menominee (r '06), Michipicoten (r '57, '80), John G. Munson **1953:** Badger, Maumee (r '07), Pathfinder (r '98), Saginaw **1957:** Commander (r '18) **1958:** John Sherwin (r '73)** **1959:** Hon. James L. Oberstar (r '72, '81), Herbert C. Jackson (r '75)

1960: Edward L. Ryerson** **1967:** Tim S. Dool (r '96), John D. Leitch (r '02) **1968:** Frontenac (r '73) **1969:** CSL Tadoussac (r '01)

1972: Roger Blough, CSL Niagara (r '99), Stewart J. Cort **1973:** Algoma Compass, Calumet, Manitowoc, John J. Boland, Rt. Hon. Paul J. Martin (r '00), Presque Isle, Tecumseh **1974:** H. Lee White, Robert S. Pierson **1975:** Sam Laud **1976:** James R. Barker, Joseph L. Block **1977:** CSL Assiniboine (r '05), CSL Laurentien (r '01), Walter J. McCarthy Jr., Mesabi Miner

1978: Radcliffe R. Latimer (r '09), American Integrity, American Spirit, Algoma Buffalo **1979:** American Courage, Algoma Transport, Edwin H. Gott, Indiana Harbor

1980: American Mariner, Burns Harbor, Edgar B. Speer, Oakglen **1981:** American Century,

Great Republic, Northern Venture, Paul R. Tregurtha **1982:** Michigan, Ashtabula **1983:** Spruceglen, Kaministiqua **1984:** Atlantic Huron (r '89, '03) **1987:** Algoma Discovery, Algoma Guardian

1991: Manitoulin (r '15) **1996:** Integrity

2000: Great Lakes Trader **2001:** Norman McLeod **2003:** NACC Argonaut (r: '18) **2004:** Algoscotia, Lake Express, Florence Spirit **2006:** Innovation **2007:** Algoberta, Algotitan, Rosaire A. Desgagnés, Argentia Desgagnés, Taiga Desgagnés, Sarah Desgagnés, Evans Spirit, McKeil Spirit **2008:** Algocanada, Algonova, John J. Carrick, Zélada Desgagnés **2009:** Sedna Desgagnés, Hinch Spirit **2010:** Nordika Desgagnés, Algoterra, Blair McKeil

2011: Algoma Mariner, Claude A. Desgagnés, NACC Alduci, NACC Quebec (r: '16) **2012:** Erie Trader, Bella Desgagnés, Baie St. Paul, Harvest Spirit **2013:** Algoma Equinox, Thunder Bay, Whitefish Bay, Baie Comeau, Acadia Desgagnés **2014:** Algoma Harvester, G3 Marquis, CSL Welland, CSL St-Laurent **2016:** Mia Desgagnés, Damia Desgagnés, NACC Capri **2017:** Algoma Strongfield, Algoma Niagara, Miena Desgagnés **2018:** Paul A. Desgagnés, Rossi A. Desgagnés, Gaia Desgagnés, Algoma Innovator, Algoma Sault **2019:** Algoma Conveyor **2020:** Michigan Trader, Algoma Intrepid

2022: Mark W. Barker, Nukumi **2023:** McAsphalt Advantage

*(r = major rebuild; * storage barge; ** in long-term lay-up)*

Saginaw getting a push away from the Algoma Steel dock at Sault Ste. Marie, ON, by the tug Adanac III. *(Nathan Leindecker)*

Badger at 70
Getting there is all the fun!

It's going to be a big year for the Lake Michigan carferry *Badger*. The Big Ship, More Fun boat is celebrating her 70th year in service. So what's planned for her platinum season? In lieu of celebrations, there will be a **Badger Birthday Bash** from 8:30-11 p.m. June 10. Instead of doing a Shoreline Cruise that evening, the *Badger* will stay at the Ludington, MI, dock, and community members will be able to tour the ship and enjoy cake and activities. Look for more details on the *Badger*'s website, *ssbadger.com*, and social media pages.

The Badger steams between Ludington, MI, and Manitowoc, WI, a distance of 62 miles, connecting U.S. Highway 10 between those two cities. She is the last coal-fired passenger vessel operating on the Great Lakes and was designated a National Historic Landmark in 2016. She is also the last vessel in service on the Great Lakes to be powered by Skinner Unaflow engines. The *Badger* is also unusual in that it is a registered historical site in two states, Michigan and Wisconsin. In 1996, the *Badger*'s propulsion system was designated a mechanical engineering landmark by the American Society of Mechanical Engineers. In 2002, she was named Ship of the Year by the Steamship Historical Society of America. The vessel was listed on the National Register of Historic Places on December 11, 2009. In January 2016, the National Park Service designated the ship a National Historic Landmark.

The *Badger* was constructed as a rail car ferry in 1952, along with her twin, *Spartan*, with a reinforced hull for icebreaking. She was originally used to carry railroad cars, passengers and automobiles between the two sides of the lake for the Chesapeake and Ohio Railway. In December 2020, the *Badger* (and *Spartan*) were sold by Lake Michigan Carferry Co. to Interlake Steamship Co., an operator of Great Lakes cargo ships that traces its legacy back to 1883 with the founding of Pickands Mather & Co.

Steam fans, get your fix now. With more emission restrictions expected in 2025, Interlake is in the early stages of investigating potential new fuel sources for the *Badger*. While grandfathered in to burn coal, simply hoping to maintain that status is not viable in the future, especially as parts for her steam plant are increasingly hard to find. **– Roger LeLievre** ◆

The Badger crossing Lake Michigan in 2022. (Brian Caswell)

Vessel Name	Engine Manufacturer & Model #	Engine Type	Total Engines	Total Cylinders	Rated HP	Total Props	Speed MPH
Acadia Desgagnés	MaK - 8M32C	Diesel	2	8	5,362 bhp	1	13.8
Albert*	Alpha -14V23L-VO	Diesel	2	14	2,030 bhp	2	13.8
Alder (USCG)	Caterpillar - 3608TA	Diesel	2	6	3,100 bhp	1 cpp	17.0
Algoberta	Wartsila 8L32	Diesel	2	8	4,622 bhp	1 ccp	13.8
Algocanada	MaK - 9M32C	Diesel	1	9	6,118 bhp	1 cpp	16.1
Algoma Buffalo	GM EMD - 20-645-E7	Diesel	2	20	7,200 bhp	1 cpp	16.1
Algoma Compass	GM EMD - 20-645-E7B	Diesel	2	20	7,200 bhp	1 cpp	16.1
Algoma Conveyor	Sulzer - 7RTA48T-B	Diesel	1	7	11,140 bhp	1	16.1
Algoma Discovery	Sulzer - 6RTA62	Diesel	1	6	15,499 bhp	1 cpp	16.41
Algoma Equinox	Wartsila 5RT-flex50-D	Diesel	1	5	11,863 bhp	1 cpp	16.1
Algoma Guardian	Sulzer - 6RTA62	Diesel	1	6	11,285 bhp	1 cpp	16.4
Algoma Harvester	Wartsila 5RT-flex50-D	Diesel	1	5	11,863 bhp	1 cpp	16.1
Algoma Innovator	Wärtsilä 5RT-flex 50-D	Diesel	1	5	6,320 bhp	1 ccp	14.0
Algoma Intrepid	Wärtsilä 5RT-flex 50-D	Diesel	1	5	6,320 bhp	1 ccp	14.0
Algoma Mariner	MAN-B&W - 6L48/60CR	Diesel	1	6	9,792 bhp	1 cpp	
Algoma Niagara	Sulzer - 7RTA48T-B	Diesel	1	7	11,140 bhp	1 cpp	16.1
Algoma Sault	Sulzer - 7RTA48T-B	Diesel	1	7	11,140 bhp	1 cpp	16.1
Algoma Strongfield	Sulzer - 7RTA48T-B	Diesel	1	7	11,140 bhp	1 cpp	16.1
Algoma Transport	MAN - 8L40/45	Diesel	2	8	10,000 bhp	1 cpp	13.8
Algotitan	Wartsila 8L32	Diesel	2	8	4,622 bhp	1 ccp	13.8
Algonova	MaK - 9M32C	Diesel	1	9	6,118 bhp	1 cpp	16.1
Algoscotia	Wartsila 6L46C	Diesel	1	6	8,445 bhp	1 cpp	16.0
Algosea	Wartsila - 6L46A	Diesel	1	6	6,434 bhp	1 cpp	15.0
Algoterra	MAN B&W SE 6L48/60B	Diesel	1	6	8,445 bhp	1 cpp	14.4
Algotitan	Wartsila 8L32	Diesel	2	8	4,622 bhp	1 cpp	13.8
Alpena	De Laval Steam Turbine Co.	Turbine	1	**	4,400 shp	1	14.1
American Century	GM - EMD - 20-645-E7B	Diesel	4	20	14,400 bhp	2 cpp	17.3
American Courage	GM - EMD - 20-645-E7	Diesel	2	20	7,200 bhp	1 cpp	16.1
American Integrity	GM EMD - 20-645-E7	Diesel	4	20	14,400 bhp	2 cpp	18.4
American Mariner	GM EMD - 20-645-E7	Diesel	2	20	7,200 bhp	1 cpp	15.0
American Spirit	Pielstick - 16PC2-2V-400	Diesel	2	16	16,000 bhp	2 cpp	17.3
Anglian Lady*	Deutz - SBA12M528	Diesel	2	12	3,480 bhp	2 cpp	15.5
Argentia Desgagnés	Wartsila C - W6L32B3	Diesel	1	6	5,362 bhp	1	15.6
Arthur M. Anderson	Westinghouse Elec. Corp.	Turbine	1	**	7,700 shp	1	16.1
Atlantic Huron	Sulzer - 6RLB66	Diesel	1	6	11,094 bhp	1 cpp	17.3
Atlantic Spirit	MaK 7M43C	Diesel	1	7	8,560 bhp	1 cpp	
Aujaq	Wartsila – 6R46	Diesel	1	6	7,278 bhp	1	
Avenger IV*	British Polar	Diesel	1	9	2,700 bhp	1 cpp	12.0
Badger**	Skinner Steeple Compound Uniflow	Steam	2	8	3,500 ihp	2	18.4
Baie Comeau	MAN B&W - 6S50ME-B9	Diesel	1	6	11,897 bhp	1	15.5
Baie St. Paul	MAN B&W - 6S50ME-B9	Diesel	1	6	11,897 bhp	1	15.5
Bella Desgagnés	Wartsila - 9L20CR	Diesel	4	9	8,320 bhp	2 azimuth	17.3
Beverly M I*	Niigata - 6L28HX	Diesel	2	6	1,971 bhp	2	16.0
Biscayne Bay (USCG)	Fairbanks Morse - 10-38D8-1/8	Diesel	2	10	2,500 bhp	1	13.8
Blair McKeil	Wartsila 6L38B	Diesel	1	6	5,833 bhp	1 cpp	
Bradshaw McKee*	GM EMD - 12-645-E5	Diesel	2	12	4,320 bhp	2	11.5
Bristol Bay (USCG)	Fairbanks Morse - 10-38D8-1/8	Diesel	2	10	2,500 bhp	1	13.8
Burns Harbor	GM EMD - 20-645-E7	Diesel	4	20	14,400 bhp	2 cpp	18.4
Calumet	Alco - 16V251E	Diesel	2	16	5,600 bhp	1	16.1
Captain Henry Jackman	Sulzer 5RT-Flex50-D	Diesel	1	5	11,722 bhp	1 cpp	15.8
Cason J. Callaway	Westinghouse Elec. Corp.	Turbine	1	**	7,700 shp	1	16.1
Chi-Cheemaun**	Caterpillar - C280-6	Diesel	4	6	9,280 bhp	2	
Claude A. Desgagnés	MaK/Caterpillar - 6M43C	Diesel	1	6	7,342 bhp	1 cpp	17.8
Clyde S. VanEnkevort*	Cat-MaK - 8M32C	Diesel	2	8	10,876 bhp	2 cpp	18.4

* = tug   ** = ferry

bhp: brake horsepower, a measure of diesel engine output measured at the crankshaft before entering gearbox or any other power take-out device

ihp: indicated horsepower, based on an internal measurement of mean cylinder pressure, piston area, piston stroke and engine speed; used for reciprocating engines

shp: shaft horsepower, a measure of engine output at the propeller shaft at the output of the reduction gearbox; used for steam and diesel-electric engines

cpp: controllable pitch propeller

Vessel Name	Engine Manufacturer & Model #	Engine Type	Total Engines	Total Cylinders	Rated HP	Total Props	Speed MPH
CSL Assiniboine	MaK/Caterpillar - 6M32C	Diesel	2	6	8,060 bhp	1 cpp	14.9,
CSL Laurentien	MaK/Caterpillar - 6M32C	Diesel	2	6	8,060 bhp	1 cpp	16.1,
CSL Niagara	MaK/Caterpillar - 6M32C	Diesel	2	6	8,060 bhp	1 cpp	17.3
CSL St-Laurent	MAN B&W 6S50ME-B	Diesel	1	6	11,897 bhp	1 cpp	15.5
CSL Tadoussac	Sulzer - 6RND76	Diesel	1	6	9,600 bhp	1	17.0
CSL Welland	MAN B&W 6S50ME-B	Diesel	1	6	11,897 bhp	1 cpp	15.5
Cuyahoga	Caterpillar - 3608	Diesel	1	8	3,000 bhp	1 cpp	12.6
Damia Desgagnés	Wärtsilä 5RT-flex 50DF	Diesel/LNG	1	5	7,305 bhp	1 cpp	15
Defiance*	GM EMD - 20-645-E7	Diesel	2	20	7,200 bhp	2	15.0
Des Groseilliers	(CCG) Alco - 16V251F	Diesel	6	16	17,700 bhp	2	18.6
Dirk S. VanEnkevort	MaK/Caterpillar – 6M32C	Diesel	2	6	8,000 bhp	1	12.7
Dorothy Ann*	GM EMD - 20-645-E7B	Diesel	2	20	7,200 bhp	2 Z-drive	16.1
Edgar B. Speer	Pielstick - 18PC2-3V-400	Diesel	2	18	19,260 bhp	2 cpp	17.0
Edward L. Ryerson	General Electric Co.	Turbine	1	**	9,900 shp	1	19.0
Edwin H. Gott	MaK - 8M43C	Diesel	2	8	19,578 bhp	2 ccp	16.7
Espada Desgagnés	B&W - 6S60MC-C	Diesel	1	5	18,605 bhp	1 cpp	18.4
Evans McKeil*	GM EMD - 16-645C	Diesel	1	16	2,150 bhp	1	11.5
Evans Spirit	Wartsila - 6L38B	Diesel	1	6	5,831 bhp	1 cpp	16.1
Everlast*	Daihatsu - 8DSM-32	Diesel	2	8	6,000 bhp	2	16.5
Federal Alster	B&W - 5S50ME-B9	Diesel	1	5	10,731 bhp	1	16.1
Federal Asahi	B&W - 6S46MC C	Diesel	1	6	10,710 bhp	1	16.1
Federal Baltic	B&W - 6S46MC-C	Diesel	1	5	10,710 bhp	1	16.1
Federal Barents	B&W - 6S46MC-C	Diesel	1	6	10,710 bhp	1	16.1
Federal Beaufort	B&W - 6S46MC-C	Diesel	1	6	10,710 bhp	1	16.1
Federal Bering	B&W - 6S46MC-C	Diesel	1	6	10,710 bhp	1	16.1
Federal Biscay	B&W - 6S46MC-C	Diesel	1	6	10,710 bhp	1	16.1
Federal Bristol	B&W - 6S46MC-C	Diesel	1	6	10,710 bhp	1	16.1
Federal Caribou	B&W - 6S46MC-C	Diesel	1	6	10,710 bhp	1	16.1
Federal Cedar	B&W - 6S46MC-C	Diesel	1	6	10,710 bhp	1	16.1
Federal Champlain	B&W - 6S46MC-C	Diesel	1	6	10,710 bhp	1	16.1
Federal Churchill	B&W - 6S46MC-C	Diesel	1	6	10,710 bhp	1	16.1
Federal Clyde	B&W - 6S46MC-C	Diesel	1	6	10,710 bhp	1	16.1
Federal Columbia	B&W - 6S46MC-C	Diesel	1	6	10,710 bhp	1	16.1
Federal Dart	B&W - 5S50ME-B9	Diesel	1	5	10,731 bhp	1	16.1
Federal Dee	B&W - 5S50ME-B9	Diesel	1	5	10,731 bhp	1	16.1
Federal Delta	B&W - 5S50ME-B9	Diesel	1	5	10,731 bhp	1	16.1
Federal Ems	B&W - 6S46MC-C	Diesel	1	6	10,686 bhp	1	16.1
Federal Hudson	B&W - 6S46MC-C	Diesel	1	6	10,710 bhp	1	15.5
Federal Hunter	B&W - 6S46MC-C	Diesel	1	6	10,710 bhp	1	15.5
Federal Katsura	Mitsubishi (Tokyo) - 6UEC52LA	Diesel	1	6	9,490 bhp	1	19.2
Federal Kivalina	B&W - 6S46MC-C	Diesel	1	6	10,710 bhp	1	16.1
Federal Kumano	B&W - 6S46MC-C	Diesel	1	6	10,710 bhp	1	16.1
Federal Kushiro	Mitsubishi - 6UEC52LA	Diesel	1	6	9,626 bhp	1	16.6
Federal Mayumi	MAN B&W - 6S46MC-C	Diesel	1	6	10,686 bhp	1	16.1
Federal Montreal	B&W - 5S50ME-B9	Diesel	1	5	10,731 bhp	1	16.1
Federal Mosel	B&W - 5S50ME-B9	Diesel	1	5	10,731 bhp	1	16.1
Federal Nagara	B&W - 5S50ME-B9	Diesel	1	5	10,731 bhp	1	16.1
Federal Nakagawa	B&W - 6S46MC-C	Diesel	1	6	10,710 bhp	1	16.1
Federal Oshima	B&W - 6S46MC-C	Diesel	1	6	10,710 bhp	1	16.1
Federal Rideau	B&W - 6S46MC-C	Diesel	1	6	10,710 bhp	1	16.1
Federal Ruhr	B&W - 5S50ME-B9	Diesel	1	5	10,731 bhp	1	16.1
Federal Sakura	Mitsubishi / Kobe - 6UEC52LA	Diesel	1	5	9,490 bhp	1	19.3
Federal Satsuki	B&W - 6S46MC-C	Diesel	1	6	9,235 bhp	1	16.1
Federal Seto	MAN B&W - 6S46MC-C	Diesel	1	6	10,711 bhp	1	16.7
Federal Shimanto	Mitsubishi - 6UEC52LA	Diesel	1	6	9,600 bhp	1	16.6
Federal St. Laurent	B&W - 5S50ME-B9	Diesel	1	5	10,731 bhp	1	16.1
Federal Welland	B&W - 6S46MC-C	Diesel	1	6	10,710 bhp	1	16.1
Federal Weser	B&W - 6S46MC-C	Diesel	1	6	10,686 bhp	1	18.0
Federal Yoshino	Mitsubishi - 6UEC52LA	Diesel	1	6	9,600 bhp	1	16.6
Federal Yukon	B&W - 6S46MC-C	Diesel	1	6	10,710 bhp	1	15.5
Ferbec	MAN B&W - 6S50MC	Diesel	1	6	9,222 bhp	1	16.7
Florence Spirit	Wartsila C - 6L38B	Diesel	1	6	5,831 bhp	1	15.5
Frontenac	Sulzer - 6RND76	Diesel	1	6	9,600 bhp	1 cpp	17.0

Vessel Name	Engine Manufacturer & Model #	Engine Type	Total Engines	Total Cylinders	Rated HP	Total Props	Speed MPH
G3 Marquis	Wartsila 5RT-flex50-D	Diesel	1	5	11,863 bhp	1 cpp	16.1
G.L. Ostrander*	Caterpillar - 3608-DITA	Diesel	2	8	6,008 bhp	2	17.3
Gaia Desgagnés	Wärtsilä 9L34DF	Diesel	1	0	6,032 bhp	1 cpp	16.8
Great Republic	GM EMD - 20-645-E7	Diesel	2	20	7,200 bhp	2 cpp	15.0
Griffon (CCG)	Fairbanks Morse - 8-38D8-1/8	Diesel	4	8	5,332 bhp	2	13.0
H. Lee White	GM EMD - 20-645-E7B	Diesel	2	20	7,200 bhp	1 cpp	15.0
Harvest Spirit	MAN-B&W - 6S35 MC Mk-7	Diesel	1	6	5,951 bhp	1 cpp	13.8
Herbert C. Jackson	MaK - 6M32E	Diesel	2	6	6,250 bhp	1 cpp	
Hinch Spirit	Yanmar - 6N330L-EN	Diesel	2	6	6,903 bhp	2	
Hollyhock (USCG)	Caterpillar - 3608TA	Diesel	2	6	6,200 bhp	1 cpp	
Hon. James L. Oberstar	Rolls-Royce Bergen - B32:40L6P	Diesel	6		8,160 shp	1 ccp	17.0
Indiana Harbor	GM EMD - 20-645-E7	Diesel	4	20	14,400 bhp	2 cpp	16.1
Iver Bright	Wärtsilä 7L32	Diesel	1	7	4,755 bhp	1	
Invincible*	GM EMD - 16-645-E7B	Diesel	2	16	5,750 bhp	2	13.8
James R. Barker	Pielstick - 16PC2-2V-400	Diesel	2	16	16,000 bhp	2 cpp	15.5
John D. Leitch	B&W - 5-74VT2BF-160	Diesel	1	5	7,500 bhp	1 cpp	16.1
John G. Munson	MaK - 6M46C	Diesel	1	6	7,000 bhp	1 cpp	16.1
John J. Boland	GM EMD - 20-645-E7B	Diesel	2	20	7,200 bhp	1 cpp	15.0
Joseph L. Block	GM EMD - 20-645-E7	Diesel	2	20	7,200 bhp	1 cpp	17.3
Joyce L. VanEnkevort*	Caterpillar - 3612	Diesel	2	12	10,200 bhp	2 cpp	
Kaministiqua	Sulzer - 4RLB76	Diesel	4	4	10,880 bhp	1cpp	15.5
Karen Andrie*	GM EMD - 8-710G7C	Diesel	2	8	4,000 bhp	2	19.0
Katmai Bay (USCG)	Fairbanks Morse - 10-38D8-1/8	Diesel	2	10	2,500 bhp	1	13.8
Kaye E. Barker	Rolls-Royce Bergen - B32:40L6P	Diesel	2	6	8,160 shp	1 ccp	17.0
Lake Express**	MTU 16V4000M70	Diesel	4	16	12,616 bhp	4 water jet	40.0
Lake Guardian	Cummins OSK38	Diesel	2	12	2,478 bhp	2	14
Laura L. VanEnkevort*	EMD 16-645-E7B	Diesel	2	16	7,000 bhp	2	12.7
Laurentia Desgagnés	B&W - 6S60MC-C	Diesel	1	5	18,605 bhp	1 cpp	18.4
Lee A. Tregurtha	Rolls-Royce Bergen B32:40L6P	Diesel	2	6	8,160 shp	1 ccp	17.0
Leo A. McArthur*	MaK - 6M25	Diesel	2	6	5,384 bhp	2 cpp	12.1
Leonard M*	Ruston P - 6RK270M	Diesel	2	6	2,097 bhp	2	13.8
Mackinaw (USCG)	Caterpillar - 3612	Diesel	3	12	9,119 bhp	2 Azipod	17.3
Manitoulin	B&W - 5L50MC	Diesel	1	5	8,113 bhp	1 cpp	16.5
Manitowoc	Alco - 16V251E	Diesel	2	16	5,600 bhp	1	16.1
Mark W. Barker	EMD - 16-710G7	Diesel	2	16	7,800 bhp	1	13.8
Martha L. Black (CCG)	Alco - 16V251F	Diesel	3	16	8,973 bhp	2	13.8
McKeil Spirit	Wartsila - 6L388	Diesel	1	6	5,831 bhp	1 cpp	16.1
Mesabi Miner	Pielstick - 16PC2-2V-400	Diesel	2	16	16,000 bhp	2 cpp	15.5
Mia Desgagnés	Wärtsilä 5RT-flex 50DF	Diesel/LNG	1	5	7,305 bhp	1 cpp	15.0
Michigan*	GM EMD - 20-645-E6	Diesel	2	16	3,900 bhp	2	13.2
Michipicoten	MaK - 6M32C	Diesel	2	6	8,160 bhp	1 cpp	14.0
Miena Desgagnés	MAN - 5G45ME-C9.5	Diesel	1	5	6,433 bhp	1	17.4
Mobile Bay (USCG)	Fairbanks Morse - 10-38D8-1/8	Diesel	2	10	2,500 bhp	1	13.8
Morro Bay (USCG)	Fairbanks Morse - 10-38D8-1/8	Diesel	2	10	2,500 bhp	1	13.8
NACC Alicudi	Daihatsu Diesel - 8DKM-28	Diesel	1	8	2,848 bhp	1	13.2
NACC Argonaut	Wartsila - 6L38B	Diesel	1	6	5,912 bhp	1 cpp	15.3
NACC Quebec	Wartsila - 6L38B	Diesel	1	6	5,831 bhp	1 cpp	15
Neah Bay (USCG)	Fairbanks Morse -10-38D8-1/8	Diesel	2	10	2,500 bhp	1	13.8
New York*	CAT 3516C	Diesel	2		4,200 bhp		
Nordika Desgagnés	B&W - 6S46MC-C	Diesel/LNG	1	6	8,955 bhp	1	17.3
Northern Spirit	MaK 7M43C	Diesel	1	7	8,560 bhp	1 cpp	
Northern Venture	MAN-B&W 6L42MC	Diesel				1 cpp	16.2
Nukumi	GM EMD 20-645-E7	Diesel	2	20	12,000	1 ccp	16.1
Oakglen	B&W - 6K67GF	Diesel	1	6	11,600 bhp	1	15.5
Ocean Explorer	Wartsila-20	Diesel	4		4,320 bhp	2 cpp	19.0
Ocean Navigator	Caterpillar 3516TA-B	Diesel	2	16	4,000 bhp	2	11.5
Ocean Voyager	Caterpillar 3516TA-B	Diesel	2	16	4,000 bhp	2	11.5
Paul A. Desgagnés	Wärtsilä 5RT-Flex 50DF	Diesel/LNG	1	5	7,302 bhp	1 cpp	16.1
Paul R. Tregurtha	MaK - 6M43C	Diesel	2	6	17,120 bhp	2 cpp	15.5
Pearl Mist	Caterpillar - 3516C-DITA	Diesel	2	16	3,386 bhp	2	
Petite Forte*	Ruston - 8ATC	Diesel	2	8	4,200 bhp	2	15.5
Philip R. Clarke	Westinghouse Elec. Corp.	Turbine	1	**	7,700 bhp	1	16.1
Pierre Radisson (CCG)	Alco - 16V251F	Diesel	6	16	17,700 bhp	1	18.4
Prentiss Brown*	GM EMD - 12-645-E2	Diesel	2	12	3,900 bhp		

Engines / *Continued*

Vessel Name	Engine Manufacturer & Model #	Engine Type	Total Engines	Total Cylinders	Rated HP	Total Props	Speed MPH
Presque Isle*	Mirrlees Blackstone Ltd. - KVMR-16	Diesel	2	16	14,840 bhp	2 cpp	
Quinte Loyalist**	Caterpillar - 3196	Diesel	2	6	770 bhp		
Radcliffe R. Latimer	MaK - 8M32C	Diesel	2	8	10,442 bhp	1 cpp	
Rebecca Lynn*	GM EMD - 16-567-BC	Diesel	2	16	3,600 bhp	2	
Robert S. Pierson	Alco - 16V251E	Diesel	2	16	5,600 bhp	1	17.8
Roger Blough	Pielstick - 16PC2V-400	Diesel	2	16	14,200 bhp	1 cpp	16.7
Rosaire A. Desgagnés	MaK/Caterpillar - 6M43	Diesel	1	6	7,344 bhp	1 cpp	17.8
Rossi A. Desgagnés	Wärtsilä 5RT-Flex 50DF	Diesel	1	5	7,302 bhp	1 cpp	16.1
Rt. Hon. Paul J. Martin	MaK/Caterpillar - 6M32C	Diesel	2	6	8,060 bhp (est)	1 cpp	
Saginaw	MaK - 6M43C	Diesel	1	6	8,160 bhp	1 cpp	16.1
Sam Laud	GM EMD - 20-645-E7	Diesel	2	20	7,200 bhp	1 cpp	16.1
Samuel de Champlain*	GM EMD - 20-645-E5	Diesel	2	20	7,200 bhp	2 cpp	17.3
Samuel Risley (CCG)	Wartsila - VASA 12V22HF	Diesel	4	12	8,836 bhp	2 cpp	17.3
Sarah Desgagnés	MaK - 7M43	Diesel	1	7	9,517 bhp	1 cpp	15.0
Sea Eagle II*	GM EMD - 20-645-E7	Diesel	2	20	7,200 bhp	2	13.8
Sedna Desgagnés	MaK/Caterpillar - 6M43	Diesel	1	6	7,344 bhp	1 cpp	17.8
Sharon M I*	Niigata - 6L38HX	Diesel	2	6	1,934 bhp	2	16.0
Sinaa	Wartsila – 6R46	Diesel	1	6	7,278 bhp	1	
Spar (USCG)	Caterpillar - 3608TA	Diesel	2	6	6,200 bhp	1 cpp	
Spruceglen	Sulzer - 4RLB76	Diesel	1	4	10,880 bhp	1 cpp	13.8
Stewart J. Cort	GM EMD - 20-645-E7	Diesel	4	20	14,400 bhp	2 cpp	18.4
Taiga Desgagnés	B&W - 6S46MC-C	Diesel	1	6	9,482 bhp	1	17.3
Thunder Bay	MAN-B&W - 6S50ME-B9	Diesel	1	6	11,897 bhp	1	15.5
Tim McKeil*	Niigata 6L38HX	Diesel	2	6	2,400 bhp	2	15.3
Tim S. Dool	MaK - 8M43C	Diesel	1	8	10,750 bhp	1 cpp	17.3
Undaunted*	Cummins - K38-M	Diesel	2	12	2,000 bhp	2	
Victory*	MaK - 6MU551AK	Diesel	2	6	7,880 bhp	2	16.1
Viking Octantis	MAN - 12V32/44CR	Diesel	4	12	25,600 bhp	2 cpp	21
Viking Polaris	MAN - 12V32/44CR	Diesel	4	12	25,600 bhp	2 cpp	21
Walter J. McCarthy Jr.	GM EMD - 20-645-E7B	Diesel	4	20	14,400 bhp	2 cpp	16.1
Whitefish Bay	MAN-B&W - 6S50ME-B9	Diesel	1	6	11,897 bhp	1	15.5
Wicky Spirit	Yanmar - 6N330L-EN	Diesel	2	6	6,903 bhp	2	
Wilfred Sykes	Westinghouse Elec. Corp.	Turbine	1	**	7,700 shp	1	16.1
Zélada Desgagnés	MaK/Caterpillar - 6M43	Diesel	1	6	7,344 bhp	1 cpp	17.8

Herbert C. Jackson's two MaK - 6M32E diesel engines. Scan the QR code to see a video taken aboard the Jackson that captures these beauties in action, along with other footage from a trip from the Soo Locks to Marquette, MI. (Nick Stenstrup)

Saltwater Fleets

Eye-catching Maxima of the Netherlands-based Royal Wagenborg fleet. (Samuel Hankinson)

A

ACE TANKERS CV, AMSTERDAM, NETHERLANDS (ace-tankers.com)

Fleet Name Vessel Name	Vessel IMO #	Vessel Type	Year Built	Engine Type	Cargo Cap. or Gross*	Overall Length	Vessel Breadth	Vessel Depth
Chem Hydra	9486180	TK	2009	D	11,939	475' 11"	75' 06"	40' 08"
Chem Lyra	9486178	TK	2009	D	11,939	475' 11"	75' 06"	40' 08"
Chem Norma	9486192	TK	2009	D	11,939	475' 11"	75' 06"	40' 08"
Chem Polaris	9416044	TK	2008	D	11,930	481' 00"	77' 09"	42' 08"

(Braken '08-'10, *Maemi* '10-'15)

ALLIANCE TANKERS, HAMILTON, BERMUDA (alliancemaritime.com)

Furuholmen	9553397	TK	2010	D	11,908	473' 02"	75' 06"	40' 08"

AMERICAN QUEEN VOYAGES, FORT LAUDERDALE, FL (aqvoyages.com)
VESSELS OPERATED BY AMERICAN STEAMBOAT OPERATING CO., NEW ALBANY, IN

Ocean Navigator	9213131	PA	2004	D	4,954*	300' 00"	50' 00"	20' 00"

Built: Atlantic Marine Inc., Jacksonville, FL (*Cape Cod Light* '04-'07, Coastal Queen 2 '07-'08, Clipper Discoverer '08-'10, Sea Discoverer '10-'17, *Victory II* '17-'22); passenger capacity 202

Ocean Voyager	9213129	PA	2004	D	4,954*	300' 00"	50' 00"	20' 00"

Built: Atlantic Marine Inc., Jacksonville, FL (*Cape May Light* '01-'09, Sea Voyager '09-'14, *Saint Laurent* '14-'16, *Victory I* '16-'22); passenger capacity 202

ARGO CORAL MARITIME LTD., ROTTERDAM, NETHERLANDS (acm-group.nl)

BBC Swift	9741152	GC	2017	D	11,436	474' 09"	74' 10"	37' 11"

(Industrial Swift '17-'20)

ARMADOR GEMI ISLETMECILIGI TICARET LTD., ISTANBUL, TURKEY (armadorshipping.com)

Pochard S	9262534	BC	2003	D	22,655	655' 10"	77' 09"	50' 02"

(Pochard '03-'14)

AUERBACH SCHIFFFAHRT GMBH & CO., HAMBURG, GERMANY (auerbach-schifffahrt.de)

Nordic Kylie	9357999	HL	2005	D	9,611	453' 00"	68' 11"	36' 01"

(Beluga Expectation '05-'11, Jule '11-'11, OXL Avatar '11-'13, Clipper Anita '13-'13, Thorco Dolphin '13-'15, *Jule* '15-'20, BBC Oklahoma '20-'21, BBC Yukon '21-'22)

B

BEATRIX ENTERPRISE CO., PIRAEUS, GREECE (beatrixenterprises.com)

Eagle	9227869	GC	2001	D	11,194	486' 01"	74' 10"	40' 00"

(Auguste Oldendorff '01-'06, Beagle IV '06-'19)

BERNHARD SCHULTE GROUP OF COMPANIES, HAMBURG, GERMANY (schultegroup.com)

Edzard Schulte	9439852	TK	2011	D	11,246	476' 02"	75' 06"	41' 01"
Elisabeth Schulte	9439840	TK	2010	D	11,246	476' 02"	75' 06"	41' 01"
Erin Schulte	9439814	TK	2009	D	11,246	476' 02"	75' 06"	41' 01"

BESIKTAS SHIPPING GROUP, ISTANBUL, TURKEY (besiktasgroup.com)

Arsland	9395989	TK	2008	D	12,164	472' 07"	75' 06"	40' 08"

(CT Dublin '08-'17)

Lagertha	9410143	TK	2009	D	12,619	530' 04"	73' 06"	42' 00"

(Halit Bey '09-'19)

BIGLIFT SHIPPING BV, AMSTERDAM, NETHERLANDS (bigliftshipping.com)

Happy Ranger	9139311	HL	1998	D	10,990	452' 09"	74' 10"	42' 06"
Happy River	9139294	HL	1997	D	10,990	452' 09"	74' 10"	42' 06"
Happy Rover	9139309	HL	1997	D	10,990	452' 09"	74' 10"	42' 06"

BLYSTAD GROUP, OSLO, NORWAY (blystad.no)
FOLLOWING VESSEL UNDER CHARTER TO SONGA SHIPMANAGEMENT

Songa Diamond	9460459	TK	2009	D	11,259	472' 05"	74' 02"	41' 00"

BRIESE SCHIFFAHRTS GMBH & CO. KG, LEER, GERMANY (briese.de)

BBC Alberta	9468102	HL	2010	D	9,611	452' 11"	68' 11"	36' 01"

(Beluga Maturity '10-'10, Beluga Firmament '10-'11, *BBC Celina* '11-'15)

BBC Arkhangelsk	9736212	HL	2020	D	11,503	482' 03"	74' 10"	
BBC Austria	9433327	GC	2009	D	7,002	392' 11"	66' 03"	32' 02"
BBC Balboa	9501667	GC	2012	D	6,310	393' 00"	66' 03"	32' 02"
BBC Europe	9266308	GC	2003	D	7,002	392' 11"	66' 03"	32' 02"
BBC Everest	9508407	HL	2011	D	8,255	412' 09"	72' 02"	35' 05"

Fleet Name / Vessel Name	Vessel IMO #	Vessel Type	Year Built	Engine Type	Cargo Cap. or Gross*	Overall Length	Vessel Breadth	Vessel Depth
BBC Gdansk	9436965	HL	2009	D	6,155	401' 09"	59' 09"	31' 02"
BBC Greenland	9427079	HL	2007	D	7,002	392' 11"	66' 03"	32' 02"
BBC Hudson	9435868	HL	2009	D	12,936	469' 07"	75' 11"	43' 08"
BBC Kibo	9508421	HL	2011	D	8,255	412' 09"	72' 02"	35' 05"
BBC Kwiatkowski	9436953	GC	2008	D	6,155	401' 09"	59' 09"	31' 02"
(Eugeniusz Kwiatkowski '08-'08)								
BBC Louise	9685097	GC	2018	D	9,670	452' 09"	70' 03"	36' 01"
BBC Mont Blanc	9508433	GC	2011	D	8,255	412' 09"	72' 02"	35' 05"
BBC Rushmore	9508469	GC	2012	D	8,255	412' 09"	72' 02"	35' 05"
BBC Russia	9700392	HL	2018	D	11,492	482' 04"	74' 10"	37' 01"
BBC Scandinavia	9362633	HL	2007	D	7,002	393' 00"	66' 03"	32' 02"
(Rysum '07-'07, BBC Scandinavia '07-'15, R Fenix '15-'16)								
BBC St. Petersburg	9736200	HL	2020	D	11,503	482' 03"	74' 10"	
(Sanfu '20-'20)								
BBC Switzerland	9433315	HL	2008	D	7,002	393' 00"	66' 03"	32' 02"
BBC Utah	9468114	HL	2011	D	9,611	452' 11"	68' 11"	36' 01"
(Beluga Flashlight '11-'11, BBC Idaho '11-'14, Isakandar '14-'15, Idaho '15-'16)								
BBC Vesuvius	9508471	GC	2012	D	8,255	412' 09"	72' 02"	35' 05"
BBC Volga	9436329	GC	2009	D	12,936	469' 07"	75' 11"	43' 08"
(Ocean Breeze '09-'09)								
BBC Weser	9347047	GC	2006	D	12,936	469' 07"	75' 11"	43' 08"
(Westerdamm '06-'06, BBC Weser '06-'10, STX Bright '10-'14)								
BBC Xingang	9508483	GC	2013	D	8,255	412' 09"	72' 02"	35' 05"
Kurt Paul	9435856	GC	2009	D	12,936	469' 07"	75' 11"	43' 08"
Sjard	9303314	GC	2007	D	12,936	469' 07"	75' 11"	43' 08"
(BBC Sjard '07-'08)								
BROSTROM AB, COPENHAGEN, DENMARK (maersktankers.com)								
Bro Agnes	9348302	TK	2008	D	12,164	472' 07"	75' 06"	40' 08"
Bro Anna	9344435	TK	2008	D	12,164	472' 07"	75' 06"	40' 08"
(Gan Gesture '08-'08)								

About the Saltwater Listings

Observers will likely spot saltwater vessels that are not included in this book. These may be newcomers to the Great Lakes/Seaway system, recent renames or new construction. This is not meant to be an exhaustive listing of every saltwater vessel that could potentially visit the Great Lakes and St. Lawrence Seaway. This list reflects vessels whose primary trade routes are on saltwater but which also regularly visit Great Lakes and St. Lawrence Seaway ports above Montreal. Fleets listed may operate other vessels worldwide than those included herein; additional vessels may be found on fleet websites, which have been included where available. Former names listed in boldface type indicate the vessel visited the Seaway under that name.

Fall colors on the St. Marys River, seen from the Polish-flagged Solina. (Jonathan Hoort)

C

CANFORNAV (CANADIAN FOREST NAVIGATION CO. LTD.), MONTREAL, CANADA *(canfornav.com)*
At press time, Canadian Forest Navigation Co. Ltd. had the following vessels under long or short-term charter. Please consult their respective fleets for details: **Andean, Barnacle, Blacky, Bluebill, Brant, Cape, Chestnut, Cinnamon, Greenwing, Labrador, Maccoa, Mandarin, Mottler, Ruddy, Shoveler, Sunda, Torrent, Tufty, Tundra, Whistler** and **Wigeon.**

CARISBROOKE SHIPPING LTD., COWES, UNITED KINGDOM *(carisbrooke.co)*

Celine C	9463566	BC	2011	D	9,530	453' 01"	68' 11"	36' 01"
(UAL Rodach '11-'12, Celine '12-'16, UAL Rodach '16-'18, Celine '18-'18)								
Jacqueline C	9429754	BC	2009	D	9,530	453' 01"	68' 11"	36' 01"
Janet C	9430129	BC	2009	D	9,530	453' 01"	68' 11"	36' 01"
Julie C	9430143	BC	2009	D	9,530	453' 01"	68' 11"	36' 01"
Vectis Pride	9626132	BC	2012	D	7,227	406' 08"	57' 01"	37' 05"
Vectis Progress	9626144	BC	2012	D	7,227	406' 08"	57' 01"	37' 05"

CARSTEN REHDER SCHIFFSMAKLER UND REEDEREI, HAMBURG, GERMANY *(carstenrehder.de)*

ABB Vanessa	9437309	BC	2009	D	9,611	455' 10"	68' 11"	36' 01"
(Beluga Frequency '09-'11, HR Frequency '11-'22)								

CELSIUS SHIPPING APS, HELLERUP, DENMARK *(celsiusshipping.com)*

Celsius Mumbai	9304332	TK	2005	D	11,623	477' 05"	77' 09"	43' 10"
(Bum Eun '05-'13)								

CLEARWATER GROUP, ROTTERDAM, NETHERLANDS *(clearwatergroup.nl)*

Carolus Magnus	9298375	TK	2007	D	12,776	539' 02"	75' 06"	42' 00"
*(MCT Breithorn '07-'15, **SCT Breithorn** '15-'17)*								
Emanuele S.	9298363	TK	2007	D	12,776	539' 02"	75' 06"	42' 00"
*(MCT Monte Rosa '07-'15, SCT **Monte Rosa** '15-'17)*								
Mirella S.	9298351	TK	2006	D	12,776	539' 02"	75' 06"	42' 00"
*(HHL Arctic '06-'06, MCT Matterhorn '06-'15, **SCT Matterhorn** '15-'17)*								
Rosy	9298387	TK	2008	D	12,776	539' 02"	75' 06"	42' 00"
*(MCT Stockhorn '08-'15, **SCT Stockhorn** '15-'17)*								

CNAN NORD SPA., KOUBA, ALGERIA *(cnan-nord.com)*

Timgad	9697337	GC	2016	D	11,494	482' 03"	74' 10"	37' 11"4

COASTAL SHIPPING LTD., GOOSE BAY, CANADA *(woodwards.nf.ca)*

Kitikmeot W.	9421219	TK	2010	D	13,097	491' 11"	75' 06"	42' 10"
(Icdas 09 '10-'18)								
Kivalliq W.	9187409	TK	2004	D	8,882	476' 08"	68' 03"	36' 09"
*(Falcon '04-'09, **Sten Fjord** '09-'18)*								

Sun rises behind Federal Nakagawa at Duluth, MN. (David Schauer)

Fleet Name / Vessel Name	Vessel IMO #	Vessel Type	Year Built	Engine Type	Cargo Cap. or Gross*	Overall Length	Vessel Breadth	Vessel Depth
Qikiqtaaluk W.	9421221	TK	2011	D	13,097	491' 11"	75' 06"	42' 10"
(Icdas-11 '10-'18)								
Tuvaq W.	9610341	TK	2012	D	5,422	369' 09"	57' 09"	30' 10"
(Bering '12-'13, San Pietro '13-'18)								

COMPAGNIE DU PONANT S.A., MARSEILLES, FRANCE *(ponant.com)*

Le Bellot	9852418	PA	2020	D	9,976	431' 04"	59' 01"	59' 09"
Built: VARD Holdings Ltd. (subsidiary of Fincantieri), Tulcea, Romania; passenger capacity184								
Le Champlain	9814038	PA	2018	D	9,976	431' 04"	59' 01"	59' 09"
Built: VARD Holdings Ltd. (subsidiary of Fincantieri), Tulcea, Romania; passenger capacity184								
Le Dumont-d'Urville	9814052	PA	2019	D	9,976	431' 04"	59' 01"	59' 09"
Built: VARD Holdings Ltd. (subsidiary of Fincantieri), Tulcea, Romania; passenger capacity184								

D-E

DANSER VAN GENT SHIPPING, DELFZIJL, NETHERLANDS *(danservangent.nl)*

Marietje Andrea	9361134	GC	2009	D	5,418	413' 10"	49' 10"	30' 02"
Marietje Deborah	9481594	GC	2011	D	5,418	413' 10"	49' 10"	30' 02"

DOORNEKAMP LINES, PICTON, ONTARIO *(doornekamplines.ca)*

Peyton Lynn C	9295531	GC	2007	D	9,909	461' 06"	77' 03"	37' 09"
(Eemsdijk '07-'18, Gesina Schepers '18-'21)								

DSHIP CARRIERS GMBH & CO., HAMBURG, GERMANY *(dship carriers.com)*

Alanis	9468085	HL	2010	D	9,611	452' 11"	68' 11"	36' 01"
*(Beluga Modification '10-'10, Beluga Faith '10-'11, **Alina** '11-'20)*								
Bruce	9741140	HL	2022	D	11,494	482' 03"	74' 10"	37' 11"
Charlie	9736236	HL	2022	D	11,494	482' 03"	74' 10"	37' 11"
Gwen	9402067	HL	2008	D	9,611	455' 10"	68' 11"	36' 01"
*(Beluga Fortune '08-'11, **Fortune** '11-'18)*								
Janis	9437311	HL	2009	D	9,611	455' 10"	68' 11"	36' 01"
(Beluga Facility '09-'11, HR Facility '11-'11, Chandra Neptune '11-'12, HR Facility '12-'15, ABB Felina '15-'18, Oslo Fjord I '18-'19)								
Josef	9467005	HL	2011	D	9,618	453' 00"	68' 11"	36' 01"
*(Beluga Fealty '11-'11, **HHL Congo** '11-'18)*								
Keith	9736195	HL	2019	D	11,494	482' 03"	74' 10"	37' 11"
(Taizhou Sanfu '19-'19)								
Melissa	9312169	HL	2005	D	9,611	453' 00"	68' 11"	36' 01"
*(**Beluga Endurance** '05-'11, Martin '11-'13, Rickmers Mumbai '13-'14, **Nordana Emilie** '14-'16, Martin '16-'16, BBC Nebraska '16-'17, **Holandia** '17-'20)*								
Mick	9736183	HL	2019	D	11,494	482' 03"	74' 10"	37' 11"

Marguerita on the lower Detroit River. (Samuel Hankinson)

Fleet Name / Vessel Name	Vessel IMO #	Vessel Type	Year Built	Engine Type	Cargo Cap. or Gross*	Overall Length	Vessel Breadth	Vessel Depth
Ronnie	9736224	HL	2021	D	11,494	474' 09"	75' 06"	37' 11"
Sophia	9467017	HL	2011	D	9,618	453' 00"	68' 11"	36' 01"
(Beluga Feasibility '11-'11)								
Stevie	9488035	HL	2010	D	9,627	454' 05"	68' 11"	36' 01"
(OXL Rebel '10-'11, Clipper Agnes '11-'13, Brattingsborg '13-'15, BBC Missouri '15-'20, Brattingsborg '20-'22)								

DUZGIT GEMI INSA SANAYI, ISTANBUL, TURKEY *(duzgit.com)*

Duzgit Endeavour	9581007	TK	2013	D	10,276	509' 09"	71' 02"	36' 05"

F-G

FEDNAV, MONTREAL, CANADA *(fednav.com)*

CANARCTIC SHIPPING CO. LTD. – DIVISION OF FEDNAV

Arvik I	9854698	BK	2021	D	22,615	619' 05"	87' 03"	51' 06"
Nunavik	9673850	BK	2014	D	22,622	619' 05"	87' 03"	51' 06"
Umiak I	9334715	BK	2006	D	22,462	619' 05"	87' 03"	51' 06"

FEDNAV INTERNATIONAL LTD. - DIVISION OF FEDNAV

Federal Asahi {2}	9200419	BC	2000	D	20,659	656' 02"	77' 11"	48' 09"
Federal Baltic	9697806	BC	2015	D	20,789	656' 01"	77' 11"	48' 09"
Federal Barents	9697820	BC	2015	D	20,789	656' 01"	77' 11"	48' 09"
Federal Beaufort	9697818	BC	2015	D	20,789	656' 01"	77' 11"	48' 09"
Federal Bering	9697832	BC	2015	D	20,789	656' 01"	77' 11"	48' 09"
Federal Biscay	9697856	BC	2015	D	20,789	656' 01"	77' 11"	48' 09"
Federal Bristol	9697844	BC	2015	D	20,789	656' 01"	77' 11"	48' 09"
Federal Caribou	9671096	BC	2016	D	20,789	656' 01"	77' 11"	48' 09"
Federal Cedar	9671101	BC	2016	D	20,789	656' 01"	77' 11"	48' 09"
Federal Champlain	9671058	BC	2016	D	20,789	656' 01"	77' 11"	48' 09"
Federal Churchill	9671060	BC	2016	D	20,789	656' 01"	77' 11"	48' 09"
Federal Clyde	9671072	BC	2016	D	20,789	656' 01"	77' 11"	48' 09"
Federal Columbia	9671084	BC	2016	D	20,789	656' 01"	77' 11"	48' 09"

Jamno assisted by tugs at Thunder Bay, ON. *(Eric Treece)*

Fleet Name / Vessel Name	Vessel IMO #	Vessel Type	Year Built	Engine Type	Cargo Cap. or Gross*	Overall Length	Vessel Breadth	Vessel Depth
Federal Dart	9805245	BC	2018	D	20,789	656' 01"	77' 11"	48' 09"
Federal Dee	9805269	BC	2018	D	20,789	656' 01"	77' 11"	48' 09"
Federal Delta	9805271	BC	2018	D	20,789	656' 01"	77' 11"	48' 09"
Federal Franklin	9866732	BC	2021	D	20,763	656' 01"	77' 11"	48' 09"
Federal Fraser {2}	9866744	BC	2021	D	20,763	656' 01"	77' 11"	48' 09"
Federal Freedom	9866756	BC	2021	D	20,763	656' 01"	77' 11"	48' 09"
Federal Frontier	9866768	BC	2021	D	20,763	656' 01"	77' 11"	48' 09"
Federal Hudson {3}	9205902	BC	2000	D	20,659	656' 02"	77' 11"	48' 09"
Federal Hunter {2}	9205938	BC	2001	D	20,659	656' 02"	77' 11"	48' 09"
Federal Katsura	9293923	BC	2005	D	19,165	624' 08"	77' 05"	49' 10"
Federal Kivalina	9205885	BC	2000	D	20,659	656' 02"	77' 11"	48' 09"
Federal Kumano	9244257	BC	2001	D	20,659	656' 02"	77' 11"	48' 09"
Federal Kushiro	9284702	BC	2003	D	19,165	624' 09"	77' 05"	49' 10"
Federal Leda	9229996	BC	2003	D	22,654	655' 10"	77' 09"	50' 02"
Federal Mayumi	9529578	BC	2012	D	20,465	655' 06"	77' 11"	48' 09"
Federal Montreal	9838474	BC	2019	D	20,763	656' 01"	78' 04"	48' 09"
Federal Nagara	9805257	BC	2018	D	20,789	656' 01"	77' 11"	48' 09"
Federal Nakagawa	9278791	BC	2005	D	20,659	656' 02"	77' 11"	48' 09"
Federal Oshima	9200330	BC	1999	D	20,659	656' 02"	77' 11"	48' 09"
Federal Rideau	9200445	BC	2000	D	20,659	656' 02"	77' 11"	48' 09"
Federal Sakura	9288291	BC	2005	D	19,165	624' 09"	77' 05"	49' 10"
Federal Satsuki	9529578	BC	2012	D	20,465	655' 06"	77' 11"	48' 09"
Federal Seto	9267209	BC	2004	D	20,659	656' 02"	77' 11"	48' 09"
Federal Shimanto	9218404	BC	2001	D	19,125	624' 09"	77' 05"	49' 10"
Federal St. Laurent {4}	9838462	BC	2019	D	20,763	656' 01"	78' 04"	48' 09"
Federal Welland	9205926	BC	2000	D	20,659	656' 02"	77' 11"	48' 09"
Federal Weser	9229972	BC	2002	D	22,654	655' 10"	77' 09"	50' 02"
Federal Yoshino	9218416	BC	2001	D	19,125	624' 09"	77' 05"	49' 10"
Federal Yukon	9205897	BC	2000	D	20,659	656' 02"	77' 11"	48' 09"

At press time, Fednav also had the following vessels under charter. Please consult their respective fleets for details: **Federal Alster, Federal Mosel, Federal Ruhr** and **Federal Yukina.**

Federal Frontier paid her first visit to Duluth, MN, in 2022. (Korey Garceau)

FORESTWAVE NAVIGATION, HEERENVEEN, NETHERLANDS *(forestwave.nl)*

Fleet Name Vessel Name	IMO #	Type	Built	Engine	Cargo/Gross	Length	Breadth	Depth
FWN Rapide	9320520	BC	2005	D	7,406	468' 02"	59' 10"	33' 04"
(Emily-C '05-'06, UAL America '06-'14)								
FWN Splendide	9320518	BC	2005	D	7,752	477' 09"	59' 10"	33' 10"
(UAL Rodach '05-'15, Jade C '15-'15)								
Trent Navigator	9631369	BC	2013	D	5,667	387' 07"	52' 02"	28' 10"
(Onego Mariner '13-'15)								
Trito Navigator	9631357	BC	2013	D	5,667	387' 07"	52' 02"	28' 10"
(Onego Navigator '13-'15)								

FRANCO COMPANIA NAVIERA SA, ATHENS, GREECE *(www.franco.gr)*
FOLLOWING VESSELS UNDER CHARTER TO GRANATH

Fleet Name Vessel Name	IMO #	Type	Built	Engine	Cargo/Gross	Length	Breadth	Depth
Barbro G	9546796	BC	2010	D	20,603	623' 04"	77' 11"	47' 11"
*(Seven Islands '10-'10, **Pacific Huron** '10-'20, **Ortolan Beta Strait** '20-'22)*								
Helena G.	9358383	BC	2007	D	22,792	655' 10"	77' 09"	50' 02"
*(**Garganey** '07-'17)*								
Isabelle G.	9285938	BC	2004	D	22,792	655' 10"	77' 09"	50' 02"
*(**Eider** '04-'18)*								
Johanna G.	9285940	BC	2005	D	22,792	655' 10"	77' 09"	50' 02"
(Redhead '05-'18)								
Maria G.	9358369	BC	2007	D	22,792	655' 10"	77' 09"	50' 02"
*(**Gadwall** '07-'17)*								

FURETANK REDERI, DONSO, SWEDEN *(furetank.se)*

Fleet Name Vessel Name	IMO #	Type	Built	Engine	Cargo/Gross	Length	Breadth	Depth
Fure Ven	9818278	TK	2019	D	17,991	491' 10"	74' 10"	39' 08"

H

HANSA TANKERS SA, BERGEN, NORWAY *(hansa-tankers.com)*

Fleet Name Vessel Name	IMO #	Type	Built	Engine	Cargo/Gross	Length	Breadth	Depth
Octonaut	9340477	TK	2007	D	11,623	477' 05"	77' 09"	43' 10"
(Bow Octavia '07-'10, AS Octavia '10-'13, Octaden '13-'21)								

HAPAG-LLOYD CRUISES, HAMBURG, GERMANY *(hl-cruises.com)*

Fleet Name Vessel Name	IMO #	Type	Built	Engine	Cargo/Gross	Length	Breadth	Depth
Hanseatic Inspiration	9817145	PA	2019	D	15,540*	456' 00"	22' 72"	23' 00"
Built: VARD Holdings Ltd. (subsidiary of Fincantieri) at Tulcea, Romania, and Langsten, Norway; passenger capacity 230								

HARREN & PARTNER GMBH, BREMEN, GERMANY *(harren-partner.de)*

Fleet Name Vessel Name	IMO #	Type	Built	Engine	Cargo/Gross	Length	Breadth	Depth
Patalya	9305180	TK	2005	D	11,935	472' 07"	75' 06"	40' 08"
Patrona I	9305178	TK	2004	D	11,935	472' 07"	75' 06"	40' 08"
(Patrona I '04-'08, Maersk Nordenham '08-'14)								

HARTMAN SEATRADE, URK, NETHERLANDS *(hartmanseatrade.com)*

Fleet Name Vessel Name	IMO #	Type	Built	Engine	Cargo/Gross	Length	Breadth	Depth
Pacific Dawn	9558464	GC	2010	D	2,981	343' 10"	51' 02"	24' 03"

HELD SHIPPING, HAREN EMS, GERMANY *(h-ship.com)*

Fleet Name Vessel Name	IMO #	Type	Built	Engine	Cargo/Gross	Length	Breadth	Depth
BBC Norfolk	9559884	GC	2011	D	6,351	433' 09"	52' 01"	31' 08"
*(Sinus Iridium '11-'11, Velocity Scan '11-'12, **Thorco Alliance** '12-'17)*								
BBC Texas	9388883	GC	2007	D	9,611	453' 00"	68' 11"	36' 01"
(Beluga Fighter '07-'11, Heino '11-'20)								

HERM. DAUELSBERG GMBH, BREMEN, GERMANY *(dauelsberg.de)*

Fleet Name Vessel Name	IMO #	Type	Built	Engine	Cargo/Gross	Length	Breadth	Depth
Puna	9546784	BC	2010	D	20,603	623' 04"	77' 11"	47' 11"
*(**Three Rivers** '10-'20)*								

HS SCHIFFAHRTS GMBH & CO., HAREN, GERMANY *(hs-schiffahrt.de)*

Fleet Name Vessel Name	IMO #	Type	Built	Engine	Cargo/Gross	Length	Breadth	Depth
BBC Eagle	9407574	GC	2008	D	8,750	456' 02"	65' 07"	37' 01"
(Apus J '08-'08, Industrial Eagle '08-'17)								
BBC Peru	9549592	GC	2012	D	9,963	479' 00"	65' 07"	37' 07"
(BBC Peru '12-'14, Thorco Chile '14-'14)								
Eider {2}	9415143	BC	2010	D	20,491	662' 02"	77' 04"	47' 11"
(Jan S '10-'15, Mistral '15-'19)								
Redhead {2}	9413901	BC	2010	D	20,491	662' 02"	77' 04"	47' 11"
*(**Hermann Schoening** '10-'15, Bora '15-'19)*								

Fleet Name / Vessel Name	Vessel IMO #	Vessel Type	Year Built	Engine Type	Cargo Cap. or Gross*	Overall Length	Vessel Breadth	Vessel Depth

I-J-K

IMM SHIPPING MANAGEMENT GMBH, BREMEN, GERMANY *(imm-shipping.de)*

| HC Melina | 9415052 | GC | 2011 | D | 6,577 | 424' 06" | 55' 09" | 32' 10" |

INTERMARINE, HOUSTON, TEXAS *(intermarine.com)*

| Industrial Color | 9810355 | HL | 2019 | D | 7,498 | 328' 00" | 68' 01" | |
(ZEA Color '19-'20, Color '20-'22)

INTERSHIP NAVIGATION CO. LTD., LIMASSOL, CYPRUS *(intership-cyprus.com)*
FOLLOWING VESSELS UNDER CHARTER TO FEDNAV LTD.

Federal Alster	9766164	BC	2016	D	22,947	655' 10"	77' 09"	50' 03"
Federal Mosel	9766188	BC	2017	D	22,947	655' 10"	77' 09"	50' 03"
Federal Ruhr	9766176	BC	2017	D	22,947	655' 10"	77' 09"	50' 03"

INTERUNITY MANAGEMENT CORP., BREMEN, GERMANY *(imc.tech)*

| Chem Tiger | 9287297 | TK | 2003 | D | 11,623 | 477' 05" | 77' 09" | 43' 10" |
| Chem Wolverine | 9340439 | TK | 2006 | D | 11,623 | 477' 05" | 77' 09" | 43' 10" |

JOHANN M.K. BLUMENTHAL GMBH & CO., HAMBURG, GERMANY *(www.bluships.com)*

| Comet | 9146106 | GC | 1997 | D | 5,999 | 351' 01" | 63' 08" | 34' 01" |
(Bay Pacific '97-'98)

JUMBO SHIPPING CO. SA, ROTTERDAM, NETHERLANDS *(jumbomaritime.nl)*

| Jumbo Vision | 9153642 | HL | 2000 | D | 7,971 | 362' 06" | 68' 05" | 44' 03" |

JUNGERHANS MARITIME SERVICES GMBH & CO., HAREN EMS, GERMANY *(juengerhans.de)*

| BBC Direction | 9347853 | GC | 2007 | D | 7,223 | 393' 01" | 65' 07" | 37' 01" |
(Industrial Dream '07-'14, BBC Vela '14-'19)
| BBC Dolphin | 9360192 | GC | 2007 | D | 7,223 | 393' 01" | 65' 07" | 37' 01" |
(Bellatrix J '09-'09, Industrial Egret '09-'12)
| BBC Echo | 9407603 | HL | 2010 | D | 8,750 | 456' 02" | 65' 07" | 37' 01" |
(Delphinus J '10-'15, Industrial Echo '15-'18)
| BBC Edge | 9407598 | HL | 2009 | D | 8,750 | 456' 02" | 65' 07" | 37' 01" |
(Industrial Edge '09-'09, BBC Pilbara '09-'13, Castor J. '13-'14, Industrial Edge '14-'16)

K-SHIPS SRL, GENOVA, ITALY

| Nike | 9431032 | TK | 2009 | D | 5,803 | 400' 03" | 55' 09" | |
(MT North Castle '09-'09, North Castle '09-'10)

KREY SCHIFFAHRTS GMBH & COMPANY KG, LEER, GERMANY *(krey-schiffahrt.de)*

| Celina | 9368326 | GC | 2008 | D | 11,894 | 469' 02" | 70' 06" | 43' 08" |
(Beluga Gravitation '08-'08, **BBC Rio Grande** '08-'11, Gabrielle Scan '11-'12, **Clipper Macau** '12-'16, **BBC Rio Grande** '16-'21))
| Erik | 9435105 | HL | 2008 | D | 9,618 | 453' 00" | 68' 11" | 36' 01" |
(BBC Louisiana '08-'17)
| Frieda | 9435117 | HL | 2008 | D | 9,618 | 453' 00" | 68' 11" | 36' 01" |
(BBC Colorado '08-'17)
| Pia | 9384318 | HL | 2007 | D | 9,618 | 453' 00" | 68' 11" | 36' 01" |
(BBC Alabama '07-'17)

L-M

LIBERTY BLUE SHIPMANAGEMENT GMBH, LEER, GERMANY *(liberty-blue.biz)*

| Onego Merchant | 9238363 | GC | 2001 | D | 6,301 | 433' 09" | 52' 01" | 31' 08" |
(Dewi Parwati '01-'03, Beluga Spirit '03-'03, Dewi Parwati '03-'08, Texel '08-'11)

MARCONSULT SCHIFFAHRT, HAMBURG, GERMANY *(mc-schiffahrt.de)*

| Onego Bayou | 9369069 | GC | 2007 | D | 7,878 | 477' 09" | 59' 10" | 33' 10" |
(Uta '07-'15, MarMakira '15-'19)

MEDITERRANEA DI NAVIGAZIONE S.P.A., RAVENNA, ITALY *(mediterraneanav.it)*

| Barbarica | 9383443 | TK | 2007 | D | 12,008 | 485' 11" | 75' 06" | 38' 09" |
| Sveva | 9156539 | TK | 1999 | D | 11,287 | 446' 01" | 75' 06" | 40' 02" |

Fleet Name Vessel Name	Vessel IMO #	Vessel Type	Year Built	Engine Type	Cargo Cap. or Gross*	Overall Length	Vessel Breadth	Vessel Depth
MINSHIP SHIPMANAGEMENT GMBH & CO. KG, SCHNAITTENBACH, GERMANY *(minship.com)*								
Lady Doris	9459955	BC	2011	D	19,814	606' 11"	77' 09"	47' 11"
(Merganser '11-'11)								
Marguerita	9717515	BC	2016	D	19,104	606' 11"	77' 09"	
Trudy	9415246	BC	2009	D	19,814	606' 11"	77' 09"	47' 11"
(Cresty '09-'09)								
Yulia	9459967	BC	2011	D	19,814	606' 11"	77' 09"	47' 11"
(Harlequin '11-'11)								
MTM SHIP MANAGEMENT LTD., SINGAPORE *(mtmshipmanagement.com)*								
MTM Antwerp	9291456	TK	2004	D	11,623	477' 05"	77' 09"	43' 10"
(Fairchem Stallion '04-'14)								
MTM Rotterdam	9477567	TK	2011	D	11,623	477' 05"	77' 09"	43' 10"
MTM Singapore	9477529	TK	2011	D	11,623	477' 05"	77' 09"	43' 10"
MTM Southport	9416032	TK	2008	D	11,930	481' 00"	77' 09"	42' 08"
(Golten '08-'10)								

N-O

Fleet Name Vessel Name	Vessel IMO #	Vessel Type	Year Built	Engine Type	Cargo Cap. or Gross*	Overall Length	Vessel Breadth	Vessel Depth
NAKKAS SHIPPING & TRADING, ISTANBUL, TURKEY *(nakkas.com)*								
Lea Atk	9566708	TK	2012	D	4,821	360' 08"	57' 02"	28' 10"
Tarsus	9883259	TK	2021	D	4,065	328' 01"	54' 06"	
NAVARONE SA MARINE ENTERPRISES, LIMASSOL, CYPRUS *(navarone.gr)*								
FOLLOWING VESSELS UNDER CHARTER TO CANFORNAV								
Andean	9413925	BC	2009	D	19,814	606' 11"	77' 09"	47' 11"
Barnacle	9409742	BC	2009	D	19,814	607' 04"	77' 09"	47' 11"
Blacky	9393149	BC	2008	D	19,814	607' 04"	77' 09"	47' 11"
Bluebill {2}	9263306	BC	2004	D	22,655	655' 10"	77' 09"	50' 02"
Brant	9393151	BC	2008	D	19,814	607' 04"	77' 09"	47' 11"
Chestnut	9477866	BC	2009	D	19,814	607' 04"	77' 09"	47' 11"
Cinnamon	9239800	BC	2002	D	18,311	611' 08"	77' 09"	46' 07"
Greenwing	9230921	BC	2002	D	18,311	611' 08"	77' 09"	46' 07"
Labrador	9415222	BC	2010	D	19,814	606' 11"	77' 09"	47' 11"
Maccoa	9413913	BC	2009	D	19,814	606' 11"	77' 09"	47' 11"
Mandarin	9239812	BC	2003	D	18,311	611' 08"	77' 09"	46' 07"
Mottler	9477828	BC	2009	D	19,814	607' 04"	77' 09"	47' 11"
Ruddy	9459981	BC	2009	D	19,814	606' 11"	77' 09"	47' 11"
Shoveler	9459979	BC	2009	D	19,814	606' 11"	77' 09"	47' 11"
Torrent	9415210	BC	2010	D	19,814	606' 11"	77' 09"	47' 11"

Pilot boat approaching Fuldaborg. *(Alain M. Gindroz)*

Fleet Name / Vessel Name	Vessel IMO #	Vessel Type	Year Built	Engine Type	Cargo Cap. or Gross*	Overall Length	Vessel Breadth	Vessel Depth
Tufty	9393163	BC	2009	D	19,814	607' 04"	77' 09"	47' 11"
Tundra	9415208	BC	2009	D	19,814	606' 11"	77' 09"	47' 11"
Whistler	9358371	BC	2007	D	22,792	655' 10"	77' 09"	50' 02"
Wigeon	9358395	BC	2007	D	22,792	655' 10"	77' 09"	50' 02"

NAVIGATION MARITIME BULGARE LTD., VARNA, BULGARIA *(navbul.com)*

Fleet Name / Vessel Name	Vessel IMO #	Vessel Type	Year Built	Engine Type	Cargo Cap. or Gross*	Overall Length	Vessel Breadth	Vessel Depth
Belasitza {2}	9498262	BC	2011	D	19,906	610' 03"	77' 09"	48' 01"
Bogdan {2}	9905710	BC	2021	D	20,848	623' 04"	77' 09"	
Kom {2}	9905708	BC	2021	D	20,848	623' 04"	77' 09"	
Ludogorets	9415155	BC	2010	D	20,491	622' 02"	77' 04"	47' 11"
(Fritz '10-'15, MarBacan '15-'16)								
Lyulin {2}	9498248	BC	2011	D	19,906	610' 03"	77' 09"	48' 01"
Oborishte {2}	9415167	BC	2010	D	20,491	622' 02"	77' 04"	47' 11"
(Luebbert '10-'15, MarBioko '15-'16)								
Osogovo {2}	9498250	BC	2010	D	19,906	610' 03"	77' 09"	47' 11"
Perelik {2}	9905722	BC	2021	D	20,848	623' 04"	77' 09"	
Rodopi {2}	9498274	BC	2012	D	19,906	610' 03"	77' 09"	47' 11"
Shipka {2}	9937282	BC	2021	D	20,848	623' 04"	77' 09"	
Strandja {2}	9564140	BC	2010	D	19,906	610' 03"	77' 09"	47' 11"
(Eastwind York '10-'10, Federal Yangtze '10-'10)								
Verila {2}	9905734	BC	2021	D	20,848	623' 04"	77' 09"	
Vezhen {2}	9937270	BC	2021	D	20,848	623' 04"	77' 09"	
Vitosha {2}	9564138	BC	2010	D	19,906	610' 03"	77' 11"	47' 11"
(Eastwind Yates '10-'10, Federal Pearl '10-'10)								

NORDIC TANKERS MARINE A/S, COPENHAGEN, DENMARK *(nordictankers.com)*

Fleet Name / Vessel Name	Vessel IMO #	Vessel Type	Year Built	Engine Type	Cargo Cap. or Gross*	Overall Length	Vessel Breadth	Vessel Depth
Nordic Ace	9800104	TK	2018	D	9,418	465' 11"	72' 02"	38' 09"
Nordic Aqua	9800116	TK	2018	D	9,418	465' 11"	72' 02"	38' 09"
Nordic Mari	9422677	TK	2009	D	11,930	481' 00"	77' 10"	42' 08"
(Clipper Mari '09-'14)								

NOVA MARINE CARRIERS SA, LUGANO, SWITZERLAND *(novamarinecarriers.com)*

Fleet Name / Vessel Name	Vessel IMO #	Vessel Type	Year Built	Engine Type	Cargo Cap. or Gross*	Overall Length	Vessel Breadth	Vessel Depth
Sider Amy	9331505	BC	2006	D	9,177	447' 06"	69' 07"	37' 01"
(Amy C '06-'18)								
Sider Bilbao	9338151	BC	2007	D	9,177	447' 06"	69' 07"	37' 01"
(Sally Ann C '07-'18)								
Sider London	9528706	BC	2007	D	9,177	447' 06"	69' 07"	37' 01"
(Charlotte C '07-'18)								

OCEANEX INC., MONTREAL, CANADA *(oceanex.com)*

Fleet Name / Vessel Name	Vessel IMO #	Vessel Type	Year Built	Engine Type	Cargo Cap. or Gross*	Overall Length	Vessel Breadth	Vessel Depth
Oceanex Avalon	9315044	CO	2005	D	14,639	481' 11"	85' 00"	45' 11"
Oceanex Connaigra	9649718	CO	2013	D	26,786	689' 00"	97' 01"	56' 01"

BBC Song on the Saginaw River. (Todd Shorkey)

Fleet Name Vessel Name	Vessel IMO #	Vessel Type	Year Built	Engine Type	Cargo Cap. or Gross*	Overall Length	Vessel Breadth	Vessel Depth
Oceanex Sanderling	7603502	RR	1977	D	21,849	364' 01"	88' 05"	57' 07
(Rauenfels '77-'80, Essen '80-'81, Kongsfjord '81-'83, Onno '83-'87, ASL Sanderling '87-'08)								

ONEGO SHIPPING & CHARTERING B.V., RHOON, NETHERLANDS *(www.onego.nl)*

Onego Deusto	9399129	GC	2008	D	6,312	433' 07"	52' 01"	38' 01"
(Beluga Skysails '08-'11, BBC Skysails '11-'19)								
Onego Duero	9580780	GC	2012	D	6,351	433' 09"	52' 01"	31' 08"
(Bastarda '12-'12, Pietro Benedetti '12-'19, Antonia '19-'21)								
Onego Maas	9535618	GC	2011	D	8,059	477' 10"	59' 10"	33' 10"
*(Thorco Copenhagen '11-'16, **BBC Brazil** '16-'17, DS Brazil '17-'19, **BBC Brazil** '19-'21)*								
Onego Rio	9258985	GC	2003	D	7,576	468' 02"	59' 09"	33' 04"
*(Frida '03-'04, **BBC England** '04-'13, BBC Ecuador '13-'14, **Thorco China** '14-'16, BBC England '16-'17, England '17-'17)*								

OSLO BULK SHIPPING, SINGAPORE *(oslobulk.com)*

Ale	9521825	BC	2012	D	17,096	492' 00"	77' 05"	41' 00"
(Raba '12-'21)								
Patagonman	9521851	BC	2012	D	17,096	492' 00"	77' 05"	41' 00"
(San '12-'22)								
Pichon	9521837	BC	2012	D	17,096	492' 00"	77' 05"	41' 00"
(Olza '12-'21)								

P

PARAKOU SHIPPING LTD., HONG KONG, CHINA *(parakougroup.com)*
FOLLOWING VESSELS UNDER CHARTER TO CANFORNAV

Cape	9498224	BC	2010	D	19,906	610' 03"	77' 09"	47' 11"
(Heloise '10-'15)								
Sunda	9498236	BC	2010	D	19,906	610' 03"	77' 09"	47' 11"
(Emilie '10-'15)								

PEARL SEAS CRUISES LLC, GUILFORD, CONNECTICUT, USA *(pearlseascruises.com)*

Pearl Mist	9412701	PA	2009	D	5,109*	325' 00"	52' 00"	15' 07"
Built: Irving Shipyards, Halifax, Nova Scotia, Canada; passenger capacity 210								

PLANTOURS CRUISES, BREMEN, GERMANY *(plantours-partner.de)*

Hamburg	9138329	PA	1997	D	15,067	472' 10"	70' 06"	33' 08"
*Built: MTW Schiffswerft GmbH, Wismar, Germany; passenger capacity 420 (**c. Columbus** '97-'12)*								

POLSTEAM (POLISH STEAMSHIP CO.), SZCZECIN, POLAND *(polsteam.com)*

Drawsko	9393450	BC	2010	D	20,603	623' 04"	77' 11"	47' 11"
Gardno	9767704	BC	2017	D	22,982	656' 02"	77' 09"	50' 02"
(Gardno '18-'18, Mont D'Iberville '18-'18)								
Irma	9180396	BC	2000	D	21,387	655' 10"	77' 05"	50' 02"
Iryda	9180384	BC	1999	D	21,387	655' 10"	77' 05"	50' 02"
Isa	9180358	BC	1999	D	21,387	655' 10"	77' 05"	50' 02"
Isadora	9180372	BC	1999	D	21,387	655' 10"	77' 05"	50' 02"
Isolda	9180360	BC	1999	D	21,387	655' 10"	77' 05"	50' 02"
Jamno	9767728	BC	2018	D	22,982	656' 02"	77' 09"	50' 02"
Juno	9422378	BC	2011	D	20,603	623' 04"	77' 11"	47' 11"
Lubie	9441984	BC	2011	D	20,603	623' 04"	77' 11"	47' 11"
Mamry	9496264	BC	2012	D	20,603	623' 04"	77' 11"	47' 11"
Miedwie	9393448	BC	2010	D	20,603	623' 04"	77' 11"	47' 11"
Narie	9767728	BC	2018	D	22,982	656' 02"	77' 09"	50' 02"
Resko	9393462	BC	2010	D	20,603	623' 04"	77' 11"	47' 11"
Solina	9496252	BC	2012	D	20,603	623' 04"	77' 11"	47' 11"
Wicko	9393474	BC	2010	D	20,603	623' 04"	77' 11"	47' 11"

POT SCHEEPVAART BV, DELFZIJL, NETHERLANDS *(pot-scheepvaart.nl)*
FOLLOWING VESSELS UNDER CHARTER TO ROYAL WAGENBORG BV

Kwintebank	9234288	GC	2002	D	6,378	433' 09"	52' 01"	36' 07"
Vikingbank	9604184	GC	2012	D	7,367	468' 00"	52' 01"	37' 09"

R

REDERI AB ALVTANK, DONSO, SWEDEN *(alvtank.se)*

Ramelia	9818280	TK	2019	D	12,770	490' 06"	74' 10"	39' 08"

REDERI AB DONSOTANK, DONSO, SWEDEN (donsotank.se)

Fleet Name Vessel Name	Vessel IMO #	Vessel Type	Year Built	Engine Type	Cargo Cap. or Gross*	Overall Length	Vessel Breadth	Vessel Depth
Solando	9428073	TK	2009	D	13,472	491' 11"	75' 06"	42' 10"
(Messinia '09-'09, **Soley-1** *'09-'13)*								

REDERIET STENERSEN AS, BERGEN, NORWAY (stenersen.com)

Sten Arnold	9371610	TK	2007	D	11,935	472' 07"	75' 06"	40' 08"
Sten Baltic	9307671	TK	2005	D	11,935	472' 07"	75' 06"	40' 08"
Stenberg	9283978	TK	2006	D	11,935	472' 07"	75' 06"	40' 08"
Sten Bergen	9407988	TK	2009	D	11,935	472' 07"	75' 06"	40' 08"
Sten Frigg	9407976	TK	2009	D	11,935	472' 07"	75' 06"	40' 08"
Sten Hidra	9358931	TK	2002	D	11,935	472' 07"	75' 06"	40' 08"
Sten Idun	9261102	TK	2002	D	11,935	472' 07"	75' 06"	40' 08"
Sten Moster	9341184	TK	2006	D	11,935	472' 07"	75' 06"	40' 08"

REEDEREI H. SCHULDT GMBH & CO., HAMBURG, GERMANY

Ocean Castle	9315537	BC	2005	D	18,825	607' 03"	77' 01"	46' 03"
*(**Federal Mattawa** '05-'15)*								

REEDEREI RUDOLF SCHEPERS, HAREN EMS, GERMANY (reederei-schepers.de)

Marguerita	9240548	GC	2002	D	7,752	477' 09"	59' 10"	33' 10"
(Hanna-C '02-'02, Corral '02-'04, Hanna C '04-'06, Opal Ace '06-'09, Hanna C '09-'12)								

RF OCEAN, LONDON, ENGLAND (rfocean.com)

RF Marina	9580986	TK	2011	D	13,239	530' 05"	75' 06"	40' 08"
(Osttank Italy '11-'11, Osttank Finland '11-'11, Adfines Sky '11-'21)								
RF Stella	9580998	TK	2011	D	13,239	530' 05"	75' 06"	40' 08"
(Osttank Denmark '11-'11, Osttank Sweden '11-'11, **Adfines Sun** *'11-'20)*								

Whistler at Picton, ON, with the tug Amy Lynn D. (Picton Terminals)

Fleet Name Vessel Name	Vessel IMO #	Vessel Type	Year Built	Engine Type	Cargo Cap. or Gross*	Overall Length	Vessel Breadth	Vessel Depth
ROYAL WAGENBORG BV, DELFZIJL, NETHERLANDS *(wagenborg.com)*								
Adriaticborg	9546497	GC	2011	D	11,894	469' 02"	70' 06"	43' 08"
Alamosborg	9466348	GC	2011	D	11,894	469' 02"	70' 06"	43' 08"
Alaskaborg	9466374	GC	2012	D	11,894	469' 02"	70' 06"	43' 08"
Albanyborg	9466300	GC	2010	D	11,894	469' 02"	70' 06"	43' 08"
Amazoneborg	9333541	GC	2007	D	11,894	469' 02"	70' 06"	43' 08"
Americaborg	9365659	GC	2007	D	11,894	469' 02"	70' 06"	43' 08"
Amstelborg	9333527	GC	2006	D	11,894	469' 02"	70' 06"	43' 08"
Amurborg	9466336	GC	2011	D	11,894	469' 02"	70' 06"	43' 08"
Aragonborg	9466312	GC	2010	D	11,894	469' 02"	70' 06"	43' 08"
Arneborg	9333539	GC	2006	D	11,894	469' 02"	70' 06"	43' 08"
Arubaborg	9466295	GC	2010	D	11,894	469' 02"	70' 06"	43' 08"
Atlanticborg	9466350	GC	2012	D	11,894	469' 02"	70' 06"	43' 08"
Avonborg	9466362	GC	2012	D	11,894	469' 02"	70' 06"	43' 08"
Azoresborg	9466051	GC	2010	D	11,894	469' 02"	70' 06"	43' 08"
Beatrix	9419280	GC	2009	D	8,911	507' 03"	56' 05"	37' 09"
(Fivelborg '09-'09)								
Ebroborg	9463451	GC	2010	D	7,196	452' 03"	52' 01"	36' 01"
Edenborg	9463449	GC	2010	D	7,196	452' 03"	52' 01"	36' 01"
Eeborg	9568328	GC	2012	D	7,680	474' 03"	52' 01"	36' 07"
Eemsborg	9423748	GC	2009	D	7,196	452' 03"	52' 01"	36' 01"
Egbert Wagenborg {2}	9802695	GC	2017	D	8,849	491' 11"	52' 02"	40' 00"
Elbeborg	9568249	GC	2011	D	7,680	474' 03"	52' 01"	36' 07"
Erieborg	9463437	GC	2009	D	7,196	452' 03"	52' 01"	36' 01"
Exeborg	9650482	GC	2011	D	7,680	474' 03"	52' 01"	36' 07"
Finnborg	9419321	GC	2011	D	8,911	507' 03"	56' 05"	37' 09"
Fivelborg	9419307	GC	2010	D	8,911	507' 03"	56' 05"	37' 09"
Flevoborg	9419292	GC	2010	D	8,911	507' 03"	56' 05"	37' 09"
Fraserborg	9419319	GC	2011	D	8,911	507' 03"	56' 05"	37' 09"
Fuldaborg	9559092	GC	2012	D	8,911	507' 03"	56' 05"	37' 09"
Ijsselborg	9456745	GC	2010	D	8,999	469' 00"	62' 00"	35' 11"
*(Ijsselborg '10-'11, Onego Houston '11-'11, Ijsselborg '11-'12, Clipper Alba '12-'15, **Nordana Sarah** '15-'16)*								
Izerborg	9456733	GC	2010	D	8,999	469' 00"	62' 00"	35' 11"
*(Anet '10-'10, Onego Bilbao '10-'11, Anet '11-'14, **Nordana Mathilde** '14-'15, **Anet** '15-'20)*								
Maxima	9882061	GC	2021	D	8,849	491' 11"	52' 02"	40' 00"
Reestborg	9592563	GC	2013	D	14,224	556' 11"	66' 11"	37' 11"
Reggeborg	9592575	GC	2014	D	14,224	556' 11"	66' 11"	37' 11"
Roerborg	9592599	GC	2014	D	14,224	556' 11"	66' 11"	37' 11"
Taagborg	9546461	GC	2013	D	14,695	565' 03"	70' 06"	43' 08"
Thamesborg	9546459	GC	2013	D	14,695	565' 03"	70' 06"	43' 08"

Federal Ems loading at Thunder Bay, ON. (Michael Hull)

Fleet Name Vessel Name	Vessel IMO #	Vessel Type	Year Built	Engine Type	Cargo Cap. or Gross*	Overall Length	Vessel Breadth	Vessel Depth
Vancouverborg	9213741	GC	2001	D	6,361	433' 10"	52' 01"	31' 08"
Victoriaborg	9234276	GC	2001	D	6,361	433' 10"	52' 01"	31' 08"
Virginiaborg	9234290	GC	2001	D	6,361	433' 10"	52' 01"	31' 08"
Vlieborg	9554781	GC	2012	D	7,367	468' 00"	52' 01"	35' 04"
Volgaborg	9631072	GC	2013	D	7,367	468' 00"	51' 09"	35' 04"

At press time, Wagenborg Shipping also had the following vessels under charter. Please consult their respective fleets for details: **Kwintebank, Morgenstond II** and **Vikingbank.**

S

SAL HEAVY LIFT GMBH, HAMBURG, GERMANY (A MEMBER OF HARREN & PARTNER GROUP) (sal-heavylift.com)

Amoenitas	9505510	HL	2010	D	11,473	439' 08"	75' 06"	37' 05"
(Palanpur '10-'12, Hyundai Phoenix '12-'13, Palanpur '13-'14)								
Calypso	9512381	HL	2011	D	11,473	439' 08"	75' 06"	37' 05"
Caroline	9501863	HL	2009	D	11,473	439' 08"	75' 06"	37' 05"
(Palmerton '09-'19)								
Hilke	9501875	HL	2010	D	11,473	439' 08"	75' 06"	37' 05"
(Palabora '10-'19)								
Imke	9501899	HL	2010	D	11,473	439' 08"	75' 06"	37' 05"
(Palau '10-'18)								

SARGEANT MARINE INC., BOCA RATON, FLORIDA, USA (sargeantmarine.com)

Amber Bay	9764520	TK	2016	D	10,377	479' 04"	72' 02"	35' 05"
(Feng Haung Ho '16-'16)								

SCOT TANKER GEMI ISLETMECILIGI A. S., ISTANBUL, TURKEY (scottanker.com)

Scot Bremen	9260835	TK	2004	D	5,145	383' 06"	59' 01"
(Wappen Von Bremen '04-'15)							
Scot Leipzig	9260847	TK	2004	D	5,145	383' 06"	59' 01"
(Demo Sperry Marine '04-'10, Wappen Von Leipzig '10-'15)							

SE SHIPPING, SINGAPORE (seshipping.com)

Potentia	9431472	HL	2009	D	9,627	454' 05"	68' 11"	36' 01"
(Brattingsborg '09-'09, **SE Potentia** '09-'20)								

SFL CORPORATION LTD., HAMILTON, BURMUDA (sflcorp.com)å

SFL Weser	9471599	TK	2008	D	11,709	498' 00"	76' 06"
(Dong Xin 2 '08-'08, Maria Victoria V '08-'21)							

SLOMAN NEPTUN SHIFFAHRTS, BREMEN, GERMANY (sloman-neptun.com)

Sloman Discoverer	9620669	GC	2012	D	9,611	452' 11"	68' 11"	36' 01"
Sloman Dispatcher	9620657	GC	2012	D	9,611	452' 11"	68' 11"	36' 01"

Hudsongracht arriving off Lake Superior at Duluth, MN. (David Schauer)

Fleet Name / Vessel Name	Vessel IMO #	Vessel Type	Year Built	Engine Type	Cargo Cap. or Gross*	Overall Length	Vessel Breadth	Vessel Depth
Sloman Helios	9466740	TK	2011	D	11,246	476' 02"	75' 06"	41' 01"
(Intrepid Canada '10-'17)								
Sloman Hera	9466714	TK	2012	D	11,246	476' 02"	75' 06"	41' 01"
Sloman Herakles	9466726	TK	2012	D	11,246	476' 02"	75' 06"	41' 01"
Sloman Hermes	9466738	TK	2012	D	11,246	476' 02"	75' 06"	41' 01"
Sloman Hestia	9776133	TK	2017	D	11,316	476' 02"	76' 05"	

SOUTH END TANKER MANAGEMENT, BARENDRECHT, NETHERLANDS *(se-tm.com)*

Selasse	9405320	TK	2008	D	7,776	426' 11"	64' 04"	35' 09"

SPLIETHOFF, AMSTERDAM, NETHERLANDS *(spliethoff.com)*

Fagelgracht	9428425	HL	2011	D	8,620	447' 10"	62' 00"	38' 03"
Floragracht	9509968	HL	2011	D	8,620	447' 10"	62' 00"	38' 03"
Floretgracht	9507611	HL	2012	D	8,620	447' 10"	62' 00"	38' 03"
Florijngracht	9428413	HL	2010	D	8,620	447' 10"	62' 00"	38' 03"
Fortunagracht	9507609	HL	2012	D	8,620	447' 10"	62' 00"	38' 03"
Heemskerkgracht	9443669	HL	2009	D	9,618	453' 00"	68' 11"	36' 01"
*(Beluga Faculty '09-'11, **HHL Nile** '11-'16)*								
Heerengracht	9435753	HL	2009	D	9,611	452' 11"	68' 11"	36' 01"
*(Beluga Fidelity '09-'11, **HHL Amur** '11-'19)*								
Houtmangracht	9435765	HL	2009	D	9,611	452' 11"	68' 11"	36' 01"
*(Beluga Fantasy '09-'11, OXL Fantasy '11-'11, **HHL Mississippi** '11-'19)*								
Hudsongracht	9433262	HL	2008	D	9,627	454' 05"	68' 11"	36' 01"
(BBC Alaska '08-'13, Elbe '13-'14, HHL Elbe '14-'19)								
Humbergracht	9433274	HL	2009	D	6,927	454' 05"	68' 11"	36' 01"
*(BBC Montana '09-'13, Tyne '13-'14, **HHL Tyne** '14-'19)*								
Maasgracht	9571492	HL	2009	D	9,524	464' 11"	62' 00"	38' 03"
Marsgracht	9571507	HL	2007	D	9,524	464' 11"	62' 00"	38' 03"
Merwedegracht	9571519	HL	2011	D	9,524	464' 11"	62' 00"	38' 03"
Minervagracht	9571521	HL	2011	D	9,524	464' 11"	62' 00"	38' 03"
Muntgracht	9571545	HL	2012	D	9,524	464' 11"	62' 00"	38' 03"

SUNSHIP SCHIFFAHRTSKONTOR KG, EMDEN, GERMANY *(sunship.de)*

Lake Erie {2}	9283540	BC	2004	D	18,825	607' 03"	77' 01"	46' 03"
*(Federal Matane '04-'11, **CL Hanse Gate** '11-'15, **Hanse Gate** '15-'19)*								
Lake Ontario	9283538	BC	2004	D	18,825	607' 03"	77' 01"	46' 03"
(Federal Manitou '04-'11)								
Lake St. Clair	9315549	BC	2004	D	18,825	607' 03"	77' 01"	46' 03"
(Federal Miramichi '04-'16)								
Spiekeroog	9506148	BC	2013	D	4,591	355' 00"	54' 06"	28' 10"

SYMPHONY SHIPPING BV, BREDA, NETHERLANDS *(symphonyshipping.nl)*

Symphony Star	9721645	HL	2015	D	6,749	401' 11"	55' 09"	35' 01"

Iryda loading grain at Gavilon Elevator in Superior, WI.
(Chris Mazzella)

T-V

TARBIT TANKERS B.V., DORDRECHT, NETHERLANDS (tarbittankers.nl)

Stella Polaris	9187057	TK	1999	D	5,396	387' 02"	55' 09"	34' 05"

TB MARINE SHIPMANAGEMENT GMBH & CO., HAMBURG GERMANY (tbmarine.de)

Harbour Fashion	9473080	TK	2011	D	11,880	473' 02"	75' 06"	40' 08"
Harbour Feature	9473092	TK	2011	D	11,880	473' 02"	75' 06"	40' 08"
(Nordtank Lerner '11-'11)								
Harbour First	9473119	TK	2011	D	11,880	473' 02"	75' 06"	40' 08"
Harbour Fountain	9473107	TK	2011	D	11,880	473' 02"	75' 06"	40' 08"
Harbour Pioneer	9572757	TK	2010	D	13,239	530' 05"	75' 06"	40' 09"
Harbour Progress	9572745	TK	2010	D	13,239	530' 05"	75' 06"	40' 09"

TRANSAL DENIZCILIK TICARET A.S., ISTANBUL, TURKEY (transal.com.tr)

Ruby-T	9457878	TK	2010	D	12,890	514' 01"	75' 02"	42' 00"

TERSAN SHIPPING LTD., ISTANBUL, TURKEY (tersanshipping.com.tr)

Alangova	9411927	TK	2008	D	7,246	406' 10"	65' 07"	32' 02"

TRANS KA AKBASOGLU HOLDING, ISTANBUL, TURKEY (akbasoglu.com)

Ali Ka	9451226	TK	2020	D	7,400	424' 10"	65' 07"	

TUFTAN OCEANIC LTD., DOUGLAS, ISLE OF MAN

Monax	9311256	TK	2005	D	11.623	477' 05"	77' 09"	43' 10"
(Fairchem Steed '05-'20)								

UNI-TANKERS A/S, MIDDELFART, DENMARK (unitankers.com)

Erria Swan	9347748	TK	2006	D	7,232	425' 08"	64' 04"	34' 01"
(Alaattin Bey '06-'07, Erria Helen '07-'12)								
Falstria Swan	9367217	TK	2006	D	3,933	337' 11"	52' 06"	28' 07"
(Ingrid Jakobsen '06-'12)								
Lillo Swan	9390329	TK	2007	D	3,300	327' 09"	49' 03"	24' 03"
(Erria Julie '07-'12)								
Tasing Swan	9403891	TK	2007	D	7,232	425' 08"	64' 04"	34' 01"
(Hamza Efe Bey '07-'08, Erria Mie '08-'12)								

UTKILEN AS, BERGEN, NORWAY (utkilen.no)

Straum	9406726	TK	2010	D	12,776	539' 02"	75' 06"	42' 00"
Susana S	9406714	TK	2009	D	12,776	539' 02"	75' 06"	42' 00"

VALLOEBY SHIPPING, MSIDA, MALTA (valloebyshipping.com)

Amur Star	9480368	TK	2010	D	8,539	421' 11"	66' 11"	37' 05"
Colorado Star	9527609	TK	2010	D	8,539	421' 11"	66' 11"	37' 09"
Ganges Star	9496692	TK	2010	D	8,539	421' 11"	66' 11"	37' 09"

Ale exits the MacArthur Lock headed for Europe. (Brendan Falkowski)

Fleet Name Vessel Name	Vessel IMO #	Vessel Type	Year Built	Engine Type	Cargo Cap. or Gross*	Overall Length	Vessel Breadth	Vessel Depth
Pechora Star	9488322	TK	2011	D	8,539	421' 11"	66' 11"	37' 09"

VANTAGE DELUXE WORLD TRAVEL, BOSTON, MASSACHUSETTS, USA *(vantagetravel.com)*
| **Ocean Explorer** | 9883194 | PA | 2021 | D | 8,228* | 432' 06" | 60' 04 | N/A |

Built: China Merchants H.I., Jiangsu, China; passenger capacity 162

VIKING CRUISES, BASEL, SWITZERLAND *(vikingcruises.com)*
| **Viking Octantis** | 9863194 | PA | 2021 | D | 30,150* | 672' 07" | 78' 09 | N/A |

Built: Fincantieri Vard Shipyard, Soviknes, Norway; passenger capacity 378
| **Viking Polaris** | 9863209 | PA | 2022 | D | 30,150* | 672' 07" | 78' 09 | N/A |

Built: Fincantieri Vard Shipyard, Soviknes, Norway; passenger capacity 378

VROON B.V., BREDA, NETHERLANDS *(vroon.nl)*
VESSEL MANAGED BY IVER SHIPS B.V., BREDA, NETHERLANDS
| **Iver Ambition** | 9439163 | TK | 2009 | D | 6,296 | 356' 00" | 61' 00" | 34' 09" |

(San Lorenzo '09-'13)
| **Iver Bright** | 9616759 | TK | 2012 | D | 6,105 | 367' 05" | 59' 09" | 32' 10" |

W-Z

W. BOCKSTIEGEL REEDEREI KG, EMDEN, GERMANY *(reederei-bockstiegel.de)*
BBC Arizona	9501253	HL	2010	D	9,618	453' 00"	68' 11"	36' 01"
BBC Campana	9291963	HL	2003	D	9,618	453' 00"	68' 11"	36' 01"
BBC Georgia	9357224	HL	2008	D	9,627	454' 05"	68' 11"	36' 01"
BBC Maine	9357200	HL	2007	D	9,627	454' 05"	68' 11"	36' 01"
BBC Oregon	9501265	HL	2010	D	9,618	453' 00"	68' 11"	36' 01"
BBC Plata	9291975	HL	2005	D	9,618	453' 00"	68' 11"	36' 01"

(Asian Voyager '05-'05)
| **BBC Zarate** | 9337236 | HL | 2007 | D | 9,627 | 454' 05" | 68' 11" | 36' 01" |

WIJNNE BARENDS, DELFZIJL, NETHERLANDS *(wijnnebarends.com)*
| **Morgenstond II** | 9367073 | BC | 2007 | D | 8,999 | 469' 00" | 62' 00" | 35' 11" |

*(**Morgenstond II** '07-'07, Beluga Legislation '07-'07, Kent Legislation '07-'09, **Beluga Legislation** '09-'10, Kent Sunset '10-'13, **Morgenstond II** '13-'13, Clipper Aurora '13-'15)*

YAWATAHAMA KISEN Y.K., YAWATAHAMA, JAPAN
FOLLOWING VESSEL UNDER CHARTER TO FEDNAV
| **Federal Yukina** | 9476977 | BC | 2010 | D | 20,465 | 655' 06" | 77' 11" | 48' 09" |

YILMAR SHIPPING & TRADING LTD., ISTANBUL, TURKEY *(yilmar.com)*
| **YM Jupiter** | 9291597 | TK | 2007 | D | 10,917 | 485' 07" | 70' 10" | 37' 01" |

ZEA MARINE, BREMEN, GERMANY
| **ZEA Servant** | 9741126 | GC | 2018 | D | 11,436 | 474' 09" | 74' 10" | 37' 11" |

Bulgarian-flagged Rodopi at the Algoma Export Dock in Sault Ste. Marie, ON. (Matt Miner)

These salties are rock stars!

By ROGER LELIEVRE

Shipwatchers around the Great Lakes and St. Lawrence Seaway may have noticed a fleet of single-named, red-painted salties hauling windmill components and other cargoes. But few probably realized the vessels, owned by dship Carriers and based in Hamburg, Germany, are named after real-life rock stars.

Four members of the legendary Rolling Stones are honored. The motor vessel Charlie is named after Charlie Watts, who passed away in 2021 and was drummer for the Rolling Stones. In the same fleet can be found Mick (Jagger), Keith (Richards), and Ronnie (Wood).

Beyond the Stones' names, there are also nautical nods to Bruce (Springsteen), Melissa (Etheridge), Janis (Joplin), Alanis (Morissette), Stevie (Nicks or Wonder?), Gwen (Stefani perhaps) and Kylie (the "Locomotion"-ing Minogue, no doubt).

dship Carriers was founded in 2014 by Thomas C. Press and is family owned. Its website says the company is 'a global provider of ocean transportation services … designed to support the specialized needs of breakbulk, heavy lift, dry bulk and project cargo clients in the oil and gas, wind energy and floating cargo industries."

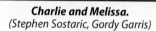

Charlie and Melissa.
(Stephen Sostaric, Gordy Garris)

KYS' crack investigative reporting team tried to track down Mr. Press to ask about the rock star-themed names but was, sadly, unsuccessful. Still, the musical theme seems to strike a chord with shipwatchers and music fans alike. ◼

Bruce is The Boss at Oswego, NY. (Ethan Severson)

Marine Museums

U.S. Navy destroyer-
turned-museum-ship
USS Edson at Bay City, MI.
(Ethan Severson)

Museum Name Vessel Name	Vessel Type	Year Built	Engine Type	Cargo Cap. or Gross*	Overall Length	Breadth	Depth
BUFFALO AND ERIE COUNTY NAVAL & MILITARY PARK, BUFFALO, NY (buffalonavalpark.org)							
Croaker	MU	1944	D	1,526*	311′07″	27′02″	33′09″
Built: Electric Boat Co., Groton, CT; former U. S. Navy Gato class submarine IXSS-246; open to the public at Buffalo, NY							
Little Rock	MU	1945	T	10,670*	610′01″	66′04″	25′00″
Built: Cramp Shipbuilding Co., Philadelphia, PA; former U. S. Navy Cleveland / Little Rock class guided missile cruiser open to the public at Buffalo, NY							
Sullivans (The)	MU	1943	T	2,500*	376′06″	39′08″	22′08″
Built: Bethlehem Shipbuilding Corp., San Francisco, CA; former U.S. Navy Fletcher class destroyer; open to the public at Buffalo, NY (laid down as USS Putnam)							
CITY OF KEWAUNEE, KEWAUNEE, WI							
Ludington	TB/MU	1943	D	249*	115′00″	26′00″	13′08″
Built: Jakobson Shipyard, Oyster Bay, NY; former U.S. Army Corps of Engineers tug is open to the public as a marine museum at Kewaunee, WI (Major Wilbur F. Browder [LT-4] '43-'47)							
DOOR COUNTY MARITIME MUSEUM & LIGHTHOUSE PRESERVATION SOCIETY INC., STURGEON BAY, WI							
John Purves	TB/MU	1919	D	436*	150′00″	27′06″	16′08″
Built: Bethlehem Steel Co., Elizabeth, NJ; former Roen/Andrie Inc. tug has been refurbished as a museum display at Sturgeon Bay, WI (Butterfield '19-'42, LT-145 '42-'57)							
DULUTH ENTERTAINMENT CONVENTION CENTER, DULUTH, MN (decc.org/william-a-irvin)							
William A. Irvin	BC/MU	1938	T	14,050	610′09″	60′00″	32′06″
Built: American Shipbuilding Co., Lorain, OH; former U.S. Steel Corp. bulk carrier last operated Dec. 16, 1978 open to the public at Duluth, MN							
ERIE MARITIME MUSEUM, ERIE, PA (flagshipniagara.org)							
Niagara	MU/2B	1988	W	295*	198′00″	32′00″	10′06″
Reconstruction of Oliver Hazard Perry's U. S. Navy brigantine from the War of 1812							
FRIENDS OF KEEWATIN, PORT McNICOLL, ON (sskeewatin.com)							
Keewatin {2}	PA/MU	1907	Q	3,856*	346′00″	43′08″	26′06″
Built: Fairfield Shipbuilding and Engineering Co. Ltd., Govan, Scotland; former Canadian Pacific Railway Co. passenger vessel last operated Nov. 29, 1965; temporarily closed to the public							
FRIENDS OF THE EDNA G, TWO HARBORS, MN (friendsofednag.org)							
Edna G	TB/MU	1896	R	154*	102′00″	23′00″	14′06″
Built: Cleveland Shipbuilding Co., Cleveland, OH; former Duluth, Missabe & Iron Range Railroad tug last operated in 1981; open to the public at Two Harbors, MN							
GREAT LAKES NAVAL MEMORIAL & MUSEUM, MUSKEGON, MI (silversidesmuseum.org)							
McLane	MU	1927	D	289*	125′00″	24′00″	12′06″
Built: American Brown Boveri Electric Co., Camden, NJ; former U.S. Coast Guard Buck & A Quarter class medium endurance cutter; on display at Muskegon, MI (USCGC McLane '27-'70, Manatra II '70-'93)							
Silversides	MU	1941	D/V	1,526*	311′08″	27′03″	33′09″
Built: Mare Island Naval Yard, Vallejo, CA; former U.S. Navy Albacore (Gato) class submarine AGSS-236; open to the public at Muskegon, MI							
GREAT LAKES SCIENCE CENTER, CLEVELAND, OH (greatscience.com)							
William G. Mather {2}	BC/MU	1925	T	13,950	618′00″	62′00″	32′00″
Built: Great Lakes Engineering Works, Ecorse, MI; former Cleveland-Cliffs Steamship Co. bulk carrier last operated Dec. 21, 1980; open to the public at Cleveland, OH							
H. LEE WHITE MARINE MUSEUM, OSWEGO, NY (hleewhitemarinemuseum.com)							
LT-5	MU	1943	D	305*	115′00″	28′00″	14′00″
Built: Jakobson Shipyard, Oyster Bay, NY; former U.S. Army Corps of Engineers tug last operated in 1989; open to the public at Oswego, NY (Major Elisha K. Henson '43-'47, U.S. Army LT-5 '47-'95, Nash '47-'95)							
HMCS HAIDA NATIONAL HISTORICAL SITE, HAMILTON, ON (hmcshaida.com)							
Haida	MU	1943	T	2,744*	377′00″	37′06″	15′02″
Former Royal Canadian Navy Tribal class destroyer G-63 / DDE-215; open to the public at Hamilton, ON							
ICEBREAKER MACKINAW MARITIME MUSEUM INC., MACKINAW CITY, MI (themackinaw.org)							
Mackinaw [WAGB-83]	IB/MU	1944	D	5,252*	290′00″	74′00″	29′00″
Built: Toledo Shipbuilding Co., Toledo, OH; former U.S. Coast Guard icebreaker was decommissioned in 2006; open to the public at Mackinaw City, MI (Launched as USCGC Manitowoc [WAG-83])							

Continued on Page 124

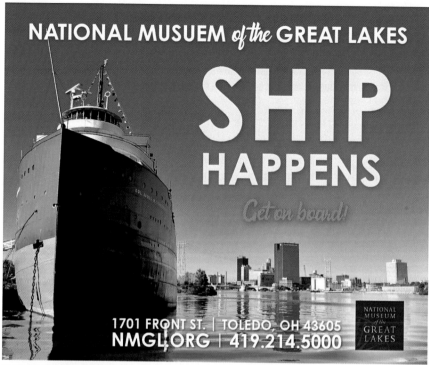
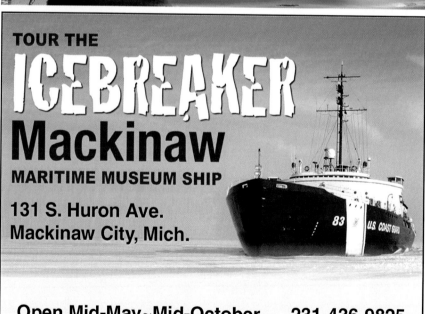

LAKEHEAD TRANSPORTATION MUSEUM SOCIETY, THUNDER BAY, ON

Alexander Henry — IB/MU — 1959 — D — 1,674* — 210'00" — 44'00" — 17'09"
Built: Port Arthur Shipbuilding Co., Port Arthur, ON; former Canadian Coast Guard icebreaker was retired in 1985; formerly at Kingston, ON, open to the public at Thunder Bay, ON

LE SAULT DE SAINTE MARIE HISTORIC SITES INC., SAULT STE. MARIE, MI *(saulthistoricsites.com)*

Valley Camp {2} — BC/MU — 1917 — — 12,000 — 550'00" — 58'00" — 13'00"
Built: American Shipbuilding Co., Lorain, OH; former Hanna Mining Co./Wilson Marine Transit Co./Republic Steel Corp. bulk carrier last operated in 1966; open to the public at Sault Ste. Marie, MI (Louis W. Hill '17-'55)

MUSÉE MARITIME DU QUÉBEC, L' ISLET, QC *(mmq.qc.ca)*

Ernest Lapointe — MU — 1941 — R — 1,179* — 185'00" — 36'00" — 22'06"
Built: Davie Shipbuilding Co., Lauzon, QC; former Canadian Coast Guard icebreaker; open to the public at L'Islet, QC

NATIONAL MUSEUM OF THE GREAT LAKES, TOLEDO, OH *(nmgl.org)*

Col. James M. Schoonmaker — BC/MU — 1911 — T — 15,000 — 617'00" — 64'00" — 33'01"
Built: Great Lakes Engineering Works, Ecorse, MI; former Shenango Furnace Co./Republic Steel Co./Cleveland-Cliffs Steamship Co. bulk carrier last operated in 1980; open to the public at Toledo, OH (Col. James M. Schoonmaker 1911-'69, Willis B. Boyer '69-'11)

Ohio — TB/MU — 1903 — D — 194* — 101'02" — 26'00" — 13'07"
Built: Great Lakes Towing Co., Chicago, IL; veteran tug is open to the public at Toledo, OH (M.F.D. No. 15 '03-'52, Laurence C. Turner '52-'73)

PORT HURON MUSEUM, PORT HURON, MI *(phmuseum.org)*

Huron — MU — 1920 — D — 392* — 96'05" — 24'00" — 10'00"
Built: Charles L. Seabury Co., Morris Heights, NY; former U.S. Coast Guard lightship WLV-526 was retired Aug. 20, 1970; open to the public at Port Huron, MI (Lightship 103 – Relief [WAL-526] '20-'36)

SAGINAW VALLEY NAVAL SHIP MUSEUM, BAY CITY, MI *(ussedson.org)*

Edson [DD-946] — MU — 1958 — T — 4,050* — 418'03" — 45'03" — 22'00"
Built: Bath Iron Works, Bath, ME; Forrest Sherman class destroyer was decommissioned in '88; from '89-'04 on display at the Intrepid Sea, Air & Space Museum, New York, NY; declared a U.S. National Historic Landmark in '90; returned to U.S. Navy in '04; open to the public at Bay City, MI

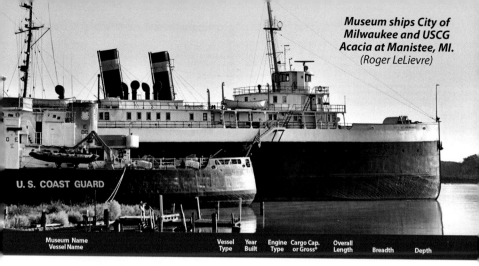

Museum ships City of Milwaukee and USCG Acacia at Manistee, MI. *(Roger LeLievre)*

U. S. COAST GUARD

Museum Name Vessel Name	Vessel Type	Year Built	Engine Type	Cargo Cap. or Gross*	Overall Length	Breadth	Depth

S.S. CITY OF MILWAUKEE – NATIONAL HISTORIC LANDMARK, MANISTEE, MI *(carferry.com)*

Acacia	BT/MU	1944	DE	1,025*	180'00"	37'00"	17'04"

Built: Marine Iron and Shipbuilding Corp., Duluth, MN; former U.S. Coast Guard bouy tender/icebreaker was decommissioned in '06 (Launched as USCGC Thistle [WAGL-406])

City of Milwaukee	MU	1931		26 cars	360'00"	56'03"	21'06"

Built: Manitowoc Shipbuilding Co., Manitowoc, WI; train ferry sailed for the Grand Trunk Railroad '31-'78 and the Ann Arbor Railroad '78-'81; open to the public at Manistee, MI

S.S. COLUMBIA PROJECT, NEW YORK, NY *(sscolumbia.org)*

Columbia {2}	PA/MU	1902		968*	216'00"	60'00"	13'06"

Built: Detroit Dry Dock Co., Wyandotte, MI; former Detroit to Bob-Lo Island passenger steamer last operated Sept. 2, 1991; moved to Buffalo, NY, Sept. 2, 2015, for further restoration and possible return to service

S.S. METEOR WHALEBACK SHIP MUSEUM, SUPERIOR, WI *(superiorpublicmuseums.org/s-s-meteor-2)*

Meteor {2}	TK/MU	1896		40,100	380'00"	45'00"	26'00"

Built: American Steel Barge Co., Superior, WI; former ore carrier/auto carrier/tanker is the last vessel of whaleback design surviving on the Great Lakes; Cleveland Tankers vessel last operated in 1969; open to the public at Superior, WI (Frank Rockefeller 1896-'28, South Park '1928-'43)

S.S. MILWAUKEE CLIPPER PRESERVATION INC., MUSKEGON, MI *(milwaukeeclipper.com)*

Milwaukee Clipper	PA/MU	1904	Q	4,272	361'00"	45'00"	28'00"

Built: American Shipbuilding Co., Cleveland, OH; rebuilt in '40 at Manitowoc Shipbuilding Co., Manitowoc, WI; former Wisconsin & Michigan Steamship Co. passenger/auto carrier last operated in 1970; undergoing restoration and open to the public at Muskegon, MI (Juniata '04-'41)

S.S. NORISLE STEAMSHIP SOCIETY, MANITOWANING, ON *(norisle.com)*

Norisle	MU	1946	R	1,668*	215'09"	36'03"	16'00"

Built: Collingwood Shipyards, Collingwood, ON; former Ontario Northland Transportation Commission passenger vessel last operated in 1974; museum is no longer open; vessel is laid up.

Continued on Page 127

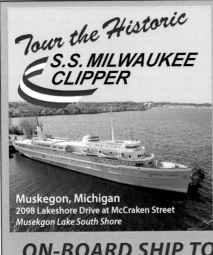

Great Lakes Museum Ship Stack Markings

Museum Ship
Alexander Henry
Thunder Bay, ON

Museum Ship
City of Milwaukee
Manistee, MI

Museum Ship
HMCS Haida
Hamilton, ON

Museum Ship Col.
James M. Schoonmaker
Toledo, OH

Museum Ship
Keewatin
Port McNicoll, ON

Museum Ship
Meteor
Superior, WI

Museum Ship
Milwaukee Clipper
Muskegon, MI

Museum Ship
USCG Mackinaw
Mackinaw City, MI

Museum Ship
USS Little Rock
Buffalo, N.Y.

Museum Ship
USS The Sullivans
Buffalo, N.Y.

Museum Ship
Valley Camp
Sault Ste. Marie, MI

Museum Ship
William A. Irvin
Duluth, MN

Museum Ship
William G. Mather
Cleveland, OH

Museum Tug
Edna G
Two Harbors, MN

Museum Tug
John Purves
Sturgeon Bay, WI

USS COD SUBMARINE MEMORIAL, CLEVELAND, OH *(usscod.org)*
Cod   MU   1943   D   1,525*   311'08"   27'02"   33'09"
Built: Electric Boat Co., Groton, CT; former U.S. Navy Albacore (Gato) class submarine IXSS-224 open to the public at Cleveland, OH

USS LST 393 PRESERVATION ASSOCIATION, MUSKEGON, MI *(lst393.org)*
LST-393   MU   1942   D   2,100   328'00"   50'00"   25'00"
Built: Newport News Shipbuilding and Dry Dock Co., Newport News, VA; former U.S. Navy/Wisconsin & Michigan Steamship Co. vessel last operated July 31, 1973; open to the public at Muskegon, MI (USS LST-393 '42-'47, Highway 16 '47-'99)

WISCONSIN MARITIME MUSEUM, MANITOWOC, WI *(wisconsinmaritime.org)*
Cobia   MU   1944   D   1,500*   311'09"   27'03"   33'09"
Built: Electric Boat Co., Groton, CT; former U.S. Navy Gato class submarine AGSS-245 is open to the public at Manitowoc, WI

Museums Ashore

Information can change without notice. Call ahead to verify location and hours.

ALGONAC CLAY MARITIME MUSEUM, 1240 ST. CLAIR RIVER DR., ALGONAC, MI – (810) 794-9015: Features many models of pleasure boats built by Chris-Craft, and includes pieces from local freighters and sailor paraphernalia. *(achistory.com)*

ANTIQUE BOAT MUSEUM, 750 MARY ST., CLAYTON, NY – (315) 686-4104: A large collection of freshwater boats and engines. Annual show is the first weekend of August. Seasonal. *(abm.org)*

ASHTABULA MARITIME & SURFACE TRANSPORTATION MUSEUM, 1071 WALNUT BLVD., ASHTABULA, OH – (440) 964-6847: Housed in the 1871/1898-built former lighthouse keeper's residence, the museum includes models, paintings, artifacts, photos, the world's only working scale model of a Hullett ore unloading machine, a Titanic display, a display of the 1876 Ashtabula Train Bridge Disaster and the pilothouse from the steamer *Thomas Walters*. Seasonal. *(ashtabulamaritime.org)*

BUFFALO HARBOR MUSEUM, 66 ERIE ST., BUFFALO, NY – (716) 849-0914: Exhibits explore local maritime history. Open all year, Thursday and Sunday only. *(llmhs.org)*

Continued on Page 129

CHICAGO MARITIME MUSEUM, 1200 W. 35th ST., RIVER LEVEL, CHICAGO, IL – (773-376-1982): This 10,000-square-foot museum offers visitors a chronological walk-through of local maritime history, including the eras of French fur traders, sail and steam-powered vessels, modern commercial Great Lakes freighters, recreational sailing and a large canoe collection. Open all year. *(chicagomaritimemuseum.org)*

DOOR COUNTY MARITIME MUSEUM & LIGHTHOUSE PRESERVATION SOCIETY INC., 120 N. MADISON AVE., STURGEON BAY, WI – (920) 743-5958: Many excellent models help portray the role shipbuilding has played in the Door Peninsula. Open all year. *(dcmm.org)*

DOSSIN GREAT LAKES MUSEUM, 100 THE STRAND, BELLE ISLE, DETROIT, MI – (313) 833-5538: Models, interpretive displays, the smoking room from the 1912 passenger steamer *City of Detroit III*, an anchor from the *Edmund Fitzgerald* and the pilothouse from the steamer *William Clay Ford* are on display. *(detroithistorical.org/main/dossin)*

ELGIN MILITARY MUSEUM, 30 TALBOT ST., ST. THOMAS, ON – (519) 633-7641: *HMCS Ojibwa*, a Cold War Oberon class submarine, is open to the public at Port Burwell, ON. *(theelginmilitarymuseum.ca)*

ERIE MARITIME MUSEUM, 150 E. FRONT ST., ERIE, PA – (814) 452-2744: Displays depict the Battle of Lake Erie and more. Open all year. *(flagshipniagara.org)*

FAIRPORT HARBOR LIGHTHOUSE & MARINE MUSEUM, 129 SECOND ST., FAIRPORT, OH – (440) 354-4825: Located in the Fairport Lighthouse, displays include the pilothouse from the *Frontenac* and the mainmast of the first *USS Michigan*. Seasonal. *(fairportharborlighthouse.org)*

GREAT LAKES LORE MARITIME MUSEUM, 367 N. THIRD ST., ROGERS CITY, MI – (989) 734-0706: The generations of men and women who sailed and made their livings on the Great Lakes are remembered here, as are their uniforms, personal possessions, and navigational and other maritime tools. *(gllmm.com)*

GREAT LAKES SHIPWRECK MUSEUM, WHITEFISH POINT, MI – (906) 635-1742 or (800)-635-1742: Exhibits include lighthouse and shipwreck artifacts, a shipwreck video theater, the restored lighthouse keeper's quarters and an *Edmund Fitzgerald* display that features the ship's bell. Seasonal. *(shipwreckmuseum.com)*

Continued on Page 130

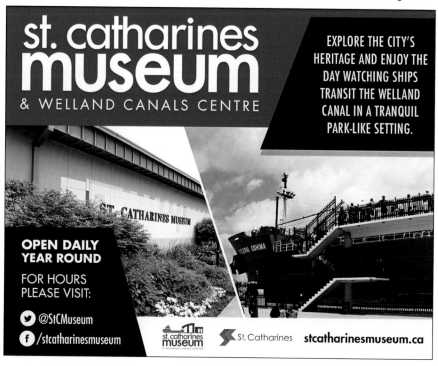

LAKE SUPERIOR MARITIME VISITOR CENTER, 600 CANAL PARK DRIVE, DULUTH, MN – (218) 720-5260: Models, artifacts and programs that explain the roles of Duluth and Superior in Great Lakes shipping, as well as the job of the U.S. Army Corps of Engineers. Open all year. *(lsmma.com)*

LE SAULT DE SAINTE MARIE HISTORICAL SITES INC., 501 E. WATER ST., SAULT STE. MARIE, MI – (906) 632-3658: The 1917-built steamer *Valley Camp* is the centerpiece of this museum. The ship's three cargo holds house artifacts, models, aquariums, photos and other memorabilia, as well as a tribute to the *Edmund Fitzgerald* that includes the ill-fated vessel's lifeboats. Seasonal. *(saulthistoricsites.com)*

LUDINGTON MARITIME MUSEUM, 217 S. LAKESHORE DRIVE, LUDINGTON, MI – (231) 843-4808: Diverse, interactive exhibits tell the stories of schooners, railroad carferries, the U.S. Coast Guard and the many other maritime activities of the region. *(ludingtonmaritimemuseum.org)*

MARINE CITY PRIDE & HERITAGE MUSEUM, 405 S. MAIN ST., MARINE CITY, MI – (810) 765-5446: Displays explore the ship and shipbuilding history of the area. Seasonal. *(marinecitymuseum.com)*

MARITIME MUSEUM OF SANDUSKY, 125 MEIGS ST., SANDUSKY, OHIO – (419) 624-0274: Exhibits explore the area's maritime history. Open all year. *(sanduskymaritime.org)*

MARQUETTE MARITIME MUSEUM, 300 N. LAKESHORE BLVD., MARQUETTE, MI – (906) 226-2006: Photos, models and maritime artifacts. Seasonal. *(mqtmaritimemuseum.com)*

MICHIGAN MARITIME MUSEUM, 260 DYCKMAN AVE., SOUTH HAVEN, MI – (269) 637-8078: Exhibits are dedicated to the U.S. Lifesaving Service/Coast Guard. The tall ship *Friends Good Will* operates during the summer. Open all year. *(michiganmaritimemuseum.org)*

MUSKOKA BOAT AND HERITAGE CENTRE, 275 STEAMSHIP BAY ROAD, GRAVENHURST, ON – (705) 687-2115: Visiting this museum, which includes many models of the early steamships to serve the area, is a great complement to a trip on the *RMS Segwun*, moored adjacent. *(realmuskoka.com/discovery-centre)*

PORT BURWELL MARINE MUSEUM & HISTORIC 1840 LIGHTHOUSE, 20 PITT ST., PORT BURWELL, ON – (519) 874-4807: Historic artifacts, a collection of lighthouse lenses, including the rotating Fresnel lenses, and period photographs are on display. Seasonal. *(bayham.on.ca/pages/museums)*

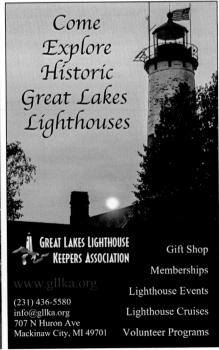

PORT COLBORNE HISTORICAL & MARINE MUSEUM, 280 KING ST., PORT COLBORNE, ON – (905) 834-7604: Wheelhouse from the tug *Yvonne Dupre Jr.* is among the museum's displays. Seasonal. *(portcolborne.ca)*

RUDY NAUTICAL MUSEUM, 23650 VAN DYKE DRIVE, CENTER LINE, MI – (586) 206-2791: Exhibits include an extensive collection of artifacts, models, works of art and research summaries. *(rudynauticalmuseum.com)*

SOMBRA MUSEUM, 3470 ST. CLAIR PARKWAY, SOMBRA, ON – (519) 892-3982: Marine room includes nautical equipment, Great Lakes and St. Clair River photos, and the Alan Mann Collection. *(sombramuseum.webs.com)*

SOO LOCKS VISITOR CENTER, SAULT STE. MARIE, MI – (906) 253-9290: Exhibits include a working model of the Soo Locks, displays and historic photos. Free; open Mother's Day weekend through mid-October. Check at the information desk for a list of vessels expected at the locks, or call 906-253-9290.

STRAITS OF MACKINAC SHIPWRECK MUSEUM, OLD MACKINAC POINT LIGHT, MACKINAC CITY, MI – (231) 436-4100: Houses artifacts recovered from the sunken *Cedarville* as well as others that tell the story of the many shipwrecks that dot the Straits of Mackinac. Seasonal. *(mackinacparks.com)*

WELLAND CANALS CENTRE & ST. CATHARINES MUSEUM, THOROLD, ON – (905) 984-8880: Museum at Lock 3 traces the development of the Welland Canal. Museum and adjacent gift shop open year-round. Check at the information desk for vessels expected at Lock 3. *(infoniagara.com)*

WISCONSIN MARITIME MUSEUM, 75 MARITIME DRIVE, MANITOWOC, WI – (920) 684-0218: Displays explore the history of area shipbuilding and also honor submariners and submarines built in Manitowoc. One of the engines of the Straits of Mackinac train ferry *Chief Wawatam* is on display. The World War II sub *Cobia* is adjacent to the museum and open for tours. Open all year. *(wisconsinmaritime.org)*

Michigan's history extends beneath the frozen surface...

Get more of Michigan's history today at hsm.pub/mhm

THE MARINER'S PORT

Like our Facebook page or check out our website to see all the action happening at the Port during the 2023 shipping season!

portofmonroe.com

Stacks and Flags

Algoma Transport's Algoma Central stack herald.
(Janey Anderson)

COLORS OF THE GREAT LAKES

Algoma Central Corp.
St. Catharines, ON

American Steamship Co.
Williamsville, NY

Andrie Inc.
Muskegon, MI

Arnold Freight Co.
St. Ignace, MI

Ashton Marine Co.
North Muskegon, MI

Bay City Boat Lines
Bay City, MI

Bay Shipbuilding Co.
Fincanteri Marine Group
Sturgeon, Bay, WI

Beaver Island Boat Co.
Charlevoix, MI

Blue Heron Co.
Tobermory, ON

Brennan Marine
LaCrosse, WI

Buffalo Dept.
of Public Works
Buffalo, N.Y.

Busch Marine Inc.
Carrollton, MI

Calumet River Fleeting
Chicago, IL

Canada Steamship Lines
Div. CSL Group
Montreal, QC

Canadian Coast Guard
Ottawa, ON

Carmeuse North America
(Erie Sand & Gravel)
Erie, PA

Central Marine Logistics Inc.
Mgr. for Cleveland-Cliffs Inc.
Griffith, IN

Chicago Fire Dept.
Chicago, IL

CJC Cruises Inc.
Detroit Princess Riverboat
Grand Ledge, MI

Cleveland Fire Dept.
Cleveland, OH

Cooper Marine Ltd.
Selkirk, OH

**Coopérative de Transport
Maritime et Aérien (C.T.M.A.)**
Cap-aux-Meules, QC

Croisières AML Inc.
Québec City, QC

Dean Construction Co.
Windsor, ON

Detroit City Fire Dept.
Detroit, MI

**Diamond Jack's
River Tours**
Detroit, MI

Duc D'Orleans Cruise Boat
Corunna, ON

**Eastern Upper Peninsula
Transportation Authority**
Sault Ste. Marie, MI

**Famous Soo Locks
Boat Tours**
Sault Ste. Marie, MI

Five Lakes Marine Towing
Sturgeon Bay, WI

Fraser Shipyards Inc.
Superior, WI

G3 Canada Ltd.
Algoma Central – Mgr.
Winnipeg, MB

Gaelic Tugboat Co.
Detroit, MI

Geo. Gradel Co.
Toledo, OH

**Gillen Marine
Construction**
Mequon, WI

Goodtime Cruise Line
Cleveland, OH

**Grand Portage /
Isle Royale Trans. Line**
Grand Portage, MN

**Great Lakes Dock
& Materials**
Muskegon, MI

Great Lakes Fleet Inc.
Key Lakes Inc. – Mgr.
Duluth, MN

**Great Lakes
Maritime Academy**
Traverse City, MI

**Great Lakes Science Center
U.S. Geological Services**
Ann Arbor, MI

Great Lakes Towing Co.
Cleveland, OH

Groupe Desgagnés Inc.
Québec City, QC

Groupe Desgagnés Inc.
Québec City, QC

Groupe Océan Inc.
Québec City, QC

Hamilton Port Authority
Hamilton, ON

Heritage Marine
Knife River, MN

Holcim U.S.
Chicago, IL

Inland Lakes Management
Chicago, IL

Inland Tug and Barge
Brockville, ON

Interlake Steamship Co.
Interlake Maritime Services - Mgr.
Middleburg Heights, OH

J.W. Westcott Co.
Detroit, MI

The King Co.
Holland, MI

Kokosing Industrial Inc.
Great Lakes Marine Div.
Cheboygan, MI

Lagasco Inc.
London, ON

Lake Erie Island Cruises
Sandusky, OH

Lakehead Tugboats Inc.
Thunder Bay, ON

Lake Michigan Carferry
Interlake Maritime Services - Mgr.
Ludington, MI

Les Barges De Matane Inc.
Matane, QC

Lower Lakes Towing Ltd.
Grand River Navigation Co.
Port Dover, ON / Traverse City, MI

Luedtke Engineering
Frankfort, MI

MacDonald Marine Ltd.
Goderich, ON

Madeline Island
Ferry Line Inc.
LaPointe, WI

Malcolm Marine
St. Clair, MI

Manitou Island Transit
Leland, MI

Marine Services Inc.
Oak Park, MI

McAsphalt Marine
Transportation
Hamilton, ON

McInnis Cement
Chartered from NACC
Montreal, QC

McKeil Marine Ltd.
Burlington, ON

McKeil Marine Ltd.
Burlington, ON

McKeil Marine Ltd.
Burlington, ON

McNally Construction
Hamilton, ON

Midwest Maritime Corp.
Franklin, WI

Miller Ferries
Put-in-Bay, OH

Ministry of Transportation
Toronto, ON

Montreal Port Authority
Montreal, QC

Muskoka Steamships
& Discovery Centre
Gravenhurst, ON

Nautica Queen
Cruise Dining
Cleveland, OH

NOAA Great Lakes
Environmental Research Lab
Ann Arbor, MI

North Shore Marine
Terminal & Logistics
Escanaba, MI

Nunavut Eastern Arctic
Shipping Inc. (NEAS)
Montréal, QC

NovaAlgoma Cement
Carriers Ltd.
St. Catharines, ON

Original Soo Locks
Boat Tours
Sault Ste. Marie, MI

Owen Sound
Transportation Co.
Owen Sound, ON

Port City Cruise Lines
Muskegon, MI

Port City Marine Services
Port City Tug Inc.
Muskegon, MI

Pure Michigan Boat
Cruises LLC
Munising, MI

Purvis Marine Ltd
Sault Ste. Marie, ON

Roen Salvage Co.
Sturgeon Bay, WI

Ryba Marine Construction
Cheboygan, MI

Shell Canada Ltd.
Calgary, AB

Shoreline Contractors Inc.
Amherst, OH

Sea Service LLC
Superior, WI

Société des Traversiers
Du Québec
Québec City, QC

St. James Marine Co.
Beaver Island, MI

St. Lawrence
Cruise Lines Inc.
Kingston, ON

St. Lawrence Seaway
Development Corp.
Massena, NY

St. Lawrence Seaway
Management Corp.
Cornwall, ON

St. Marys Cement Group
Port City Marine Services, Mgr.
Burlington, ON

Sterling Fuels Ltd.
Hamilton, ON

Thunder Bay
Tug Services Ltd.
Thunder Bay, ON

Toronto Fire Services
Toronto, ON

Toronto Port Authority
Toronto, ON

Toronto Tug & Transport Ltd.
Toronto, ON

University of Minnesota Duluth
Great Lakes Observatory
Duluth, MN

U.S. Army
Corps of Engineers
Cincinnatti, OH

U.S Coast Guard
9th Coast Guard District
Cleveland, OH

U.S. Environmental
Protection Agency
Chicago, IL

U.S. Fish & Wildlife
Service
Alpena, MI

U.S. Oil
Div. U.S. Venture Inc.
Appleton, WI

Vane Brothers Co.
Baltimore, MD

VanEnkevort Tug & Barge
Escanaba, MI

White Lake
Dock & Dredge Inc.
Montague, MI

Willy's Contracting Co.
Southhampton, ON

SALTWATER FLEETS ON THE SEAWAY

Ace Tankers CV
Amsterdam, Netherlands

Alliance Tankers
Hamilton, Bermuda

American Queen Voyages
Fort Lauderdale, FL

Argo Coral Maritime Ltd.
Rotterdam, Netherlands

Beatrix Enterprises Co.
Piraeus, Greece

Bernhard Schulte Group
Hamburg, Germany

Besiktas Shipping Group
Istanbul, Turkey

BigLift Shipping
Amsterdam, Netherlands

Bilka Shipping Co.
Istanbul, Turkey

Blystad Group
Oslo, Norway

**Briese Schiffahrts
GmbH & Co. KG**
Leer, Germany

Brostrom AB
Copenhagen, Denmark

Canfornav Inc.
Montreal, QC, Canada

Carisbrooke Shipping Ltd.
Cowes, United Kingdom

**Carsten Rehder
Schiffsmakler & Reederei**
Hamburg, Germany

Celsius Shipping ApS
Hellerup, Denmark

ClearWater Group
Rotterdam, Netherlands

Cnan Nord Spa
Kouba, Algeria

**Coastal Shipping Ltd.
Div. Woodward Group**
Goose Bay, NL, Canada

Compagnie Du Ponant SA
Marseilles, France

Danser Van Gent
Delfzul, Netherlands

Duzgit Gemi Insa Sanayi
Istanbul, Turkey

Fednav
Montreal, QC, Canada

Forestwave Navigation
Heerenveen, Netherlands

Franco Compania Naviera SA
Athens, Greece

Furetank Rederi
Donso, Sweden

Hansa Tankers SA
Bergen, Norway

Hapag-Lloyd Cruises
Hamburg, Germany

Harren & Partner Schiffahrts GmbH
Bremen, Germany

Hartman Seatrade
Urk, Netherlands

Held Shipping
Haren Ems, Germany

Herm. Dauelsberg GmbH
Bremen, Germany

HS Schiffahrts
Haren-Ems, Germany

IMM Shipping Management GmbH
Bremen, Germany

Intermarine
Houston, Texas

Interunity Management Corp.
Bremen, Germany

Johann M.K. Blumenthal GmbH & Co.
Hamburg, Germany

Jumbo Shipping Co. SA
Rotterdam, Netherlands

Jungerhans Maritime Services GmbH
Haren EMS, Germany

K-Ships SRL
Genova, Italy

Krey Schiffahrts GmbH & Co.
Leer, Germany

Liberty Blue Shipmanagement
Leer, Germany

Marconsult Schiffarht
Hamburg, Germany

Mediterranea Di Navigazione SPA
Ravenna, Italy

Minship Shipmanagement GMBH & Co.
Schnaittenbach, Germany

MTM Ship Management Ltd.
Singapore

Navigation Maritime Bulgare Ltd.
Varna, Bulgaria

Nordic Tankers Marine A/S
Copenhagen, Denmark

Nova Marine Carriers S.A.
Lugano, Switzerland

Oceanex Inc.
Montreal, QC, Canada

Onego Shipping & Chartering
Rhoon, Netherlands

Oslo Bulk Shipping
Singapore

Parakou Shipping Ltd.
Hong Kong, China

Pearl Seas Cruises LLC.
Guilford, CT, USA

Peter Dohle Schiffahrts
Hamburg, Germany

Phoenix Shipping and Trading SA
Piraeus, Greece

Plantours Cruises
Bremen, Germany

Polsteam Polish Steamship Co.
Szczecin, Poland

Pot Scheepvaart BV
Delfzijl, Netherlands

RF Ocean
London, United Kingdom

Rederi AB Alvtank
Donso, Sweden

Rederi AB Donsotank
Donso, Sweden

Rederiet Stenersen AS
Bergen, Norway

Reederei H. Schuldt Gmbh & Co.
Hamburg, Germany

Reederei Rudolf Schepers
Haren EMS, Germany

Royal Wagenborg Shipping
Delfzijl, Netherlands

Sargeant Marine Inc.
Boca Raton, FL, USA

Scot Tanker Gemi Isletmeciligi A.S.
Istanbul, Turkey

SFL Corporation Ltd.
Hamilton, Burmuda

Sloman Neptun Shiffarhts
Bremen, Germany

South End Tanker Management
Barendrecht, Netherlands

Spliethoff
Amsterdam, Netherlands

Sunship Schiffahrtskontor KG
Emden, Germany

Tarbit Tankers B.V.
Dordrecht, Netherlands

TB Marine Shipmanagement GmbH & Co.
Hamburg, Germany

Team Tankers Management AS
Hellerup, Denmark

Transmarine Management APS
Copenhagen, Denmark

Uni-Tankers International
Middelfart, Denmark

Utkilen A.S.
Bergen, Norway

Valloeby Shipping
Msida, Malta

Vantage Deluxe World Travel
Boston, MA

Viking Cruises
Basel, Switzerland

Vroon B.V.
Breda, Netherlands

W. Bockstiegel Reederei KG
Emden, Germany

Wijnne Barends
Delfzijl, Netherlands

Yilmar Shipping and Trading Ltd.
Istanbul, Turkey

Zea Marine
Bremen, Germany

REEDERI and **SCHIFFFAHRT** means shipping and **GmbH** means a company with limited liability in German. **SCHEEPVAART** means shipping in Dutch. **TICKARET** is Arabic for commerce or trade.

FLAGS OF REGISTRY

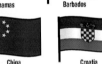

Bahamas | Barbados | Belgium | Bermuda | Bulgaria | Canada

China | Croatia | Cyprus | Denmark | Finland | France

Germany | Greece | Hong Kong | India | Ireland | Isle of Man

Israel | Italy | Japan | Liberia | Lithuania | Malta

Monaco | Netherlands | Norway | Panama | Philippines | Poland

Singapore | Spain | St. Vincent and The Grenadines | Sweden | Switzerland | Taiwan

Turkey | Ukraine | United Kingdom | United States | Vanuatu

FLEET HOUSEFLAGS

Algoma Central Corp.
St. Catherines, ON

American Steamship Co.
Williamsville, NY

Andrie Inc.
Muskegon, MI

Ashton Marine Co.
North Muskegon, MI

BigLift Shipping
Amsterdam, Netherlands

Canada Steamship Lines Inc. (CSL)
Montreal, QC

Canadian Coast Guard
Ottawa, ON

Canfornav Inc.
Montreal, QC

Central Marine Logistics Inc. Mgr. for Cleveland-Cliffs Inc.
Griffith, IN

Famous Soo Locks Boat Tours
Sault Ste. Marie, MI

Fednav
Montreal, QC

G3 Canada Ltd. Algoma Central – Mgr
Winnipeg, MB

Gaelic Tugboat Co. Diamond Jack's Tours
Detroit, MI

Great Lakes Fleet Inc. Key Lakes Inc. - Mgr.
Duluth, MN

Great Lakes Maritime Academy
Traverse City, MI

Great Lakes Towing Co.
Cleveland, OH

Groupe Desgagnés Inc.
Québec City, QC

Groupe Océan Inc.
Québec City, QC

Inland Lakes Management Inc.
Alpena, MI

Interlake Steamship Co Interlake Maritime Services - Mgr.
Middleburg Heights, OH

J.W. Westcott Co.
Detroit, MI

Key Lakes Inc. Great Lakes Fleet - Mgr.
Duluth, MN

Lake Michigan Carferry Interlake Maritime Services - Mgr.
Ludington, MI

Lower Lakes Towing Ltd. Grand River Navigation Co.
Port Dover, ON / Traverse City, MI

McAsphalt Marine Transportation Ltd.
Hamilton, ON

McKeil Marine Ltd.
Burlington, ON

Original Soo Locks Boat Tours
Sault Ste. Marie, MI

Polsteam Polish Steamship Co.
Szczecin, Poland

Port City Marine Services Port City Tug Inc.
Muskegon, MI

Purvis Marine Ltd.
Sault Ste. Marie, ON

Royal Wagenborg Shipping
Delfzijl, Netherlands

Spliethoff
Amsterdam, Netherlands

St. Lawrence Seaway Development Corp.
Massena, NY

St. Lawrence Seaway Management Corp.
Cornwall, ON

U.S. Army Corps of Engineers
Cincinnati, OH

U.S. Coast Guard
Cleveland, OH

U.S. Environmental Protection Agency
Chicago, IL

Vane Brothers Co.
Baltimore, MD

VanEnkevort Tug & Barge
Escanaba, MI

Vroon B.V. Iver Ships Mgr.
Breda, Netherlands

Extra Tonnage

Ports • Cargoes
Locks • Canals

"A pirate's life for me," says the crew of the John G. Munson.
(Roger LeLievre)

JOHN G. MUN

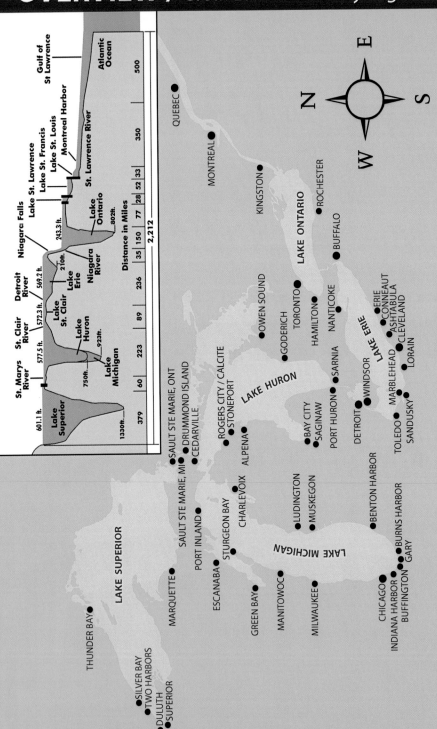

PORTS / *Loading & Unloading*

The primary U.S. iron ore and limestone destinations are Cleveland and Chicago, along with Gary, Burns Harbor and Indiana Harbor, IN; Detroit; and Toledo, Lorain, Ashtabula and Conneaut, OH. In Canada, Nanticoke, Hamilton and Sault Ste. Marie, ON, are major ore-receiving ports. Coal is carried by self-unloaders to power plants in the United States and Canada. Most grain loaded on the lakes is destined for export via the St. Lawrence Seaway, although some is carried to Toledo, OH, and Buffalo, NY. Cement from Alpena and Charlevoix, MI, is delivered to terminals from Lake Superior to Lake Ontario. Tankers bring petroleum products to cities such as Cleveland; Green Bay, WI; Cheboygan, MI; and Detroit. Self-unloaders carry limestone, coal, road salt and sand throughout the region. Steel coils are moved from mills in Sault Ste. Marie and Hamilton, ON, to ports on the lower lakes.

Taconite ore is loaded for delivery to lower lakes steel mills at Duluth, Two Harbors, and Silver Bay, MN, as well as Superior, WI, and Marquette, MI. Limestone-loading ports are Port Inland, Cedarville, Drummond Island, Calcite and Stoneport, MI, and Marblehead, OH. Coal ports are Superior, WI; South Chicago, IL; and the Ohio ports of Toledo, Sandusky and Conneaut. Petroleum is loaded aboard vessels at Sarnia, ON, and East Chicago, IN. Grain export ports include Duluth, MN; Milwaukee and Superior, WI; and the Ontario ports of Thunder Bay, Sarnia and Owen Sound.

Philip R. Clarke (foreground) loading blast furnace trim at Duluth, MN, with her sister ship Arthur M. Anderson in the background. (David Schauer)

AVERAGE RUNNING TIMES

Times listed are for downbound passages. Reverse for upbound times. Times vary with speed / weather / traffic.

LAKE SUPERIOR

Duluth/Superior – Soo Locks	26 hrs
Marquette – Soo Locks	12 hrs
Thunder Bay – Soo Locks	12 hrs

ST. MARYS RIVER

Soo Locks – DeTour, MI	6 hrs
DeTour – Port Huron	19 hrs

LAKE HURON

DeTour – Mackinac Bridge	2 hrs
DeTour – Port Huron	15 hrs
Harbor Beach – Port Huron	4 hrs

LAKE MICHIGAN

Gray's Reef Light – Gary, IN	22 hrs

LAKE ERIE

Detroit River Light – Toledo	1.75 hrs
Detroit River Light – Southeast Shoal	3 hrs
Southeast Shoal – Long Point	9 hrs
Long Point – CIP 15 (off Port Weller)	3 hrs
Detroit River Light – Port Colborne piers – CIP 16 (Welland Canal)	15 hrs

LAKE ONTARIO

Welland Canal (Port Weller) – Hamilton	2 hrs
Welland Canal (Port Weller) – Cape Vincent, NY (call-in points at Newcastle, mid-lake and Sodus Point)	12 hrs

Edwin H. Gott unloading taconite pellets at Gary, IN. (Roger LeLievre)

AGRICULTURAL PRODUCTS – Wheat, grain, soybeans, canola, flax and oats are shipped on the Great Lakes. Some is used domestically, but most is shipped to international markets.

BLAST FURNACE TRIM – Raw crushed taconite.

BOTTOM ASH – Part of the non-combustible residue of combustion in a power plant boiler, furnace or incinerator. Bottom ash has been used as structural fill material for the construction of highway embankments and/or the backfilling of abutments, retaining walls or trenches.

BUNKER C – A special grade of heavy fuel oil, also known as No. 6 fuel.

CEMENT CLINKER – A material, made by heating ground limestone and clay, that is ground up to a fine powder to produce cement.

CLINKER – The incombustible residue that remains after the combustion of coal.

COAL – Both eastern (high sulfur, used in industry) and western (low sulfur, burned at power plants) coal are shipped aboard Great Lakes vessels.

COKE – A byproduct of blended coals baked in ovens until mostly pure carbon is left. Coke is used to generate the high heat necessary to make steel in blast furnaces.

COKE BREEZE – Byproduct of coke production

DOLOMITE – Rock similar to limestone but somewhat harder and heavier.

FLUXSTONE – Taconite pellets premixed with limestone, so no limestone needs to be added in a blast furnace.

HOT BRIQUETTE IRON (HBI) – HBI is created by reducing iron ore with natural gas to feed blast or electric arc furnaces to make steel.

IRON FINES – Fines (ore less than 6mm in diameter) are created as a result of mining, crushing and processing the larger pieces of ore. See **SINTER**.

LIMESTONE – Common sedimentary rock consisting mostly of calcium carbonate used as a building stone and in the manufacture of lime, carbon dioxide and cement.

LIQUID ASPHALT – The last product taken from an oil refinery. The thick, black product is mixed with small stones to make pavement material.

MILL SCALE – Byproduct of the shaping of iron and steel.

PETROLEUM COKE – Petroleum coke (petcoke) is the bottom end of oil refining – the parts of crude oil that will not vaporize in the refining process. It is mostly used as fuel (often with coal) in power plants.

PIG IRON – Crude iron that is the direct product of the blast furnace and is refined to produce steel, wrought iron or ingot iron.

POTASH – A compound used for fertilizer.

SALT – Most salt shipped on the Great Lakes is used on roads and highways during the winter to melt ice.

SINTER – Broken taconite pellets, a.k.a. taconite pellet chips and fines. Small, but still useful in the blast furnace.

SLAG – Byproduct of the steelmaking process is used in the production of concrete and as seal coat cover, a base for paving, septic drain fields and railroad ballast.

TACONITE – A low-grade iron ore, containing about 27 percent iron and 51 percent silica, found as a hard rock formation in the Lake Superior region. It is pelletized for shipment to steel mills (see below).

TRAP ROCK – Rock, usually ground fairly fine, for use as foundations and roads or walkways. It is mined near Bruce Mines, ON, and loaded there.

About taconite pellets

The high-grade iron ore (around 60 percent pure) that was mined on the ranges around Lake Superior was mostly exhausted in the tremendous mining efforts of World War II through the early 1950s. There was still plenty of iron ore in the ground, but it was only about 20-30 percent pure. To mine and ship that ore in its natural form would have been expensive, so engineers developed the taconite pelletization process to increase the iron content of the product coming off the ranges.

Pellets have a number of positive attributes. Their iron content (and the content of other elements) can be precisely controlled, so the steel mills know exactly what they are getting. Pellets are relatively moisture free compared with raw iron ore, so they are less prone to freeze in rail cars, storage piles or dock pockets. This means the pellets can be shipped for a much longer season, so companies need fewer rail cars and ships to carry the same amount of pellets, thus saving money on labor and infrastructure. Pellets are also uniform in size, shape and mass, making them very easy to handle on conveyor belt systems, which makes for speedy, precise ship loading and unloading using a shipboard self-unloading system, again cutting costs.

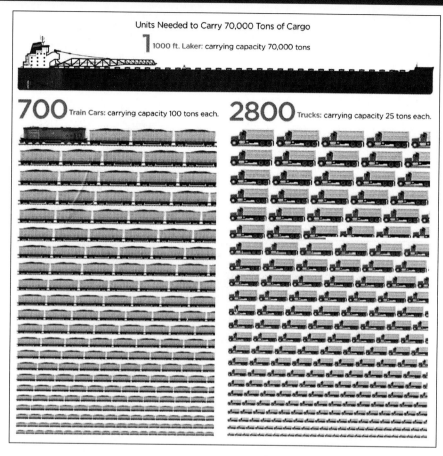

Units Needed to Carry 70,000 Tons of Cargo

1 1000 ft. Laker: carrying capacity 70,000 tons

700 Train Cars: carrying capacity 100 tons each.

2800 Trucks: carrying capacity 25 tons each.

A Great Lakes freighter can sail **607 miles** on **1 gallon** of fuel per ton of cargo.

A 1,000-footer can haul as much as **3 million tons** of cargo in a single shipping season.

In terms of energy efficiency and greenhouse gas emissions, a recent study found that the Great Lakes-Seaway fleet is nearly 7 times more fuel-efficient than trucks and 1.14 times more fuel-efficient than rail. It would take 3 million train trips to carry the total cargo transported by the Great Lakes-Seaway fleet. It would take 7.1 million truck trips to carry the total cargo transported by water. That would increase existing truck traffic by 35-100 percent depending on the highway.

The Soo Locks at Sault Ste. Marie, MI, on the St. Marys River overcome a 21-foot difference in water levels between Lake Superior and lakes Huron, Michigan and Erie. The first canal on the U.S. side was built from 1853-55. Several larger locks followed, spurred by the building of even larger ships.

Under the jurisdiction of the U.S. Army Corps of Engineers, the locks operate on gravity, as do all locks in the St. Lawrence Seaway system. No pumps are used to empty or fill the lock chambers; valves are opened, and water is allowed to seek its own level. All traffic passes through the locks toll-free. Traffic is directed by radio to the appropriate lock according to size, other vessels in the locks area and the time the captain first calls in to the lockmaster. All vessels longer than 730 feet

The Soo Locks, photographed through a zoom lens from outside the no-drone-zone near the locks complex. (Chuck Zentmeyer)

and/or wider than 76 feet are restricted by size to the **Poe**, or second, lock. Smaller vessels go to the **MacArthur Lock**, closest to the viewing platform. Vessels are under engine and thruster control at all times, with crews ready to drop mooring lines over bollards on the lock wall to stop their movement.

As soon as the vessel is in position, the engines are stopped and mooring lines are made fast. If the vessel is being lowered, valves at the lower end of the lock chamber are opened to allow the water inside to flow out. If the vessel is being raised, valves at the upper end of the chamber are opened to allow water to enter. When the water reaches the desired level, the valves are closed, the protective boom is raised, the gates are opened, and the vessel leaves the lock.

Frontenac enters the MacArthur Lock while Lee A. Tregurtha departs the Poe Lock heading toward Lake Superior. (John C. Knecht)

MacArthur Lock

Named after World War II Gen. Douglas MacArthur, the MacArthur Lock is 800 feet long (243.8 meters) between inner gates, 80 feet wide (24.4 meters) and 31 feet deep (9.4 meters) over the sills. The lock was built in 1942-43 and opened to traffic on July 11, 1943. Vessel size is limited to 730 feet long (222.5 meters) by 76 feet wide (23 meters).

Poe Lock

The Poe Lock is 1,200 feet long (365.8 meters) and 110 feet wide (33.5 meters), and has a depth over the sills of 32 feet (9.8 meters). Named after Col. Orlando M. Poe, it was built in the years 1961-68. The lock's vessel size limit is 1,100 feet long (335.3 meters) by 105 feet wide (32 meters).

Canadian Lock

The Canadian Lock at Sault Ste. Marie, ON, has its origin in a canal constructed in 1797 by the North West Co. That lock remained in use until destroyed in the War of 1812. It was replaced by a new lock in 1895, which was rebuilt after a wall failure in 1987 and reopened in 1998. The present lock, which is 253 feet long and operated by Parks Canada, is used by pleasure craft, tugs and tour boats.

FUN AT THE ANNUAL ENGINEERS DAY

Every year on the last Friday of June, the public is invited by the U.S. Army Corps of Engineers to visit areas of the Soo Locks complex usually off limits. Engineers Day draws thousands and is accompanied by other events that weekend, including tours, an art show and a popular Boatnerd picnic. (Roger LeLievre)

New Lock Construction

In late 2019, $75 million for a new Soo Lock was approved as part of a $1.4 trillion spending measure passed by the U.S. House and Senate. It was fully funded in January 2022 with an additional $479 million to finish the work and is expectd to be completed by 2030. The new lock mirrors the Poe at 1,200 feet long, 110 feet wide and 32 feet deep. It is being built where the long-obsolete Davis and Sabin locks were located.

CALL-IN POINTS / St. Marys River

The St. Marys River flows out of the southeast corner of Lake Superior in a southeasterly direction to Lake Huron. Vessels transiting the St. Marys River system are under the jurisdiction of Soo Traffic, part of the U.S. Coast Guard at Sault Ste. Marie, MI, and must radio their positions on VHF Ch. 12 (156.600 MHz) at predetermined locations. Vessels in the vicinity of the Soo Locks fall under the jurisdiction of the lockmaster, who must be contacted on VHF Ch. 14 (156.700 MHz) for lock assignments.

Call-in points (bold type on map) are not the same for upbound and downbound traffic. Approximate running times between call-in points are at left; times may vary due to other traffic and weather. Because of their size, 1,000-footers take more time to transit than smaller vessels.

Arrival times at the Soo Locks are available at the Information Center located in the locks park. Upbound vessels must make a pre-call to Soo Traffic one hour before entering the river at DeTour, and downbound traffic is required to make a one-hour pre-call above Ile Parisienne.

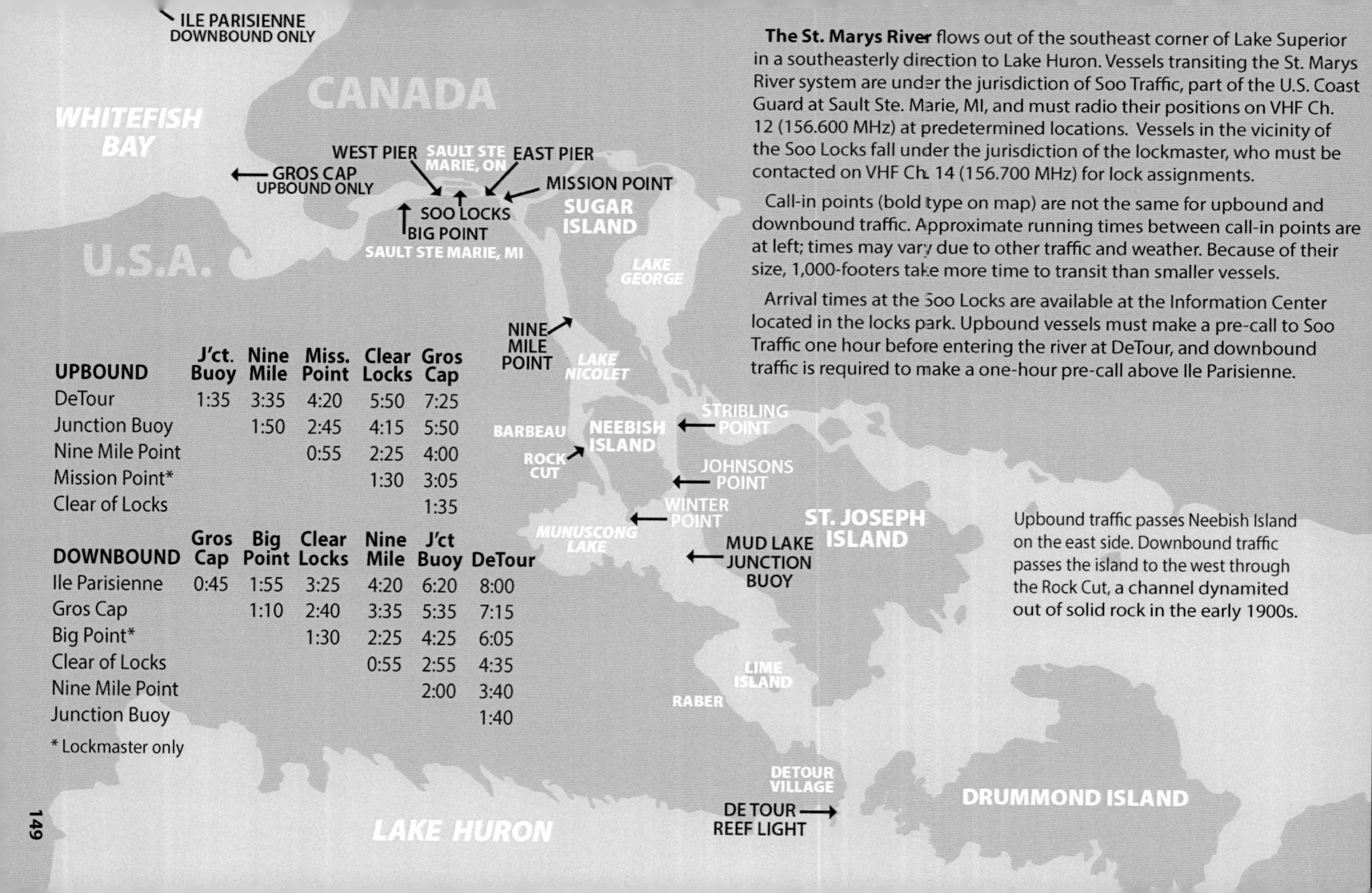

Upbound traffic passes Neebish Island on the east side. Downbound traffic passes the island to the west through the Rock Cut, a channel dynamited out of solid rock in the early 1900s.

UPBOUND

	J'ct. Buoy	Nine Mile	Miss. Point	Clear Locks	Gros Cap
DeTour	1:35	3:35	4:20	5:50	7:25
Junction Buoy		1:50	2:45	4:15	5:50
Nine Mile Point			0:55	2:25	4:00
Mission Point*				1:30	3:05
Clear of Locks					1:35

DOWNBOUND

	Gros Cap	Big Point	Clear Locks	Nine Mile	J'ct Buoy	DeTour
Ile Parisienne	0:45	1:55	3:25	4:20	6:20	8:00
Gros Cap		1:10	2:40	3:35	5:35	7:15
Big Point*			1:30	2:25	4:25	6:05
Clear of Locks				0:55	2:55	4:35
Nine Mile Point					2:00	3:40
Junction Buoy						1:40

* Lockmaster only

149

Vessels transiting the St. Clair River, Lake St. Clair and the Detroit River are under the jurisdiction of Sarnia Traffic and must radio their positions at predetermined locations. Call-in points (bold type on map) are not the same for upbound and downbound traffic. Average running times between call-in points are below. *

UPBOUND	Buoys 1&2	Black River	Stag Isl.	Salt Dock	Light X-32	Crib Light	Grassy Isl.
Detroit River Lt.	8:10	7:50	7:20	6:00	4:20	4:00	1:35
Grassy Island	6:45	6:25	5:55	4:35	2:55	2:35	
St. Clair Crib	4:10	3:50	3:20	2:00	0:25		
Light X-32	3:50	3:30	3:00	1:35			
Salt Dock	2:10	1:50	1:20				
Stag Isl. Upper	0:50	0:35					
Black River	0:20						

DOWNBOUND	Det. River	Grassy Isl.	Belle Isl.	Crib Light	Light 23	Salt Dock	Black River	7&8
30 min. above buoys 11 & 12	9:05	7:35	6:25	5:10	3:55	3:10	1:20	0:40
Buoys 7 & 8	8:15	6:55	5:45	4:30	3:15	2:30	0:40	
Black River	7:45	6:15	5:05	3:50	2:35	1:50		
Salt Dock	5:55	4:25	3:15	2:00	0:45			
Light 23	5:10	3:40	2:30	1:10				
St. Clair Crib	3:55	2:25	1:10					
USCG Belle Isle	2:40	1:10						
Grassy Isl.	1:30							

* Times can change if vessels stop for fuel or are delayed by other traffic.

BUOYS 11 & 12 DOWNBOUND ONLY →

BUOYS 7 & 8 DOWNBOUND ONLY →

BUOYS 1 & 2 UPBOUND ONLY →

LAKE HURON

SARNIA

PORT HURON

IMPERIAL FUEL D

BLACK RIVER ←

STAG ISLAND UPPER UPBOUND ONLY →

SHELL FUEL DOCK ←

ST. CLAIR

ST. CLAIR EDISON POWER PLANT RECOR POINT →

MARINE CITY

SALT DOCK →

ALGONAC

HARSENS ISLAND

← **LIGHT 23** DOWNBOUND ONLY

← **X(RAY) 32** UPBOUND ONLY

ST. CLAIR CRIB LIGHT →

LAKE ST. CLAIR

USCG BELLE ISLE DOWNBOUND ONLY

J.W. WESTCOTT MAILBOAT

DETROIT

MISTERSKY FUEL

WINDSOR

ROUGE RIVER →

STERLING FUEL

GRASSY ISLAND →

← FIGHTING ISLAND

GROSSE ILE →

LIVINGSTONE CHANNEL →

← AMHERSTBURG CHANNEL

DETROIT RIVER LIGHT →

N

W E

S

LAKE ERIE

MONROE

PELEE PASSAGE

POINT PELEE

PELEE ISLAND

SOUTHEAST SHOAL

LOCKS & CANALS / *Welland Canal*

The 28-mile (44 km) **Welland Canal** is the fourth version of a waterway link between Lake Ontario and Lake Erie, first built in 1829. The present canal was completed in 1932, deepened in the 1950s as part of the Seaway project and further straightened in 1973. Today its eight locks, all Canadian, lift ships 326 feet (100 meters) over the Niagara Escarpment.

Each of the seven Welland Canal locks has an average lift of 46.5 feet (14.2 meters). All locks (except Lock 8) are 859 feet (261.8 meters) long, 80 feet (24.4 meters) wide and 30 feet (9.1 meters) deep. Lock 8 is 1,380 feet (420. 6 meters) long.

The largest vessel that may transit the canal is 740 feet (225.5 meters) long, 78 feet (23.8 meters) wide and 26.5 feet (8.08 meters) in draft. **Locks 1, 2** and **3** are at Port Weller and St. Catharines, ON, on the Lake Ontario end of the waterway. At Lock 3, the Welland Canals Centre and St. Catharines Museum also house an information desk (which posts a list of vessels expected at the lock), a gift shop and restaurant.

At Thorold, ON, **Locks 4, 5** and **6**, twinned to help speed passage of vessels, are controlled with an elaborate interlocking system for safety. These locks (positioned end to end, they resemble a short flight of stairs) have an aggregate lift of 139.5 feet (42.5 meters). Just south of locks **4**, **5** and **6** is **Lock 7**. **Lock 8**, 7 miles (11.2 km) upstream at Port Colborne, ON, completes the process, making the final adjustment to Lake Erie's level.

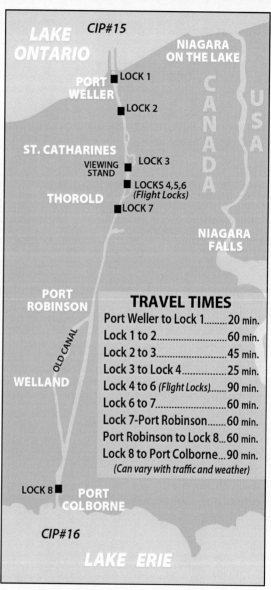

TRAVEL TIMES

Port Weller to Lock 1	20 min.
Lock 1 to 2	60 min.
Lock 2 to 3	45 min.
Lock 3 to Lock 4	25 min.
Lock 4 to 6 *(Flight Locks)*	90 min.
Lock 6 to 7	60 min.
Lock 7-Port Robinson	60 min.
Port Robinson to Lock 8	60 min.
Lock 8 to Port Colborne	90 min.

(Can vary with traffic and weather)

In 1973, a new channel was constructed to replace the section of the old canal that bisected the city of Welland. The Welland Bypass eliminated long delays for canal navigation and for road and rail traffic. Two tunnels allow auto and train traffic to pass beneath the canal.

The average passage time for the canal is 8-11 hours, with the majority of the time spent transiting Locks 4-7. All vessel traffic though the Welland Canal is regulated by a control center, Seaway Welland, which also remotely operates the locks and the traffic bridges over the canal. Vessels passing through the Welland Canal and St. Lawrence Seaway must carry a qualified pilot at all times.

NACC Quebec, in the St. Lawrence River, with Crossover Island astern. (Emmett Hawkes)

The St. Lawrence Seaway is a waterway extending some 2,038 miles (3,701.4 km) from the Atlantic Ocean to the head of the Great Lakes at Duluth, MN, including Montreal harbor and the Welland Canal. More specifically, it is a system of locks and canals (U.S. and Canadian), built between 1954 and 1958 at a cost of $474 million and opened in 1959, that allows vessels to pass from Montreal to the Welland Canal at the western end of Lake Ontario. For the Montreal-Lake Ontario section, the average transit time is 24 hours upbound and 22 hours downbound. The difference is mainly due to the current in the St. Lawrence River. The vessel size limit within this system is 740 feet (225.6 meters) long, 78 feet (23.8 meters) wide and 26 feet (7.9 meters) draft. It takes 8-10 days for a ship to go from Lake Superior to the Atlantic Ocean.

LOCK DIMENSIONS

Length	766 feet (233.5 meters)
Width	80 feet (24 meters)
Depth	30 feet (9.1 meters)

Closest to the ocean is the **St. Lambert Lock**, which lifts ships some 15 feet (4.6 meters) from Montreal harbor to the level of the Laprairie Basin, through which the channel sweeps in a great arc 8.5 miles (13.7 km) long to the second lock. The **Côte Ste. Catherine Lock**, like the other six St. Lawrence Seaway locks, is built to the dimensions shown in the table above. The Côte Ste. Catherine lifts ships from the level of the Laprairie Basin 30 feet (9.1 meters) to the level of Lake Saint-Louis, bypassing the Lachine Rapids. Beyond it, the channel runs 7.5 miles (12.1 km) before reaching Lake Saint-Louis.

The **Lower Beauharnois Lock**, bypassing the Beauharnois Power House, lifts ships 41 feet (12.5 meters) and sends them through a short canal to the **Upper Beauharnois Lock**, where they are lifted 41 feet (12.5 meters) to reach the Beauharnois Canal. After a 13-mile (20.9 km) trip in the canal and a 30-mile (48.3 km) passage through Lake Saint Francis, vessels reach the U.S. border and the **Snell Lock**, which has a lift of 45 feet (13.7 meters) and empties into the 10-mile (16.1 km) Wiley-Dondero Canal.

After passing through the Wiley-Dondero, ships are raised another 38 feet (11.6 meters) by the **Dwight D. Eisenhower Lock**, after which they enter Lake St. Lawrence, the pool upon which nearby power-generating stations draw for their turbines located a mile to the north.

At the western end of Lake St. Lawrence, the **Iroquois Lock** allows ships to bypass the Iroquois Control Dam. The lift here is only about 1 foot (0.3 meters). Once in the waters west of Iroquois, the channel meanders through the Thousand Islands to Lake Ontario, the Welland Canal and beyond.

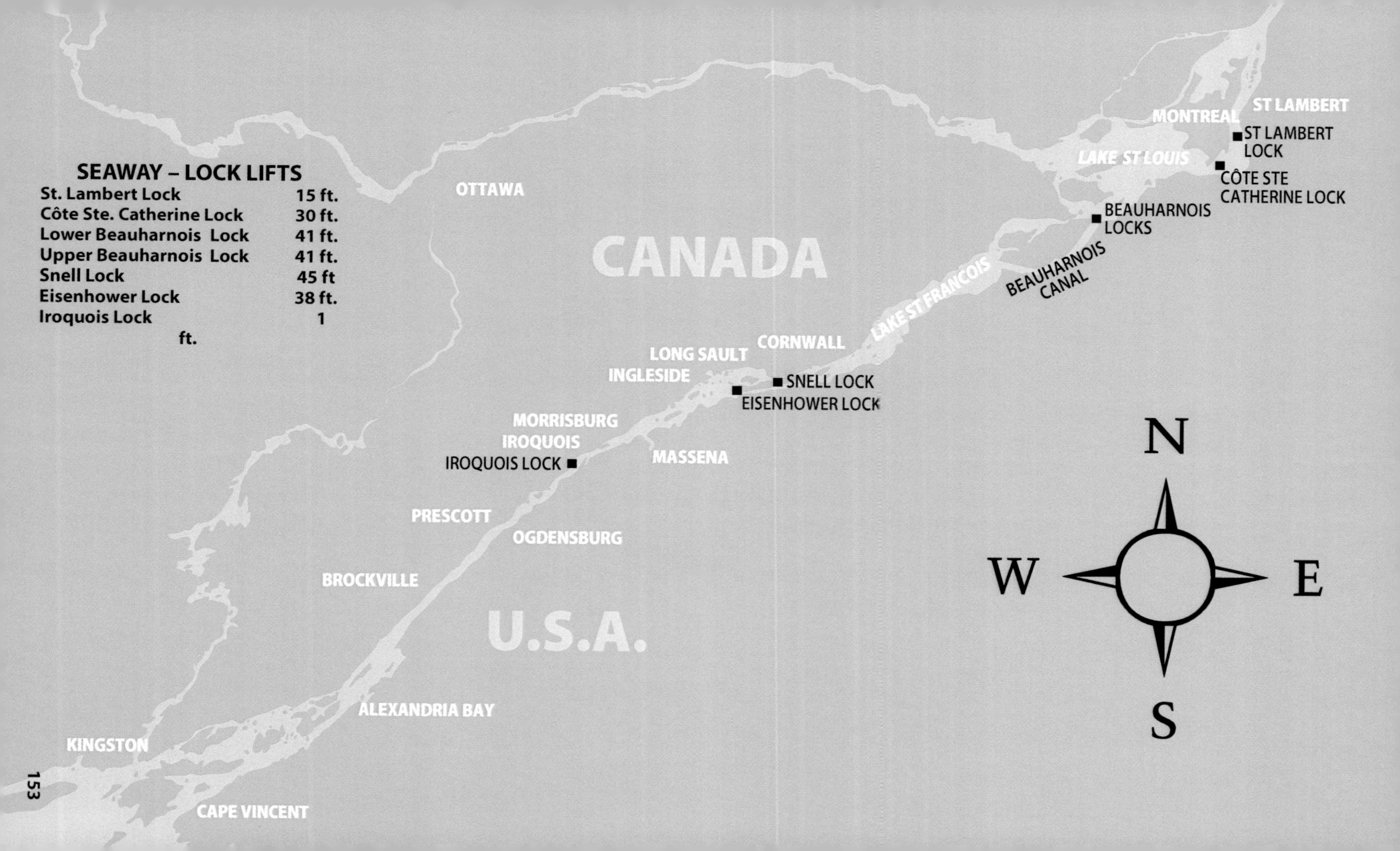

N E
W S

ST LAMBERT
ST LAMBERT LOCK
MONTREAL
CÔTE STE CATHERINE LOCK
LAKE ST LOUIS
BEAUHARNOIS LOCKS
BEAUHARNOIS CANAL

LAKE ST FRANCOIS

CANADA

OTTAWA

SNELL LOCK
EISENHOWER LOCK
CORNWALL
LONG SAULT
INGLESIDE
MASSENA

MORRISBURG
IROQUOIS
IROQUOIS LOCK

PRESCOTT
OGDENSBURG

U.S.A.

BROCKVILLE

ALEXANDRIA BAY

KINGSTON

CAPE VINCENT

SEAWAY – LOCK LIFTS

St. Lambert Lock	15 ft.
Côte Ste. Catherine Lock	30 ft.
Lower Beauharnois Lock	41 ft.
Upper Beauharnois Lock	41 ft.
Snell Lock	45 ft
Eisenhower Lock	38 ft.
Iroquois Lock	1
	ft.

There are about 100 major cargo carriers, including tug/barge combinations, engaged in regular Great Lakes/Seaway trade. They are supplemented by a variety of international vessels, also known as salties.

The Great Lakes shipping season runs from March 25 to Jan. 15, when the Soo Locks close for maintenance and most vessels tie up for the winter.

A vessel traveling from the Atlantic Ocean to Lake Superior through the St. Lawrence Seaway and the Soo Locks rises nearly 600 feet though a stairstep-like series of locks. The first lift, a total of 224 feet, is provided by the seven St. Lawrence Seaway locks that begin at Montreal. The Welland Canal raises vessels an additional 326 feet. The Soo Locks at Sault Ste. Marie, MI, complete the process with a 21-foot lift.

A red-and-white flag flying from a vessel's mast indicates a pilot is on board. Saltwater vessels must pick up Great Lakes pilots at various points in their voyage.

Menominee (with tug Olive L.
Moore) unloading at the Wirt
Stone Dock in Bay City, MI.
(Ben VanOchten)

Mighty ships and a big Seaway lift

No tolls are charged at the Soo Locks. However, tolls are charged for the Welland Canal and St. Lawrence Seaway locks.

In the spring and fall, a small fleet of icebreakers operated by the U.S. and Canadian coast guards, as well as commercial tugs, helps keep shipping channels open.

The St. Marys River, running 80 miles (128.7 km) from Ile Parisienne at its north end to DeTour Reef Light at its south end, connects Lake Superior with Lake Huron. It includes two engineering marvels, the Soo Locks at Sault Ste. Marie, MI, and the West Neebish Cut at Barbeau, MI, a channel dynamited out of solid rock that allows traffic to pass to the west side of Neebish Island.

One ship can move enough wheat to make bread for every resident of New York City for nearly a month.

One short blast of a vessel's horn while in a lock means "cast off lines."

Largest vessel on the Great Lakes, Paul R. Tregurtha, at 1,013.5 feet long, compared to the 1,250-foot-tall Empire State Buillding. A 1,000-footer can haul as much as 3 million tons of cargo in one shipping season.

Empire State Building 1250 ft.

M/V Paul Tregurtha 1013.5 ft.

155

Crowded morning at Toronto. Viking Octantis, Bogdan and an American Queen Voyages passenger ship are all in port. *(Toronto Port Authority)*

Three boats at once at Superior, WI. From left, CSL Laurentien, Stewart J. Cort and Frontenac. *(Vanessa Kaari)*

FOLLOWING THE FLEET

AIS (Automatic Identification System): All major vessels are now equipped with AIS, an automatic tracking system. With sites such as **MarineTraffic.com** or **ais.boatnerd.com**, it's possible to find vessel positions and see other information, including speed and destination.

With an inexpensive VHF scanner, boatwatchers can tune to ship-to-ship and ship-to-shore traffic using the following frequency guide.

Calling/distress only	Ch. 16 – 156.800 MHz	Calling/distress only
Commercial vessels only	Ch. 06 – 156.300 MHz	Working channel
Commercial vessels only	Ch. 08 – 156.400 MHz	Working channel
DeTour Reef – Lake St. Clair Light	Ch. 11 – 156.550 MHz	Sarnia Traffic - Sect. 1
Long Point Light – Lake St. Clair Light	Ch. 12 – 156.600 MHz	Sarnia Traffic - Sect. 2
Montreal – Mid-Lake St. Francis	Ch. 14 – 156.700 MHz	Seaway Beauharnois – Sect. 1
Mid-Lake St. Francis – Bradford Island	Ch. 12 – 156.600 MHz	Seaway Eisenhower – Sect. 2
Bradford Island – Crossover Island	Ch. 11 – 156.550 MHz	Seaway Iroquois – Sect. 3
Crossover Island-Cape Vincent	Ch. 13 – 156.650 MHz	Seaway Clayton – Sect. 4 St. Lawrence River portion
Cape Vincent – Mid-Lake Ontario	Ch. 12 – 156.600 MHz	Seaway Sodus – Sect. 4 Lake Ontario portion
Seaway Pilot Office – Cape Vincent	Ch. 14 – 156.700 MHz	Pilotage traffic
Mid-Lake Ontario – Welland Canal	Ch. 11 – 156.550 MHz	Seaway Newcastle – Sect. 5
Welland Canal	Ch. 14 – 156.700 MHz	Seaway Welland – Sect. 6
Welland Canal-Long Point Light	Ch. 11 – 156.550 MHz	Seaway Long Point – Sect. 7
Montreal traffic	Ch. 10 – 156.500 MHz	Vessel traffic
Soo Traffic	Ch. 12 – 156.600 MHz	Vessel control, Sault Ste. Marie, MI
Lockmaster, Soo Locks	Ch. 14 – 156.700 MHz	Soo Lockmaster (WUE-21)
Coast Guard traffic	Ch. 21 – 157.050 MHz	United States Coast Guard
Coast Guard traffic	Ch. 22 – 157.100 MHz	United States Coast Guard
U.S. mailboat, Detroit, MI	Ch. 10 – 156.500 MHz	Mailboat *J. W. Westcott II*

The following prerecorded messages help track vessel arrivals and departures.

Boatwatcher's Hotline	(218) 722-6489	Superior, Duluth, Two Harbors, Taconite Harbor and Silver Bay, MN
CSX coal docks/Torco dock	(419) 697-2304	Toledo vessel information
Eisenhower Lock	(315) 769-2422	Eisenhower Lock vessel traffic
Michigan Limestone dock	(989) 734-2117	Calcite, MI, vessel information
Michigan Limestone dock	(906) 484-2201	Press 1 – Cedarville, MI, passages
Presque Isle Corp.	(989) 595-6611	Stoneport vessel information ext. 7
Seaway Vessel Locator	(905) 688-6462	St. Lawrence Seaway vessel traffic
Soo Locks Visitor Center Hotline	(906) 202-1333	Current Soo Locks traffic information
Welland Canal Traffic	(905) 688-6462	Welland Canal traffic

WHISTLE TALK

1 SHORT: I intend to leave you on my port side (answered by same if agreed upon).

2 SHORT: I intend to leave you on my starboard side (answered by same if agreed upon). (Passing arrangements may be agreed upon by radio. If so, no whistle signal is required.)

1 PROLONGED: Vessel leaving dock.

3 SHORT: Operating astern propulsion.

1 PROLONGED, SOUNDED AT INTERVALS OF NOT MORE THAN 2 MINUTES: Vessel moving in restricted visibility.

1 SHORT, 1 PROLONGED, 1 SHORT: Vessel at anchor in restricted visibility (optional). May be accompanied by the ringing of a bell on the forward part of the ship and a gong on the aft end.

3 PROLONGED & 2 SHORT: Salute (formal)

1 PROLONGED & 2 SHORT: Salute (commonly used)

3 PROLONGED & 1 SHORT: International Shipmasters' Association member salute

5 OR MORE SHORT BLASTS SOUNDED RAPIDLY: Danger

spotlight

- **Ships**
- **Sailors**
- **Adventures**

Wintry wave from the bow of the Great Lakes Trader in December 2022.
(Jane Herrick)

By SAMUEL HANKINSON

When the Interlake Steamship Co. announced more than three years ago its intention to build a new vessel, the shipping community had a lot of questions. What kind would it be? What would it carry? What would it be named? The "what" began as Hull No. 788 at Fincantieri Bay Shipbuilding, Sturgeon Bay, WI, and the name became *Mark W. Barker*. As to what it would it carry, the answer was a bit more complicated, since the *Mark W. Barker* was built for versatility.

The vessel's construction was well-documented, as were her fit out, trials and first cargoes. *Know Your Ships* was present at her christening at Cleveland in September 2022, where the vessel was open for public tours before and after the ceremonial bottle break.

Although plenty of tug/barges have entered the fold and Canadian programs have resulted in full-scale fleet renewals, the *Barker* is the first Great Lakes bulk carrier to be built on the Great Lakes in more than 35 years. She's also the first new vessel in Interlake's fleet since 1981.

In many ways, the *Barker*'s operation is like writing a new book on Great Lakes shipping. A partnership among Cleveland-based businesses, the vessel was built to haul salt from Cargill's mine on the Cuyahoga River. Cargill's dock is tricky to reach, so Interlake built the *Mark W. Barker* with a single square-shaped flat-bottomed cargo hold to increase cargo capacity. This is unique, as most Great Lakes self-unloaders have V-shaped cargo holds. Two front-end loaders assist the ship in unloading bulk cargo, which is discharged via a bow-mounted self-unloading boom repurposed from the scrapped, World War II-era steamer *American Victory*.

The *Mark W. Barker* also has five large, hydraulically controlled, stackable MacGregor hatches,

Bottle of bubbly, expertly smashed by Megan November. (Bill Kloss)

THAT NEW BOAT SMELL

Mark W. Barker arriving at Monroe, MI. (Paul C. LaMarre III)

Left to right, James R. Barker, Kaye E. Barker and Mark W. Barker at the christening.

more commonly seen on ocean-going vessels. The flat holds and wide hatch openings create possibilities for the vessel to carry oversized project cargo on top of the hatches and in the cargo hold. This essentially makes the *Barker's* book of business unlimited, but likely cargoes in 2023 and beyond may include containers and wind tower components.

The Mark W. Barker is named after Interlake's current president and second-generation leader of the family-owned-and-operated fleet. It is the third Interlake ship to be named after a member of the Barker family, behind

Continued on Page 162

A Bobcat moves a salt cargo to the conveyor gates set into the Barker's flat-bottomed hold. (David Schauer)

1,004-foot-long *James R. Barker* (Mark's father) and 767-foot *Kaye E. Barker* (Mark's mother).

***Mark W. Barker* was** named one of 2023's Most Significant Ships by *Workboat.com*. She's a one-of-a-kind vessel capable of handling whatever the future of Great Lakes shipping has in store.

Across the border, Canada Steamship Line's *Nukumi* has made waves of her own on the St. Lawrence River and Canadian East Coast. The new

Stern view of the Barker at Cleveland. *(Scott Tish)*

ship is the result of a partnership between Windsor Salt and CSL to use a state-of-the-art self-unloader to service the Mines Seleine salt mine on the Gulf of St. Lawrence.

This self-unloader features a single-point loading system that simplifies loading by reducing the number of times the vessel needs to shift while taking on cargo. Salt is received from the shoreside ship loader at a fixed hopper located on the *Nukumi*'s main deck and is transferred to a traveling reversible shuttle conveyor that loads the salt into the ship's cargo holds. The ship's shuttle boom arrangement also reduces the need for shifting positions during discharge.

Other design elements that make the *Nukumi* more environmentally conscious included Diesel-electric Tier 3 engines, a unique hull design that will decrease carbon emissions and improve energy efficiency, a ballast water treatment system designed to reduce the transfer of invasive species and quieter machinery that will lessen vessel noise to protect marine mammals.

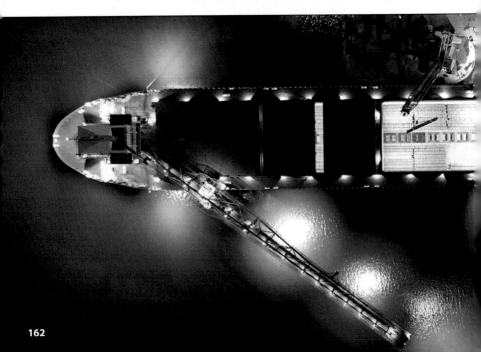

CSL's unique salt-carrying Nukumi at Cote-Ste-Catherine. (René Beauchamp)

Nukumi inherited the salt run from her now-scrapped fleetmate *Salarium,* originally named *Nanticoke.* CSL took over the cargo in 2009 from Algoma Central when the latter retired the *Saunière.* The name of the ship was submitted by a Windsor Salt employee as part of a company-wide naming contest and refers to a legendary figure of the indigenous Mi'kmaq people. *Salarium* (which translates to "a payment made in salt" in French), and *Saunière* (salter) had very literal names, making the *Nukumi* the first ship in this trade pattern to not be named after her line of work.

The *Nukumi* took home awards for Bulk Ship of the Year 2022, and designer EMS-Tech Inc. was awarded the 2022 Best Ship Loading/Unloading System Award at the International Bulk Journal Awards in Rotterdam, Netherlands. Due to her trade routes, this salt ship may be a rare sight west of Montreal. ◆

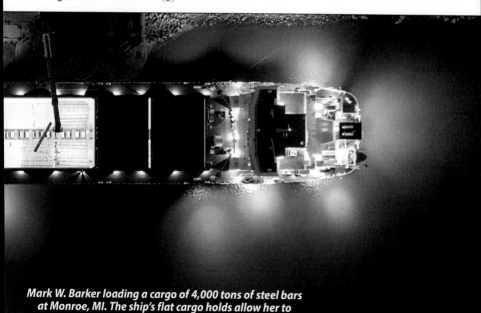

Mark W. Barker loading a cargo of 4,000 tons of steel bars at Monroe, MI. The ship's flat cargo holds allow her to carry such loads. (Paul C. LaMarre III)

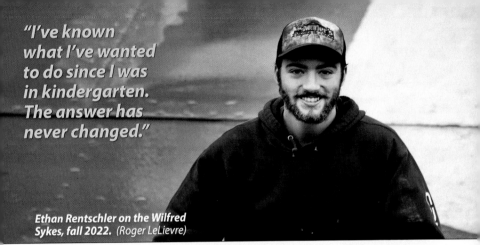

> "I've known what I've wanted to do since I was in kindergarten. The answer has never changed."

Ethan Rentschler on the Wilfred Sykes, fall 2022. (Roger LeLievre)

Goodbye high school, hello Great Lakes!

By ROGER LeLIEVRE

Ethan Rentschler never doubted what he wanted to be when he grew up. "I've known what I've wanted to do since I was in kindergarten," Rentschler remembers. "The answer has never changed." After a youth spent on tugboats at Duluth-Superior, most recently aboard those belonging to Heritage Marine, in May 2022 the 18-year-old drove Heritage's tug *Edward H.* to his graduation ceremony at the Duluth Entertainment Convention Center on the waterfront clad in cap, gown and his well-worn work boots. Two days later, and after an appropriate graduation party send-off aboard the tug by friends and family, he joined the engine room crew of the veteran steamer *Wilfred Sykes* as an ordinary seaman/wiper.

"Wrench" comes by his interest in lake boats naturally. His parents, Dan and Sarah Rentschler, met aboard the *Roger Blough* in the late 1990s when she was a passenger porter and he was second mate. Dan went on to captain the *Edgar B. Speer* for 10 years and now pilots saltwater ships on the Great Lakes for the Western Great Lakes Pilots Association.

Ethan's dad couldn't be prouder, and remembers the first time his son showed an interest in boats. "He was riding in the car, and he recognized a ship at the CN Dock in Duluth. With his limited vocabulary he said 'da da boat.' Everyone thought he would follow his dad, but there were signs he would do something a little different. The chief engineer on one of the lakers let Ethan start the main engine. He was so proud. After that experience, he decided to dress as a Pielstick V18 engine, like the main engines on the *Speer*, for Halloween. His mom turned a box into an engine for a costume. The next year he wanted to be a chief engineer for Halloween. Mom fixed up a pair of coveralls and put smudges on his face. Dad found the biggest wrench in the engine room, traced it onto scrap plywood and painted it silver. The

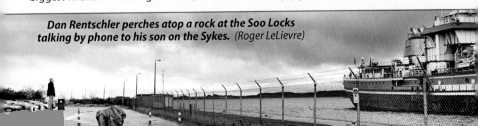

Dan Rentschler perches atop a rock at the Soo Locks talking by phone to his son on the Sykes. (Roger LeLievre)

Wilfred Sykes paid a rare visit to Cleveland in 2022. (John Puda)

big wrench is still hanging in the garage. The signs were there in second grade."

Growing up on the waterfront, Rentschler learned the basics of sailoring. By age 15, he had earned his merchant marine credential, followed at 16 by a license to sail from the Coast Guard. On busy days when he was needed to help crew the tug, Rentschler would call the school for an excused absence. "The school was pretty understanding of that," he recalls. "The high school and my mom pushed me to keep on task and stay on top of school. The way I saw it, I was never going to go to college ever."

He says working on the 1942-built *Sykes*, one of the few remaining steamships on the lakes, has lived up to expectations. "I am fortunate to be on a good ship with a good crew and food," he reports. "I'd highly suggest anyone my age who wants to give it a try to go for it. It's a great opportunity to be able to work on a true steamboat."

Ethan Rentschler on the Thomas K., with his eye set on the Sykes. (Scott Bjorklund)

When he was 16, Rentschler bought his first boat, one of the grocery launches that once served ships at Duluth, MN, built in 1948 as the *Carol Jean* at the Knudsen Brothers Shipbuilding & Dry Dock Co. in Superior, WI, the forerunner of today's Fraser Shipyards. "I named her the *Thomas K* after my Grandpa," says Rentschler. His grandfather was second mate for U.S .Steel, and his great-grandfather also sailed, which makes Ethan Rentschler a fourth-generation Great Lakes seaman.

He's not only continuing to learn the skills needed to be a sailor, he's also got a pretty good handle on sailing for someone so young. "When you run into a new situation, it's always pretty nerve-wracking, but you've got to just trust the people around you," Rentschler said. "You've got to trust yourself, too, and let it happen."

In his off time, he's never very far from the water. On an early 2022 winter break from the *Sykes*, he relaxed by breaking ice at Duluth, MN, on the *Edward H*. "It's funny how you couldn't get Ethan up for school, but he can get up at 0430 to break ice," recalls his dad.

"Everyone on the Great Lakes is hiring"

GLMA Cadets Chart Maritime Industry's Future

By JACK HURT

Training vessel State of Michigan

There is no better view on the Great Lakes than from the pilothouse, taking in the splendor of the inland seas while moving the raw materials upon which multiple nations rely. These ships are captained and crewed by experienced mariners who understand the importance of their trade. But how does one get a job piloting or operating the engines of a Great Lakes freighter? If you ask someone who works on one, odds are they are a product of the Traverse City, MI-based Great Lakes Maritime Academy (GLMA).

Established in 1969, the school is one of seven maritime academies in the United States (plus two in Canada) that specialize in training cadets for a Great Lakes or oceans career. GLMA presents a fast-track route to a licensed position, compared to those who "hawsepipe" their way up through the ranks. GLMA offers two programs – one for engineering officers and another for deck officers. The engineering program provides cadets with hands-on training in keeping engines and other machinery running smoothly. The deck program immerses cadets in the responsibilities of deck officers, including navigating through tight harbors, narrow rivers, fog, storms and on the open lakes. The school has about 200 cadets at present.

While GLMA produces high-quality officers from both programs, the deck program is renowned nationwide, with cadets from as far away as California, Hawaii and Louisiana attending GLMA to master the skills of marine navigation.

For some, attending GLMA to become a skilled pilot was a last-second decision. For others, a career on the water had been planned for a long time. "I always knew I wanted to become a deck officer from the time I decided to pursue a career aboard ships," said Daniel Lindner, a 21-year-old deck cadet from Stevens Point, WI, who sailed on the *Walter J. McCarthy Jr.* last summer. "I first learned of GLMA while I was still in middle school, and I knew I wanted to end up there ever since."

Brianna Linderholm (Noah Pulitzer)

The curriculum for deck cadets is filled with intense classes and training that ranges from basic knot-tying to celestial navigation. But the learning isn't confined to classrooms, as cadets must complete three sea projects during their time at GLMA. The first takes place aboard the school's 224-foot-long training ship *State of Michigan*, formerly used by the U.S. Navy for submarine surveillance during the Cold War and later by the U.S. Coast Guard for drug enforcement in the Caribbean. The last other two projects are internships with companies on the Great Lakes and oceans.

Sea projects allow cadets to accumulate the required 300 sea days to test for their licenses while also providing a taste of life afloat and a chance to apply the theories and methods taught in

Logan Vasicek
(Joy Fett)

lectures to real world situations.

"**Once you get out** on your sea project, all of the information you learn comes together and clicks," said 20-year-old deck cadet Brianna Linderholm of Superior, WI, whose latest sea project was completed aboard the *State of Michigan*. "You're out there using it in real scenarios."

Once a cadet completes the three sea projects, the hardest part of the curriculum begins – license prep. During the second-to-last semester of their time at GLMA, cadets will take a class dedicated to preparing for the strenuous U.S. Coast Guard license examinations. "It's very structured," said Lindner. "It's made up of daily tests with a pass/fail format that strictly adheres to the USCG regulations which we'll experience when we're taking the real exams. It's demanding and the workload is high."

Shortly after cadets pass testing, they will "ring off watch" from GLMA with a bachelor of science degree in maritime technology as well the appropriate licenses for their program. It's after the bell has tolled for the final time that the transition from a cadet to a licensed sailor is complete, and the search for employment begins. New graduates won't need to search for long. With a recent spike in retirements and the difficulty of selling younger people on the benefits of life away from home, job opportunities aren't scarce. There's a shortage of licensed sailors on the Great Lakes and oceans, and GLMA is playing a vital part in trying to put a dent in it.

"GLMA is important because they're regional," said Key Lakes fleet engineer Aaron Pitrago. "In the end, we have a better chance of getting people that will stay here with us. This is a very critical time in the industry. We're seeing changes in cargo routes, admissions. … We got to a point where, the way the system was designed, people stayed forever. Then we had a massive baby boomer exit, which left us with a lack of unlicensed sailors. The cyclic part (of the industry) hasn't helped either."

Once graduates find a job, they'll be assigned to a freighter for their first hitch, which, for a freshly licensed sailor, can be daunting with the safety net of being a cadet gone. "When you are licensed and on the job, you're in the hot seat," said GLMA graduate and third mate Logan Vasicek, who chose to work for the Interlake Steamship Co. after considering offers from other fleets. "It's up to you to make decisions, and there's no longer someone else there to guide you at every moment."

"In terms of a shortage, the industry has certainly been impacted by the COVID pandemic and the resulting workplace shift toward remote and hybrid work," said Chrissy Kadleck, director of communications at Interlake Maritime Services. "That trend is particularly challenging for our industry, as mariners are required to work on and, in many cases, live aboard vessels. That shift has collided with the fact that our industry has struggled to maintain and grow the number of skilled unlicensed personnel, positions such as able seaman (AB) and qualified member of the engine department (QMED)."

Daniel Lindner
(Scott Bjorklund)

GLMA has always played a critical role in the Great Lakes shipping industry. But with the demand for licensed sailors rising, it will be more important than ever. "Everyone on the Great Lakes is hiring," said GLMA Sea Projects Specialist Patrick Podolan. "Our engineering cadets are hands-on. I had one chief engineer contact me and say, 'I think your cadets come out prepared and ready for life at sea.' If any graduate wants a job, they have one waiting for them." ◆

TICKET TO PARADISE

Great Lakes Cruise Market Red-Hot

By **ROGER LeLIEVRE**

No question about it, 2022 proved the biggest year for cruise ships on the Great Lakes in decades. Nine such vessels visited numerous inland ports, and at least two more were expected in 2023.

Viking Octantis in the Welland Canal.
(Chris de Laat)

The gleaming white, 672-foot-long *Viking Octantis*, which opened the Great Lakes to the high-quality Viking Cruise Lines brand, turned heads wherever she went. And she wasn't the only one. Another new visitor in 2022 was Vantage Deluxe World Travel's *Ocean Explorer*, checking in at 432 feet in length. Familiar visitors from past seasons were American Queen Voyages' *Ocean Navigator (*the former *Victory II)* and *Ocean Voyager* (ex *Victory I*), as well as *Pearl Mist ,* another repeat customer.

Coming in 2023 will be Hapag-Lloyd's newest ship, the 230-passenger *Hanseatic Inspiration,* and *Octantis* will welcome a sister ship, *Viking Polaris,* to the Great Lakes for the 2023 cruise season.

The newer and larger ships reflect growing interest in Great Lakes cruising. *Conde Nast Traveler* magazine, for example, highlighted Great Lakes cruises on its list of "22 Best Places to Go in 2022."

Great Lakes cruise lines use relatively small ships. *Viking Octantis* carries 378 passengers plus crew, compared with a modern oceangoing cruise ship's capacity of 3,000 or more.

With more than 150,000 passenger visits to ports large and small generating an economic impact of about $125 million, 2022 was a record-setting season for the Great Lakes region. In 2023, passenger visits are expected to increase by 15 percent to nearly 170,000 and the total economic impact is expected to hit $180 million, according to the organization Cruise the Great Lakes, a coalition of cruise lines, ports and travel bureaus. Ports around the Great Lakes have been hurrying to modernize or build new facilities to take advantage of the increased trade and influx of tourism dollars.

Continued on Page 170

VIKING OCTANTIS

French-flagged Le Dumont d'Urville at Parry Sound, ON. (Eric Treece)

Ocean Explorer, operated by Vantage Deluxe World Travel. (Roger LeLievre)

American Queen Voyages' Ocean Voyager. (Roger LeLievre)

"There's a huge pent-up demand for cruising," said David Lorenz, vice president of Travel Michigan. "There's a bigger pent-up demand for cruising travel than most categories of travel, and I think the reason for that is people want to be treated in a slightly different way after COVID-19."

The Great Lakes were gaining traction as an appealing destination prior to 2020, and the global pandemic only accelerated the growing interest in U.S. and Canadian destinations, considered close to home for by North Americans. The entrance of Viking into the region expands the definition of a Great Lakes cruise from quaint, sleepy sails into lakeside ports to expedition-style voyages with active excursion options and science-based enrichment.

Viking tries to appeal to the academic minded. It offers lectures, workshops, documentaries, presentations and guided tours. *Viking Octantis* even boasts specially designed submersibles to view underwater caves. The yellow-painted submarines are named – fittingly – John and Paul. Many of the Viking cruises are already sold out.

Stephen Burnett, executive director of the Great Lakes Cruise Association, said expedition cruising in the Great Lakes places the emphasis on experiences ashore, many well off the beaten path.

"Cruise operators may offer their guests opportunities to discover remote regions and get up close and personal with the natural environment – the unique flora and fauna of each port of call – and learn of the territories with a team of experts," he said. "Visitors may engage in ambitious hikes, view endemic wildlife, learn of the history of indigenous peoples, indulge in local cultures and attend lectures from naturalists and scientists."

From charming tourist-laden retreats such as Mackinac Island in Michigan to the remote nature of the Georgian Bay region in Ontario, the ports of the Great Lakes are extremely varied. This is an excellent selling point, as clients can choose an itinerary based on their preferences (hiking and kayaking versus souvenir shopping in town).

The Great Lakes aren't a cheap option, despite the ability to avoid long flights or overseas jet lag. Couples can expect to spend about $10,000, on average, for an eight-day cruise. Viking is closer to the $800-plus per person, per night, with a eight-day "Great Lakes Explorer" standard itinerary starting from $6,495 per person.

Meanwhile, the long-established St. Lawrence Cruise Lines, continues to offer small-ship cruises on is *Canadian Empress* from Kingston, ON, to points east, with a variety of interesting stops that include Upper Canada Village and daylight transits of the St. Lawrence Seaway Locks so passengers don't miss a second of the breathtaking scenery. ◼

ST. JOUGHNUTS AT THE DOCK

By JOSHUA HEBEISEN

On the southeast shore of Lake Michigan, a tasty treat awaits sailors at a community quickly earning a reputation as "The Sweetest Port on the Lakes." Around 50 vessels visit St. Joseph-Benton Harbor, MI, each year, typically delivering cargoes such as cement and stone. But there's a twist: On nearly every visit, a personal delivery for the ship's crew waits courtesy of Harbormaster Michael Moran – a box of tasty pastries. But this isn't just any baker's dozen – this is the sweet, sugary, downright delicious treat known around the lakes as the savory "St. Joughnuts."

Moran's interest in the shipping industry began following a trip to the Soo Locks as a teenager. Fascinated by the giant freighters, the Indiana native enlisted in the U.S. Coast Guard and served for several years while stationed in St. Joe, where he has lived ever since. After more than a decade of photographing ships there, Moran was spotted by the Rieth-Riley Construction dock boss while taking pictures through the company's fence in September 2020. The boss came over to introduce himself and was impressed by the future harbormaster's maritime aptitude. He soon invited Moran onto the property in exchange for keeping an eye on the company's operations. It was a perfect fit. The St. Joseph and Benton Harbor Shipping News Facebook page would soon be created, with more than 5,700 followers receiving daily updates on port activity.

Trevor Schick, third mate on the Sam Laud, scoffs at calories, snaps a selfie.

Inspired by a Texas port delivering cupcakes to vessels, Moran decided to do something similar for St. Joe's own sailors. Lucky crewmembers on cement tug/barge *G.L. Ostrander/Integrity* would soon be treated to piping-hot donut holes on a cold spring day in April 2021. A tradition had begun, and what was supposed to be a one-time treat would soon take on a "hole" new life of its own. By June, nearly every boat coming into port received its own donut delivery. And it's not just the sailors who get a sugar rush – Moran makes sure to order enough sweets for the dock

St. Joughnuts coming up! (Robb Quinn)

crews, harbor supervisors, and company truck drivers. "I don't want anyone to feel left out," he says.

The preferred pastry venue is Red Coach Donuts, a bakery located in nearby Stevensville. MI, and a favorite of the locals. "They didn't know they would become synonymous with ships when I started, but they started noticing a pattern in my buying," Moran laughs. "Now the shop embraces it." His average order is an assortment of two or three dozen fresh-baked pastries, depending on the size of the vessel's crew. Some dock personnel even put in a request for their favorite items – cinnamon twists and sprinkled cake donuts are frequently set aside for certain individuals. The goodies are boxed, bagged and driven down to the harbor by Moran himself.

> ## The box of St. Joughnuts doesn't last long, and some captains have even been known to come on deck themselves to personally "secure" the package ...

In less than two years, the tasty tradition has cooked up a boatload of community engagement." In years prior," Moran recalls, "the boats were out of sight, out of mind… it was rare to see anyone gather to watch an arrival. Now there are people who gather at almost every arrival. They talk about the boats and the donuts and the traditions. Boats salute in port again." Red Coach now has an envelope in their shop for public donations to help offset the cost of Moran's orders. And coming full circle – like a donut – Moran himself was appointed the first St. Joseph Harbormaster in half a decade.

For sailors, the fresh-baked snack generates considerable excitement whenever St. Joe appears on the schedule. The box of donuts doesn't last long, and some captains have even been known to come on deck themselves to personally "secure" the package as it comes aboard. With all the time Great Lakes mariners spend away from their friends and families, Moran says, it means a lot for them to know that someone is thinking of them ashore. Sailors even vacation to the area with their families to take them to the bakery that gives a sense of home away from home. Always with mariners in mind, Moran's program has expanded recently to occasionally deliver warm meals to vessels without a designated cook in the galley. "It takes a decent amount to make donuts happen," he said, "and making a full meal happen takes a lot of effort. That said, seeing the smiles on the crews' faces makes it worth the effort."

And for the name? Credit the crew of the motor vessel *Manitowoc*, whose punny AIS destination of "St. Joughnuts" quickly caught on around the lakes. Said Trevor Schick, third mate on the motor vessel *Sam Laud*, at the mention of donuts waiting ashore: "St. Joughnuts? I thought those were a fairy tale!"

"No, sir," replied Moran, "The St. Joughnuts are very real. And I hope you enjoy them!"

Michael Moran (left) is the St. Joughnut man. (Mark Ostruszka)

It takes a steady hand to wheel the Badger. Luckily, bosun Cory Ottgen is on the job. *(Roger LeLievre)*

Sailors Keep Ships Moving

Riding the bosun's chair down to the dock. *(David Schauer)*

HON. JAMES L. OBERSTAR

THE INTERLAKE STEAMSHIP CO.

Skinny Santa on the Joseph L. Block needs a trip to the galley! (Paul Scinocca)

John Rice after thawing a frozen deck line on Lake Superior aboard the Edwin H. Gott. (Selfie)

Historic Gallery

Canada Steamship Lines' package
freighter Weyburn exits the
Eisenhower Lock on the then-new
St. Lawrence Seaway in 1960. Oil
Transporter is bringing up the rear.
(Gordon F. Bugbee / Marine Historical
Society of Detroit Archives)

Package freighter Fort Henry was known as one of the speediest ships on the lakes. She was built in 1955 and scrapped in 1984. (Marine Historical Society of Detroit Archives)

Paterson fleet's Senator of Canada in the Welland Canal, 1959. This lovely vessel was scrapped in 1984. (J.R. Williams)

USCG cutters Naugatuck, Arundel and Mackinaw break ice at the Sugar Island ferry dock, Sault Ste. Marie, MI, in January 1974. (Roger LeLlevre)

Tug America and G.A. Tomlinson at Toledo, OH, in the 1950s. (Paul C. LaMarre III Coll.)

J. Burton Ayers in Columbia Transportation Co. colors, St. Clair River, 1985. She sails today as Cuyahoga. (Jim Jackson)

S.T. Crapo, St. Marys River. The 1927-built vessel was sold for scrap in 2022. (Tom Manse)

The 1900-vintage Howard L. Shaw on the Detroit RIver in 1967, seen from the Ambassador Bridge. Her hull is one of three sunk in 1969 to form a breakwall for Toronto's Ontario Place. (J.R. Williams)

Christmas on the Arthur M. Anderson
c. the 1960s. (John Vournakis)

Arthur B. Homer in 1980, her last season of operation, coming off
Lake St. Clair downbound. She would be scrapped six years later,
at 807 feet long the largest laker to be cut up. (Graham Grattan)

Tug Brochu assists Canadian Mariner at Port-Cartier, QC. (Graham Grattan)

Ernest R. Breech on the Rouge River in 1973, flanked by Moshill and Myron C. Taylor. (Roger LeLievre)

Birchglen meets T.R. McLagan in the Welland Canal, 1983. (Jim Jackson)

Canadian Century and Algowood. *(Know Your Ships Coll.)*

Mapleglen arriving at Goderich, ON, with grain, assisted by MacDonald Marine tugs. *(Graham Grattan)*

Canadian Provider enters the MacArthur Lock while Quebecois leaves the Poe Lock in 2003. *(Roger LeLievre)*

Richard Trimble unloading ore at Conneaut, OH, in 1973. U.S. Army Corps of Engineers floating plant is in the foreground. *(Dick Wicklund)*

Wilson Marine Transit's Edward S. Kendrick. She was scrapped in Spain in 1973. *(Peter Vander Linden)*

U.S. Steel steamer William E. Corey at a Cleveland coal dock. The Corey's hull survives as a breakwall at Port Credit, ON. She last sailed as Ridgetown in 1970. (Jim Hoffman Coll.)

John O. McKellar assisted by tug Roger at Milwaukee on Dec. 15, 1955.
(Milwaukee Press, Roger LeLievre Coll.)

Republic Steel Corp.'s Charles M. White is followed down the St. Marys River by Pickands Mather's J.L. Mauthe c. the late 1970s. The White was one of three World War II C-4 troop/cargo ships converted to lake steamers in the early 1950s. All three were scrapped in the early 1980s. J.L. Mauthe of 1953 still sails as the barge Pathfinder. (Tom Manse)

Canadian bulk carrier Menihek Lake assisted by the tug Peninsula at Thunder Bay, ON. (Know Your Ships Coll.)

Collingwood and Franquelin moored at a Kingston, ON, grain elevator. (Peter Vander Linden Coll.)

Pointe Noire being overtaken by the speedy CSL package freighter Fort York on Lake St. Clair in 1980. (Graham Grattan)

Vessels of the Misener fleet were once familiar sights on the Great Lakes. Above image shows John O. McKellar and John A. France stopped in the ice above Nine Mile Point on the St. Marys River. They would be part of a downbound convoy waiting for upbound traffic to clear before heading down the upbound channel east of Neebish Island. (Graham Grattan) *Lower photo shows the Royalton (i) above Six Mile Point, about four miles from where the two Misener boats were photographed.* (Gordon Bugbee)

GREAT LAKES GLOSSARY

AAA CLASS – Vessel design popular on the Great Lakes in the early 1950s. *Arthur M. Anderson* is one example.

AFT – Toward the back, or stern, of a ship.

AMIDSHIPS – The middle point of a vessel, referring to either length or width.

ARTICULATED TUG/BARGE (ATB) – Tug-barge combination. The two vessels are mechanically linked in one axis but with the tug free to move, or articulate, on another axis.

BACKHAUL – The practice of carrying a revenue-producing cargo (rather than ballast) on a return trip from hauling a primary cargo.

BARGE – Vessel with no engine, either pushed or pulled by a tug.

BEAM – The width of a vessel at its widest point.

BILGE – Lowest part of a hold or compartment, generally where the rounded side of a ship curves from the keel to the vertical sides.

BLAST FURNACE TRIM (BFT) – Raw crushed taconite ore used to adjust the silica content in a blast furnace.

BOW THRUSTER – Propeller mounted transversely in a vessel's bow under the waterline to assist in moving sideways. A stern thruster may also be installed.

BRIDGE – The platform above the main deck from which a ship is steered/navigated. Also: PILOTHOUSE or WHEELHOUSE.

BULK CARGO – Goods, loose or in mass, that generally must be shoveled, pumped, blown or scooped out of a vessel.

BULKHEAD – Wall or partition that separates rooms, holds or tanks within a ship's hull.

BULWARK – The part of the ship that extends fore and aft above the main deck to form a rail.

DATUM – Level of water in a given area, determined by an average over time.

DEADWEIGHT TONNAGE – Deadweight tonnage (DWT) is a measure of how much weight a ship can carry. It is the sum of the weights of cargo, fuel, fresh water, ballast water, provisions, passengers and crew.

DECK SPRINKLERS – The reason for spraying water on a vessel's deck is to help cool the upper part of a boat and prevent hogging (bending due to temperature differences above and below the waterline). With decks exposed to the sun all day, the surface can get very hot. The hull of the boat underwater stays cooler. Hogging can affect cargo capacity and the depth to which a boat can load.

DISPLACEMENT TONNAGE – The displacement or displacement tonnage of a ship is its weight. As the term indicates, it is measured indirectly, using Archimedes' principle, by first calculating the volume of water displaced by the ship, then converting that value into weight.

DRAFT – The depth of water a ship needs to float. Also, the distance from keel to waterline.

FIT OUT – The process of preparing a vessel for service after a period of inactivity.

FIVE-YEAR INSPECTION – U.S. Coast Guard survey, conducted in a drydock every five years, of a vessel's hull, machinery and other components.

FLATBACK – Lakes slang for a non-self-unloader.

FOOTER – Lakes slang for a 1,000-foot vessel.

FOREPEAK – The space below the forecastle.

FREEBOARD – The distance from the waterline to the main deck.

GEARLESS VESSEL – One that is not a self-unloader.

GROSS TONNAGE – The internal space of a vessel, measured in units of 100 cubic feet (2.83 cubic meters) = a gross ton.

HATCH – An opening in the deck through which cargo is lowered or raised. A hatch is closed by securing a hatch cover over it.

IMO # – Unique number issued by the International Maritime Organization, or IMO, to ships for identification. Not all vessels have an IMO number.

INTEGRATED TUG/BARGE (ITB) – Tug-barge combination in which the tug is rigidly mated to the barge. *Presque Isle* is one example.

IRON DECKHAND – Mechanical device that runs on rails on a vessel's main deck and is used to remove and replace hatch covers.

JONES ACT – A U.S. law that mandates that cargoes moved between American ports be carried by U.S.-flag, U.S.-built and U.S.-crewed vessels.

KEEL – A ship's steel backbone. It runs along the lowest part of the hull.

LAID UP or **LAY-UP** – Out of service.

NET REGISTER TONNAGE – The internal capacity of a vessel available for carrying cargo. It does not

Exterior hull markings

The Plimsoll line is a reference mark located on a ship's hull that indicates the maximum depth to which the vessel may be safely immersed when loaded with cargo. This depth varies with a ship's dimensions, type of cargo, time of year and the water densities encountered in port and at sea. In the 1860s, after increased loss of ships due to overloading, government regulations were proposed by Samuel Plimsoll, a British Member of Parliament. The Plimsoll mark, or line, was adopted in 1876. Since that time, every vessel has been required to have a line painted amidships on both sides of the hull to act as a visual indicator of the limit to which the ship can be loaded. It is a diamond with a horizontal line drawn through it. The letter T painted on a ship's side indicates the best place for tugs to push.

Left symbol warns of a bow or stern thruster below. The one at right indicates a bulbous bow and how far it extends in front of the hull.

Plimsoll line with draft markings in meters and feet at left. Symbols at left indicate draft in saltwater (SW) and freshwater (FW).

include the space occupied by boilers, engines, shaft alleys, chain lockers or officers' and crew's quarters. Net register tonnage is usually referred to as registered tonnage or net tonnage and is used to calculate taxes, tolls and port charges. It is used in situations where a vessel's earning capacity is important, rather than its mere size.

PROJECT CARGO – Dimensionally challenging, heavy, complex pieces of equipment which often involve engineering, extensive planning and specialized transport equipment. Examples include blades for wind turbines, large storage tanks, oil and gas drilling equipment and factory production equipment. Often referred to as heavy lift cargo.

RIVER CLASS – Group of vessels built in the 1970s to service smaller ports and negotiate narrow rivers.

SELF-UNLOADER – Vessel able to discharge its own cargo using a system of conveyor belts and a movable boom.

SINTER FEED – Crushed taconite.

STEM – The extreme forward end of the bow.

STEMWINDER – Vessel with all cabins aft.

STRAIGHT DECKER – Non-self-unloading vessel.

TACONITE – Processed, pelletized iron ore. Easy to load and unload, this is the primary type of ore shipped on the Great Lakes and St. Lawrence Seaway. Also known as pellets.

TRACTOR TUG – Highly maneuverable tug propelled by either a Z-drive or cycloidal system rather than the traditional screw propeller.

TOLL – Fee charged against a ship, cargo and passengers for a complete or partial transit of a waterway covering a single trip in one direction.

TURKEY TRAIL – Route from North Channel (above Manitoulin Island) into the St. Marys River, named for the many courses which zigzag through the area's islands, shoals and ports.

TURNAROUND – The time it takes between the arrival of a vessel and its departure.

VESSEL AGENT – An agent represents a saltwater vessel's owner or operator at each port of call, and takes care of the needs of the vessel and its crew.

195

VESSEL LOG / *Record your own ship sightings*

Date	Vessel Name	Date	Vessel Name

Date	Vessel Name

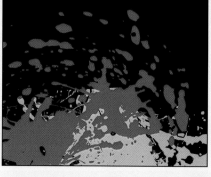

Lee A. Tregurtha downbound at Mission Point in Sault Ste. Marie, MI, with ore for Dearborn, MI. A fleet of waterfowl heads upbound. (Glenn Blaszkiewicz)

ADVERTISER INDEX   *Thank you!*

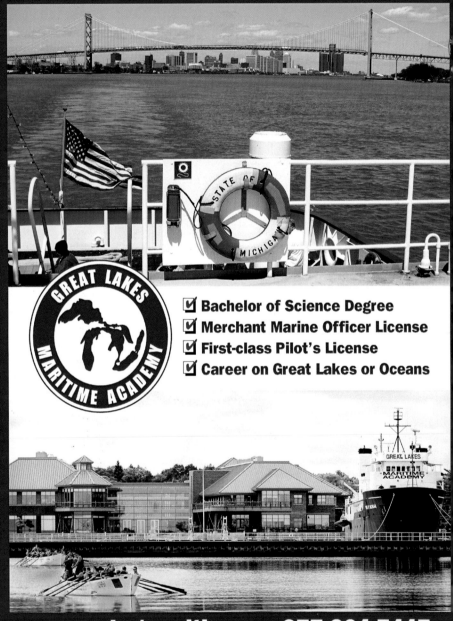